The International Humanitarian Order

One of the genuinely remarkable but relatively unnoticed developments of the last half-century is the blossoming of an international humanitarian order – a complex of norms, informal institutions, laws, and discourses that legitimate and compel various kinds of interventions by state and nonstate actors with the explicit goal of preserving and protecting human life. For those who have sacrificed to build this order, and for those who have come to rely on it, the international humanitarian order represents a towering achievement and the best evidence of an international community and the possibility of moral progress. Yet there is also cause for sobriety. What kind of international humanitarian order is being imagined, created, and practiced? To what extent are the international agents of this order deliverers of progress or disappointment?

Featuring previously published and original essays, this collection offers a critical assessment of the practices and politics of global ethical interventions in the context of the post-cold war transformation of the international humanitarian order. After an Introduction that introduces the reader to the concept and the significance of the international humanitarian order, Section I explores the braided relationship between international order and the UN, while Section II critically examines international ethics in practice. The Conclusion reflects on these and other themes, asking why the international humanitarian order retains such a loyal following despite its flaws, what is the relationship of this order to power and politics, how such relationships implicate our understanding of moral progress, and how the international humanitarian order challenges both practitioners and scholars to rethink the meaning of their vocations.

Michael N. Barnett is the Harold Stassen Chair of International Relations at the Humphrey Institute of Public Affairs and Professor of Political Science at the University of Minnesota.

Security and Governance Series
Edited by Fiona B. Adamson
School of Oriental and African Studies, University of London
Roland Paris
University of Ottawa
Stefan Wolff
University of Nottingham

Editorial Board:

This series reflects the broadening conceptions of security and the growing nexus between the study of governance issues and security issues. The topics covered in the series range from issues relating to the management of terrorism and political violence, non-state actors, transnational security threats, migration, borders, and "homeland security" to questions surrounding weak and failing states, post-conflict reconstruction, the evolution of regional and international security institutions, energy and environmental security, and the proliferation of WMD. Particular emphasis is placed on publishing theoretically informed scholarship that elucidates the governance mechanisms, actors, and processes available for managing issues in the new security environment.

Rethinking Japanese Security
Peter J. Katzenstein

State Building and International Intervention in Bosnia
Roberto Belloni

"In this outstanding and convenient collection of previously published papers one of the leading scholars of the international humanitarian order takes stock of developments that have been vastly consequential since the end of the Cold War. In developing his arguments Michael Barnett is intellectually incisive and politically astute. This book is required reading for all who are interested in the profound changes that have affected world politics during the last two decades."

Peter J. Katzenstein, Walter S. Carpenter, Jr.
Professor of International Studies,
Cornell University

"Over the past fifteen years, Michael Barnett has emerged as the most thoughtful American scholarly voice on the dilemmas of humanitarianism. In these penetrating essays, he ranges widely, probing the role of political pragmatism and the impulse for moral transcendence in shaping contemporary humanitarianism."

Jack Snyder, Robert and Renée Belfer
Professor of International Relations,
Columbia University

"Relying on personal experience and academic prudence, Barnett's collection does a wonderful job of interrogating the rise of the International Humanitarian Order. Always insightful but never losing balance and perspective, Barnett refreshingly focuses on the intermeshing of ethics and power and, in so doing, overcomes the one-sidedness of much of the thinking on this topic."

David Chandler, Professor of International Relations,
University of Westminster

The International Humanitarian Order

Michael N. Barnett

Routledge
Taylor & Francis Group

LONDON AND NEW YORK

First published 2010
by Routledge
2 Park Square, Milton Park, Abingdon, Oxon OX14 4RN

Simultaneously published in the USA and Canada
by Routledge
270 Madison Avenue, New York, NY 10016

*Routledge is an imprint of the Taylor & Francis Group,
an informa business*

© 2010 Michael N. Barnett

Typeset in Times New Roman by
RefineCatch Limited, Bungay, Suffolk
Printed and bound in Great Britain by
TJ International, Padstow, Cornwall

British Library Cataloguing in Publication Data
A catalogue record for this book is available from the British Library

Library of Congress Cataloging-in-Publication Data
A catalog record has been requested for this book

ISBN10: 0–415–77631–7 (hbk)
ISBN10: 0–415–77632–5 (pbk)
ISBN10: 0–203–86297–X (ebk)

ISBN13: 978–0–415–77631–8 (hbk)
ISBN13: 978–0–415–77632–5 (pbk)
ISBN13: 978–0–203–86297–1 (ebk)

Contents

Acknowledgments

The essays in this volume, in many respects, were collectively produced. I have been fortunate to benefit from an academic community that values the free exchange of ideas, and has always been willing to tell me when my half-baked ideas needed longer cooking time or should be disposed down the drain. I have been doubly fortunate, though, to have collaborated with several friends that have forever changed the way I think about the world and whose influence is present on nearly every page. Although now nearly two decades have passed, Alex Wendt and I collaborated on a couple of pieces on Third World militarization (which I credit as being Alex's finest empirically oriented work), and our exchanges over the years have been deeply influential. I have been lucky to work with Emanuel Adler on the subject of security communities, and I became, I realized only later, a disciple of the idea of cognitive evolution (though I am still too cynical to be completely persuaded). Martha Finnemore and I found that we were passionate about the oddities of international organizations, and our passions fueled several collaborations and nurtured many of the ideas that are contained in the essays in this volume. And, lastly, Bud Duvall, who has had a hold over my intellectual development for over two decades and whose intellectual integrity, honesty, and ethics have caused me to struggle with basic questions of power in world affairs. In addition to their influence over the ideas contained in these essays, I also learned much from them regarding the craft of writing, an all too overlooked but absolutely essential feature of the scholarly enterprise.

My family has been my not so silent partner and to them I owe more than words can express. One family member, though, deserves special recognition—Judith Shampaine, who has occupied the ground between mother-in-law and mother for longer than I can remember, whose sense of the world contains elements of magic, and whose inexplicable belief in the possibility that I can do better has kept me moving forward. Thank you.

I would like to thank the following for permission to reprint their material:

"Bringing in the new world order: liberalism, legitimacy, and the United Nations," first published in *World Politics*, 49, 4, July, 526–551, 1997, Cambridge University Press.

"The new United Nations politics of peace: from juridical sovereignty to empirical sovereignty," reproduced from *Global Governance: A Review of Multilateralism and International Organizations*, 1, 1. Copyright © 1995 by Lynne Rienner Publishers, Inc. Used with permission of the publisher.

"The United Nations and global security: the norm is mightier than the sword," first published in *Ethics and International Affairs*, 9, 37–54, 1996, Wiley-Blackwell.

"Humanitarianism with a sovereign face: UNHCR in the global undertow," first published in *International Migration Review*, 35, 1, 244–276, Wiley-Blackwell.

"The UN Security Council, indifference, and genocide in Rwanda," first published in *Cultural Anthropology*, 12, 1, 551–578, 1997, Wiley-Blackwell.

"UNHCR and the ethics of repatriation," *Forced Migration Review*, April, 2001, *http://www.fmreview.org/FMRpdfs/FMR10/fmr10.11.pdf*). Reproduced with kind permission.

"Building a republican peace: stabilizing states after war," *International Security*, 30, 4, Spring, 87–112, 2006, reproduced with kind permission of MIT Press Journals.

"Humanitarianism transformed," first published in *Perspectives on Politics*, 3, 4, December, 723–740, 2005, Cambridge University Press.

1 Introduction
The international humanitarian order

The international humanitarian order concerns the protection of those in immediate peril and the prevention of unnecessary suffering. It includes norms, informal institutions, laws, and discourses that legitimate and compel various kinds of interventions with the explicit goal of preserving and protecting life. There are now a surfeit of conventions and treaties that are designed to protect the fundamental right of all peoples—the right to life. International human rights, humanitarian, and refugee law were distant cousins for most of the last century, but over the last two decades they have become intertwined, reinforcing each other and creating an increasingly dense normative structure. In 2005 the UN World Summit acknowledged a "responsibility to protect" populations who are the victims of campaigns of extermination. Although much less famous than the doctrine of a responsibility to protect, a "right to relief" has been around much longer and has more teeth—there now exist fairly ingrained expectations that the international community should deliver life-saving assistance to those endangered by natural or humanly made disasters. A multitude of slogans and rallying cries—including "never again" and the "humanitarian imperative"—accompany graphic and heart-wrenching photos of victims of violence. These norms, laws, and institutions are nestled in discourses of compassion, responsibility, and care, which, in turn, are attached to claims regarding the kinds of obligations the "international community" has to its weakest members.

The international humanitarian order also includes a metropolis of organizations, some of which are dedicated to the goal of reducing suffering and others that will lend a hand under the right circumstances. Nongovernmental organizations such as Doctors without Borders, the International Committee of the Red Cross, CARE International, and Oxfam are perhaps most closely identified with this order because they have been around for decades. They assert that it is their job to be on the front line when danger strikes and lives are at stake, and are treated by the media and popular culture as icons of heroic compassion. Over the last hundred years states have created a multitude of international organizations to assist vulnerable and neglected peoples. Most famous are the United Nations and its specialized agencies, including the World Food Program, UN peacekeeping, the UN High Commissioner for

Refugees, UNICEF, and the World Health Organization. States, though they rarely get much credit, have been increasingly central to this order. For decades they have been its principal patron, and over the last two decades they contributed in more direct ways, including dispatching their militaries to deliver aid and protect civilians during emergencies. Even the private sector has become more visibly involved in humanitarian action. Corporations are increasingly expected to demonstrate a "social responsibility," integrating welfare concerns into their profit-oriented strategies, and appear most willing to do so when they believe that consumers are looking.

The international humanitarian order extends beyond "humanitarianism." Humanitarianism is generally understood as assistance that occurs in the context of disasters; consequently, it is most readily applied to emergency relief and post-conflict recovery. However, the international humanitarian order includes other professional fields and communities of practice such as human rights, development, and public health. And, you don't have to be either a professional or even a card-carrying humanitarian to be part of the humanitarian order. All that is required is dedicated action to saving lives, reducing suffering, preventing harm, and improving the lot of humankind. Those who are committed to humanity, however defined, abbreviated, and circumscribed, are part of that order. In general, there now exists a "humanitarian government . . . [T]he administration of human collectivities in the name of a higher moral principle that sees the preservation of life and the alleviation of suffering as the highest value of action."[1]

The international humanitarian order is most easily identified when contrasted with the international security and economic orders. What distinguishes the contemporary international security order from the long, bloody, history of war and conflict is the self-conscious attempt by states and others to try and create international institutions with the explicit purpose of managing, curtailing, and preventing organized violence and its effects. Toward that end states have established various kinds of institutions and arrangements, including preventive diplomacy, multilateral conferences, and arms control regimes. What distinguishes the contemporary international economic order from the extensive history of long-distance trade and economic exchange is the self-conscious attempt by states and others to create global rules to manage and liberalize the global economy. Toward that end states have established regimes for regulating finance, capital, labor, and trade. What distinguishes the international humanitarian order from all previous acts of compassion is the self-conscious and explicit attempt by states and non-state actors to create international mechanisms to reduce suffering and improve human welfare. Toward that end states and non-state actors have created international refugee and human rights regimes, banned landmines, created campaigns to improve global health, and attacked global poverty.

The international humanitarian order has expanded significantly over the last two decades. Before giving some sense of the magnitude of the change it is important to note that the international humanitarian order rivals in age these other orders. Historically speaking, the origins of the international humanitarian order reside in the combustible mix of technological, economic, religious, and ideological changes of the late eighteenth and early nineteenth centuries.[2] In many respects the abolitionist movements of the early nineteenth century were the inaugural event, predating the establishment of the International Committee of the Red Cross and international humanitarian law by nearly a half-century, and over the last century there has been a steady accumulation of norms, rules, and institutions whose purpose is to protect human life.[3] But arguably the greatest burst of activity occurred following the end of the Cold War. There was more money available for various forms of emergency relief, rights and democracy promotion, post-conflict recovery, and the prevention and treatment of disease. There were more organizations, some private, others non-profit, some local, others global, involved in matters of humanitarian governance. The best sign of the expanding population was the growing interest in various forms of coordination that were intended to bring coherence to an increasingly dense and ever-expanding sector. Yet perhaps the most impressive change occurred in the growing, interlocking, and increasingly nested networks for the prevention of suffering, due in large part to changing knowledge regarding what kinds of interventions were desirable and necessary in order to improve human life. The world was complex, the task of building states after war was complex, preventing suffering was complex, and all this complexity required new forms of knowledge that not only identified what were the critical pieces but also how all the pieces fit together. Global governance became increasingly dedicated to humanitarian practices and humanitarian governance was now global.

I am rather astonished to be assembling a volume on the transformation of the post-Cold War international humanitarian order, for two reasons. I did not set out with a grand plan or research agenda. Instead, the essays resulted from a modified path dependence, where one topic snowballed into another. In fact, it was only recently that I even noticed the existence of an international humanitarian order; at the time that I wrote these articles I understood myself to be exploring the loosely connected areas of international order, peacekeeping, peacebuilding, and humanitarianism. Also, the international humanitarian order is of a considerable distance from my "first" scholarly career. My dissertation was on the politics of warmaking and statemaking in the Middle East. By the early 1990s I knew my way a lot better around Cairo and Tel-Aviv than New York; I knew the history of the Arab League a lot better than the history of the United Nations; I knew a lot more about the causes and consequences of war than about the prospects of peacekeeping and peacebuilding; and I had considerable familiarity with Third World militarization and almost no knowledge of humanitarianism.

What changed? The end of the Cold War shifted the geopolitical plates in ways that elevated the United Nations and handed it a growing role in my areas of research. The 1990 Iraqi invasion of Kuwait became a matter of "international peace and security" and was handled at the UN Security

Council. During the Cold War the U.S. and the Soviet Union played their war games in the Third World, but once the superpowers settled their differences they asked the United Nations to clean up their mess. Third World security dynamics also changed dramatically, as Third World regimes who once counted on the United States or the Soviet Union to preserve their regime security against their domestic rivals now had a United Nations pushing reconciliation, democratization, and human security. The players and the terms of the debate changed remarkably as a consequence of the end of the Cold War, and I followed the action to the United Nations to better understand the evolving global governance of Third World security. I had the opportunity to study these emerging dynamics up close and personal for a year beginning in late summer 1993 at the United States Mission to the United Nations, and I became increasingly knowledgeable about the rapidly developing peacekeeping sector.

Then in the late 1990s I developed an interest in refugee studies and suddenly found myself keeping company with scholars and practitioners of humanitarianism. Again, the reasons were circumstantial. Because of my experiences at the U.S. Mission to the United Nations and research on the Rwandan genocide (I will say more later), I became deeply interested in the global institutions that were assigned responsibility for protecting the world's most vulnerable populations. Also, the international policy and scholarly community increasingly treated refugee flows as part of international security, mass displacement as both a consequence and a cause of conflict, and refugee repatriation and resettlement as an essential cornerstone for any stable peace. The intersecting interests in global governance and refugees directed me to the door of the United Nations High Commissioner of Refugees, which became my gateway to the complex connections between security and humanitarianism. I found myself in a completely different world; in fact, my world turned upside down. Whereas once I treated the growing connection between security and humanitarianism as an instance of the humanization of security, always a good thing, aid workers were warning me about the dangers of securitization of humanitarianism. I began looking at the post-Cold War transformation of humanitarianism, realized that I could not talk about "after" without having a good sense of what came "before," and so started a project on the history of humanitarianism. Only recently did I look backwards, connect the practices of peacekeeping, peacebuilding, and humanitarianism, and discover a body—the international humanitarian order.

While the essays were written against the backdrop of a changing international humanitarian order, I must re-state that the international humanitarian order was not born in 1990 but rather has a long history. Indeed, even a slight awareness of that history should disabuse anyone from thinking that the observed developments and dilemmas, causes and consequences, of the international humanitarian order are novel. At best the emerging international order was part rupture from, part return to, and part continuation of all that came before. The desire to save failed states sounds and looks a lot like nineteenth century civilizing missions. The dilemmas that beset humanitarian relief were present during the Cold War, during World War Two, during World War One, and during various colonial interventions. There is very little that is new under the sun, even if each day brings something different.

International (humanitarian) orders and constructivist international relations theory

I have explored various aspects of the international humanitarian order with the aid of constructivist international relations theory. I am not a constructivist, although in a discipline that feels the same need to place scholars into existing boxes as zoologists to classify animals and botanists plants, my work tends to get labeled in this way. I am not entirely comfortable with this designation. Theory is a tool and not a religion, and I have drawn from whatever tools might be useful for understanding the issues at hand and am not worried about being labeled a heretic. Moreover, while I owe a tremendous debt to those international relations theorists who are closely identified with constructivist international relations, I found myself gravitating more toward those eminent social scientists that worked at the intersection of culture and action, including Max Weber, and political theorists who offered a complex and at times uncomfortable understanding of the relationship between history and ethics, including Hannah Arendt. I do not entirely reject the label, though. Constructivism has helped me both explore my existing research questions and, most importantly, formulate the questions I want to ask. Consequently, I want to briefly address how constructivism influenced my approach to the international humanitarian order, and, in turn, how the international humanitarian order exposes some shortcomings in current trends in constructivism.

The "problem of order" has been central to the study of international relations since the discipline's founding, but the unexpected and rapid end of the Cold War invested the topic with considerable urgency and import. It is mildly ironic that the school of international relations, namely realism, which prided itself on a keen awareness of "reality" and intimate knowledge of Soviet–American conflict dynamics could have been caught completely flat-footed by the end of the Cold War. Although few, if any, international relations theorists predicted the collapse of the superpower rivalry and the demise of the Soviet Union, the failure to see this "black swan" proved particularly damaging to a school of thought whose authority rested on its presumed expertise regarding patterns of war and peace. To compound matters, when during the Cold War realists speculated about possible endings they imagined scenarios from bad to worse, from major power war to nuclear destruction.

Realists also seemed particularly ill-suited to explain the emerging organization and architecture of the post-Cold War order. Certainly any international order would be built on the foundation of national interests, but states were actively debating what were their national interests. It was trivially true to claim that most states wanted to survive most of the time, and empirically inaccurate to claim that states maximized power. If anarchy and the distribution of military power did not determine the content of the national interest, then what other forces did? States also appeared to be influenced by the distribution of ideas, including the kind of world they wanted to replace what had existed for nearly fifty years. Perhaps more important were domestic debates over the national identity. Consider the United States. Although enjoying a "unipolar moment," it was not acting like a fire-breathing deity. Instead, it was articulating principles of multilateralism, consensus building, and democracy that many American officials insisted were consistent with American values and various scholars argued had guided American foreign policy officials after World War Two, the last time the United States could indulge envisioning a new international order.[4] Moreover, as the United States and others were debating who they were and what they wanted, they did so while considering how "we" differ from "them." In some cases states easily categorized the world, drawing from long-established fault lines, like civilized vs. uncivilized. In other cases states had difficulty figuring out where they belonged because they had a difficult time deciding who they were. Ever since the end of the Cold War, Turkey has been undergoing a vibrant national debate regarding whether it is European and part of the "West" or Islamic and part of the "East," choices that were heavily structured by a "Europe" that had strong views regarding Turkey's status as an "other" and the kind of transformation it would have to undergo if it was to become a member of the European club.

The failure of realist theories provided openings for others, including liberalism, neoliberal institutionalism, and the English School, but arguably no theory benefited more from the end of the Cold War than constructivism. An embryonic constructivism began making a name for itself because it was asking the right questions at the right time and possessed an epistemology that offered the promise of answering them. Established theories assumed that interests were exogenous and fixed; that international institutions, law, and norms resulted from the bargains forged between (powerful) states; and that these brokered arrangements, at most, regulated the behaviour of states, thus representing little more than an intervening variable. Constructivism, on the other hand, made as a matter of empirical inquiry the identities and interests of actors, offered a more complex understanding of the emergence and evolution of international norms, and imagined how the underlying normative structure could constitute the very organization of world affairs. It offered, in short, an alternative way of thinking about the making, remaking, and unmaking of international order, pulling attention away from the distribution of power (realism) and the distribution of information (neoliberal institutionalism) and toward the distribution of knowledge (constructivism).[5]

Section I explores various themes in the making of the post-Cold War order. It begins with a consideration of legitimacy. All international orders require some legitimacy if they are to have any staying power and shape the behavior of its members, and the unraveling of one order and the emergence of another provides an insider's look at the process of legitimation.[6] "Bringing in the new world order" (Chapter 2) highlights several related issues regarding legitimacy. Liberal principles increasingly constituted the post-Cold War order, pivoting around markets, democracy, and human rights. Given a century of institution-building and international governance founded on liberal principles, it was no great surprise that liberalism was one of the primary beneficiaries of the demise of the Soviet Union; its hegemony, however, was, and while many objected to Francis Fukuyama's taunt regarding the "end of history," there were no immediate contenders in sight.[7] One of the defining features of the post-Cold War period was the extent to which liberalism had its "coming out party"; proponents unapologetically pushed liberalism in all areas of life, and states were now explicitly judged in terms of how liberal they were. Liberalism's rapid rise, however, required some intellectual and political labor—all political orders are produced through on-going contestations. In the early 1990s there were various commissions, study groups, and reports that contributed to that debate and were particularly powerful voices. Furthermore, political orders need to be legitimated, and while legitimation processes can occur in various locales, some formal and others informal, the post-Cold War debate regarding the ideal characteristics of the members and the rules of the club took place at the world's principal legitimation forum, the United Nations.[8]

This emerging international order also revealed the extent to which norms have two different kinds of effects, each making a distinctive and necessary contribution to production of order.[9] Regulative norms constrain the behaviour of already existing actors, shaping what they do and how they do it. The UN, as an institution, has various tools that it can deploy to give incentives for states to settle their difference through negotiation and not war. After the end of the Cold War the UN developed new conflict-reducing tools and expanded existing ones: the Secretary-General began sending more special representatives to hot spots around the world; states established contact and "friends" groups, relatively small clubs that herded rival parties toward conflict resolution; and, most famously, a rapidly expanding UN peacekeeping apparatus that deployed blue helmets around the world for the purpose of monitoring an existing cease-fire or peace agreement. These developments were consistent with a UN culture that privileged quiet diplomacy over loud sabre-rattling. Yet the UN was not completely resistant to using force. Beginning in the 1990s it took up the cause of peace enforcement, a euphemism for becoming a party to the war. Although Somalia, Haiti, and Bosnia caused UN officials to return to first principles, the continuing desire to protect civilians during times of war meant that the UN had to consider the use of military force. The article "The United Nations and global security" (Chapter 4), examines the UN's 1990s infatuation with coercive diplomacy and argues that the UN's comparative advantage is in its deployment and manipulation of norms.

Norms also can have constitutive effects, shaping who are the actors, and what are their identities, interests, and social capacities, and thus represent a second prop for maintaining international order. Specifically, whereas the view that norms constrain isolates the distribution of external incentives that compel states and nonstate actors to comply with existing norms, the view that norms are also constitutive considers how they shape the identities, interests, and practices of actors in ways that are potentially consistent with the demands of social order. There are several ways to think about this process. One is norm diffusion, which tends to focus on the structures and processes that are responsible for spreading a set of beliefs, practices, and interests across a population.[10] Another is socialization, which tends to focus on the processes that change the identity of an actor so that it is consistent with other members of the dominant group.[11] These processes can be impersonal, having their effects without any intention on the part of any actor. Yet they also can be quite personal. Core members of the group will often try and get peripheral and new members to identify with the group for the reason that it is a more cost-effective way to maintain order. Toward that end, actors can either try to directly shape the identity and interests of the actors or alter the normative landscape so that it creates incentives for actors to orient themselves in a particular direction.[12] Although scholars of norm diffusion, socialization, and strategic social construction have tended to focus on communication and persuasion as means of transmission and constitution (perhaps an unintended influence of liberal approaches), it is important to remember the ever-present role of force. Arguably modern international history's most effective mechanism of norm diffusion and socialization was imperialism and colonialism.[13] In general, world orders are sustained by a combination of interests and identities, environmental forces and self-understandings.

The shifting conception of international order had a dramatic impact on the governance of the international security and humanitarian orders. There was a change in the prevailing belief regarding what kinds of arrangements would best maintain international stability. Whereas during the Cold War the general view was that international order could be stabilized through deterrence and the military balance of power, with reinforcing braces from an austere interpretation of sovereignty, after the Cold War an emerging view was that international peace and security was best founded on states that had domestic legitimacy, and domestic legitimacy, in turn, depended on the trifekta of democracy, markets, and rights. The language of human security now began to creep into discussions, not quite pushing aside more traditional conceptions of security but certainly altering the landscape.[14] This emerging view regarding how to build a better peace system helped to create the categories of weak and failing states and constitute them as a "problem" for international security and a matter of global governance.[15]

Because failed and weak states were now seen as a threat to themselves and others, the international security sector began to develop new kinds of tools, techniques, and templates for helping states get back on their feet and make the transition from civil war to civil society.[16] Drawing largely from the English School, "The new United Nations politics of peace" (Chapter 3) represented a relatively early effort to consider how second-generation peace-building operations were both reflective of and helping to produce a change in the meaning and practice of international order. Such practices have deepened and institutionalized over the last fifteen years, and the liberal order has produced a nearly identifiable brand of peacebuilding—liberal peace-building.[17] Liberals might be identified with extolling the virtues of autonomy, independence, and liberty, but not when it comes to peacebuilding. Liberal peacebuilding is a highly invasive project; the expanded list of factors associated with a stable peace meant that nearly all features of state and society were fair game for external intervention.[18] Along the way some began to notice that liberal peacebuilding appeared to be better at re-igniting conflict rather than producing reconciliation, noting that societies emerging from war do not have the institutional mechanisms or sufficient trust to ensure that competition, the hallmark of a liberal polity, will stay nonviolent and not turn deadly. In response, some downplayed the importance of liberalism and emphasized the importance of institution and state-building, which, in fact, expanded rather than curtailed peacebuilding's ambitions.[19] "Building a republican peace" (Chapter 8) represents my attempt to think through alternative peacebuilding principles, emphasizing the importance not of the ends that new states and societies should embrace but rather a set of principles that will hopefully lead to a more inclusive participatory process that also limits the dangers that one faction will gain control of the state.

The "international community" assumed new kinds of "responsibilities" that legitimated and demanded new kinds of interventions. Although the emerging international order was connected to state interests (how could it be otherwise?), one of the striking features of these expanded responsibilities was that they rested on the discourse of obligation and not on the discourse of interests. Advocates of new kinds of responsibilities and interventions always felt the need to refer to the language of obligation and rights and not the language of interests (for instance, weak states breed international terrorism and instability), but ultimately the strongest and most compelling arguments in favor of intervention claimed that sovereignty was changing in ways that increased our mutual responsibilities. Famously, the International Commission on Intervention and State Sovereignty argued that sovereignty meant responsibility and that when the state is unable to fulfill its responsibilities, then that responsibility is inherited by the international community. An international community worthy of its name required that the strongest members look after the weakest.[20] The international humanitarian order, almost by definition, divided the world between those who were too weak to help themselves and those who now had responsibilities to save them.

These changes in the conception, meaning, and practices of international order heralded the emergence of one of the post-Cold War's central buzz-words: global governance. There were several important developments directly related to governance practices in the international security and humanitarian orders. Whereas once it was largely a state-centric governance model, now a panoply of actors, including states, international organizations, and even nongovernmental organizations were part of governance structures.[21] Responsibility for restoring sovereignty and protecting human security increasingly fell to a growing layer of international bureaucrats.[22]

Also, paralleling the earlier distinction between regulative and constitutive norms, scholars and practitioners employed the concept of global governance in two distinctive ways. The dominant definition revolved around the coordination of people's activities in ways that achieve more desirable outcomes. Governance, in this view, involves resolving conflicts and/or overcoming inefficiencies between actors in situations of interdependent choice. Yet governance is not only about regulating what already exists and producing more cooperation at lesser cost, it also includes other aspects that are examined in various ways in this volume.

- What is the social purpose of governance? Is governance designed to maintain stability or promote a particular conception of progress? Is progress defined only in terms of an increase in wealth or does it also include the development of new kinds of relationships between the haves and have-nots, the fortunate and the unfortunate?
- What areas of life are to be governed? One of the impressive features of modern global governance is the steady expansion of the areas of life that need to be governed, from economic productivity, to human rights, to reproductive rights. Is this steady expansion due simply to the technical requirements of the issue? How are these areas understood in relationship to one another? During the Cold War the international and the domestic order were considered to be relatively independent domains, but since the end of the Cold War areas once delegated to the state are now seen as part of a "collective responsibility" and thus can be governed by a more complex architecture. What is the relationship between global governance and international order? Does an expansion of global governance activities blur the boundaries between economic, security, and humanitarian orders?
- How is a particular meaning of humanitarianism fixed and accepted? Humanitarianism can mean emergency relief in order to keep people alive or broader interventions to try and mitigate the underlying causes of suffering. How does one meaning become increasingly hegemonic?
- Who governs whom? How, when, and in what ways did international nongovernmental organizations become integrated into the architecture of global governance? How does their integration help to produce the subjects that need to be governed? Do self-defined humanitarians need

a world of vulnerable populations imagined to be too weak to help themselves?

Any discussion of international order and governance involves consider-ations of power—and the international humanitarian order and humani-tarian governance are no exceptions—even though they are frequently treated as if they have ethical purity and are a remedy to power (a percep-tion that members of this order certainly perpetuate and benefit from). Power exists in all social relationships and the fundamental question is not whether power exists, a formulation that I find nonsensical, but rather the forms of power that exist, the mechanisms by which they operate, how the different forms cohabit in any concrete social formation, and the effects that they have on the capacity for peoples to determine their fate.[23]

Consider the analysis of the UNHCR in "Humanitarianism with a sover-eign face" (Chapter 5). The UNHCR exhibits compulsory power because it can directly shape the behavior of states. It can name and shame governments who violate international refugee law, and thus improve the circumstances of refugees. UNHCR protection officers can confer or deny refugee status, a matter of life or death for many refugees. UNHCR also exhibits institutional power because it shapes indirectly the behavior of states through its agenda setting capacities and ability to frame "problems" as part of its jurisdiction and competence. Pushing to expand the category of refugees to include those once seen outside its jurisdiction provides opportunities for new kinds of interventions and extends new forms of protections to those who might otherwise be exposed to the elements.

In addition to compulsory and institutional power, the case of the UNHCR also raises the presence of productive power, how underlying discourses produce social kinds, make possible, imaginable, and desirable certain kinds of actions, and distribute unevenly social capacities to actors that are situated in distinct social positions. Changes in global discourses had a palpable impact on the debate at the UNHCR regarding what kind of organization it is—whether it is a representative of states, of refugees, or some combination of the two. The development of new social practices, including new forms of intervention during times of war, also shaped the ontological debate. In other words, practices helped to shape identity and identity helped to shape prac-tices. UNHCR was also a beneficiary of a growing trend toward more and more interventions justified on the grounds that they would improve human welfare. Indeed, whereas once scholars and practitioners valued non-intervention because it was central to sovereignty and maintaining inter-national stability, after the Cold War the exact opposite argument grew in favor: relaxing sovereignty to allow for various forms of intervention was central for creating and maintaining international order. This changing fortune was particularly evident in the area of humanitarian intervention: during the Cold War most states reflexively condemned any act of so-called humanitarian intervention, but afterwards an emerging central concern was underprovision—many deserving cases were now "orphaned." UNHCR accumulated considerable institutional authority after the end of the Cold War, authority it claimed would immediately benefit refugees. Yet to what extent did this scaling up of decisional authority make it more difficult for refugees to control their fates? Did UNHCR justify its authority on the grounds that refugees, by definition, were helpless? What happens when global governance becomes scaled up, bureaucratized, and treated as an increasingly complex system? Does authority shift from local actors to public international bureaucracies? What are the normative implications of such a shift?

My attempt to understand how productive power operates in the international humanitarian order forced me to engage international ethics in two ways that I discovered were out of sync with their prevailing treatment by scholars of global governance. I was less concerned with how particular practices measured up to some quasi-Platonic conception of international ethics and more concerned with the cultural and historical production of ethics. Many scholars of international ethics rely on transhistorical conceptions of what is just, fair, and good to evaluate international actions and outcomes, particularly evident in utilitarian writings on global poverty and neo-Kantian writings on international human rights. There is nothing objectionable about such exercises; in fact, they can guard against moral complacency or self-satisfaction because they suggest that we can do better and are an important source for our moral imagination. However, it is equally important to understand how a people define what is proper and good at any historical moment. Whereas some religious doctrines and natural rights might always find slavery sinful, for most of human history it was seen as part of the natural (if unfortunate) order of things. An implication of attempting to understand how individuals and collectives define what counts as ethically defensible action is that we become much more sensitive to how the same behavior that we might condemn might be defensible to those engaged in such practices.

I will have more to say in the conclusion regarding whether or not developments in the international humanitarian order are indicators of moral progress, but for the moment I feel compelled to explain why my writings gravitated from a slightly hopeful register during the mid-1990s to a more serious investigation of the "dark side" of the very humanitarian institutions that were supposed to rescue the vulnerable and humanize a state-centric world. Much like aid workers from the pre-Rwanda days who assumed that just showing up would produce good outcomes, a fair bit of scholarship assumed that the institutionalization of the international humanitarian order was a victory of ethics over power. Sometimes moral institutions disappoint, but even their disappointments were often excused because they have little power in comparison to states—colorfully illustrated by Richard Holbrooke's recent observation that it makes no more sense to blame the UN for Rwanda than it does to blame Madison Square Garden for the poor performance of the New York Knicks.[24]

Yet trailing behind these studies in ethical progress were those who were not so certain that every step toward ethics was a victory for progress. Some scholars worried that: the search for justice might undermine the more fundamental need for order; the expansion of "oughts" only deepened the world's hypocrisy; unsavory actors were manipulating these norms to further their goals; these principled actors were only able to have an effect when states let them, and when states said "no" these principled actors found themselves constrained to the point of being co-opted; and aid organizations can act just like the typical organization because it is constantly searching for resources. These dissents raised important issues regarding the effects of the international humanitarian order, but they largely presumed that those who staffed these organizations were who they said they were: devout practitioners of principled action.[25] It seemed no more polite to question their motives than to question those of Mother Teresa's.

I began to wonder after considerable soul-searching in response to one of the twentieth century's darkest chapters: the genocide in Rwanda. At the time of the genocide I was working at the U.S. Mission to the United Nations and assigned to cover Rwanda (in addition to other sub-Saharan peacekeeping operations). Like many others at that moment, I had grave doubts regarding whether a humanitarian intervention might stop the genocide, and worried that the UN was, once again and just like in Somalia and Bosnia, about to be a sacrificial lamb. Fearing the Security Council would send an undermanned and token peacekeeping force to certain defeat at the same moment that the United States had just finished its withdrawal from Somalia and ten Belgian peacekeepers had been killed at the beginning of the genocide, I and others spent considerable energy debating how to justify non-intervention.

About a year after the genocide I began to question why I was so intent on arguing that not intervening was ethical even in the face of genocide, and a few months after that I learned that high-ranking UN officials, including Secretary-General Boutros-Ghali and Under-Secretary for Peacekeeping Operations General Kofi Annan, had been receiving detailed recommendations from Force Commander General Romeo Dallaire, including a fairly well-conceived plan for intervention. This was news. During the first weeks of the genocide the Secretary-General's office consistently and repeatedly told the Security Council that it had not received any concrete suggestions from Dallaire, intimating that he was too overwhelmed by events to develop any contingency plan. Why the Secretary-General's office would withhold information that would provide fuel for an intervention became something of an obsession of mine for the next several years.[26] I had my doubts that the Security Council would have acted differently had Dallaire's recommendations become part of the debate, and I also am not as confident as others that an intervention would have worked. But, in many respects, that was beside the point—the point was that UN officials were acting just like state officials. I could understand why the United States, for instance, wanted to stay away from the genocide; indeed, there was no great mystery why most states would choose to sit out and why those who supported intervention were keen to volunteer other countries' soldiers. But why would UN officials—who present themselves as acting in the name of the international community and as defenders of the genocide convention—believe that it was proper and correct to ignore genocide? As I discuss in "The UN Security Council, indifference, and genocide in Rwanda" (Chapter 6), my answers orbited around the transfiguration of ethics once they are institutionalized, and how changes in bureaucratic rules can subtly but consequentially change the moral compass used by the staff of humanitarian institutions to decide what is the right thing to do.

This conclusion forced me to go beyond the general trend in constructivist theorizing that focused on how principled actors have softened the sharp-elbowed world of interests, civilized states, and transformed the very structure of world politics. I became more interested in the origins of the principles of these principled actors and how their principles evolve in unexpected and not necessarily desirable ways, a central theme of the article "Humanitarianism transformed" (Chapter 9). If ethical scruples are shaped by the environment and the environment is defined by powerful actors such as self-regarding states, then the environment contains mechanisms that can and do force principled actors to develop in ways that potentially increases their "fitness" to survive in the same environments that they want to change.[27] There are many examples of the possibility of the practical ethics of aid agencies becoming politicized, mainstreamed, and tamed as a consequence of external pressures and the attempt by humanitarian actors to find a pragmatic path. As I argue in "Humanitarianism with a sovereign face" (Chapter 5), the UNHCR continually accommodated itself to the interests and ethics of states. This does not mean that it no longer tried to represent the interests of refugees, but it does suggest that its interpretation of what are those interests might be more aligned with the view from states than they are the view from refugees. Exactly how so, and with what implications, is explored in the piece "UNHCR and the ethics of repatriation" (Chapter 7). ICRC's principles, and especially its vow of silence, was itself a response to a world of sovereign states, and the Red Cross movement later became defined by patriotic nationalism that suffocated cosmopolitanism.[28] NGOs (and international organizations) might themselves be helping to reproduce and expand the very world order that they claim to resist. In fact, many humanitarian agencies worry that their agendas are serving the interests of powerful states, that they are furthering a liberal world order that advantages some over others, and that they are part of governance structures that place them in positions of power over the very people they claim to want to emancipate. As I argue in "Humanitarianism transformed" (Chapter 9), they are right to be worried.

The Introduction brushes against two themes that will get more attention in the conclusion—progress and power. Although the international humanitarian order is often considered to be a measure of progress, one of the striking features of the debates in its core constituencies is the general malaise, caused in part because of a recent history of setbacks, struggles, and accumulating self-doubts. Yet the order retains a loyal following. Why? One possibility is that the order reflects not only the needs of those in distress but also the needs of those who can give—needs that are not material but rather spiritual. The international humanitarian order, in other words, is connected not only to cosmopolitanism but also to transcendentalism and the desire to find an other-worldly meaning in everyday practices and to maintain a sense of enchantment in a world of disenchantment. If so, the international humanitarian order becomes the place where individuals express and locate the possibility of progress.

Such aspirations, however, can create the dangerous delusion that the international humanitarian order operates free from power and politics. Yet, as discussed earlier, the order did not somehow, miraculously, solve power; instead, different forms of power tend to dominate. The presence of power in the international humanitarian order, I argue, is best captured by the concept of paternalism. The siren of progress alongside the presence of power can create considerable anxiety for practitioners—shaking their confidence that they are acting properly. This anxiety, I will suggest, is welcome, opening the possibility of space for those who are frequently defined as unable to help themselves. The international humanitarian order also challenges scholars to engage the world of ethics and practice, an engagement that also is guaranteed to unleash anxiety among scholars who too often find comfort in being distant from the world that they want to study.

Notes

1 Didier Fassin, "Humanitarianism: a Nongovernmental Government," in Michael Feher, ed., *Nongovernmental Politics* (New York: Zone Books, 2007), p. 151.
2 I develop this argument in Michael Barnett, *In a World of Hurt* (Ithaca: Cornell University Press, forthcoming).
3 For related claims, see the application of biopolitics to humanitarianism by Peter Redfield, "Triage, Sacrifice, and the Sacrificial International Order," in M. Barnett and T. Weiss, eds., *Humanitarianism in Question: Politics, Power, Ethics* (Ithaca: Cornell University Press, 2008); and Jean-Herve Bradol, "The Sacrificial International Order," in Fabrice Weissman, ed., *In the Shadow of "Just Wars": Violence, Politics, and Humanitarian Action* (Ithaca: Cornell University Press, 2004). For a fascinating study of biopolitics without the Foucault, see Matthew Connelly, *Fatal Misconception: The Struggle to Control World Population* (Cambridge, MA: Harvard University Press, 2008).
4 Jeff Legro, *Rethinking the World: Great Power Strategies and International Order* (Ithaca: Cornell University Press, 2007); Elizabeth Borgwardt, *A New Deal for the World: America's Vision for Human Rights* (Cambridge, MA: Harvard University Press, 2007); G. John Ikenberry, *After Victory* (Princeton: Princeton University Press, 2000); G. John Ruggie, ed., *Multilateralism Matters* (New York: Columbia University Press, 1992).

5 This is not the place to review the controversies, interpretations, and strands. For a sampling, see Alexander Wendt, *A Social Theory of International Politics*; Martha Finnemore and Kathryn Sikkink, "International Norms and Political Change," in P. Katzenstein et al., eds., *Explorations and Controversies in World Politics* (Cambridge, MA: MIT Press, 1999), 247–78; Emanuel Adler, "Constructivism," in *Handbook of International Relations* (T. Risse, Beth Simmons, eds., Thousand Oaks, California: Sage Press, 2000), 95–118; John Ruggie, "What Makes the World Hang Together?" Neo-utilitarianism and the Social Constructivist Challenge," International Organization, 52, 1998, 855–85. Martha Finnemore and Kathryn Sikkink, "Taking Stock: The Constructivist Research Program in International Relations and Comparative Politics," *Annual Review of Political Science*, 4, 2001, 391–416; Emanuel Adler, "Seizing the Middle Ground: Constructivism in World Politics," *European Journal of International Relations*, 3, 3, September 1997, 291–318; Stephan Guzzini, "A Reconstruction of Constructivism in International Relations," *European Journal of International Relations*, 6, 2, June 2000, 147–182; and Ian Hurd, "Constructivism," in Chris Reus-Smit and Duncan Snidal, eds., *The Oxford Handbook of International Relations* (New York: Oxford University Press, 2008), 298–316.

6 For good statements on international legitimacy, see Chris Reus-Smit and Ian Clark, eds., "Special Issue: Resolving International Crises of Legitimacy," *International Politics*, 44, 2–3, 2007; Ian Clark, *International Legitimacy and World Society* (New York: Oxford University Press, 2007); and Hilary Charlesworth and Jean Marc Coicaud, eds., *Fault Lines of International Legitimacy* (New York: Cambridge University Press, 2009).

7 On end of history, see Francis Fukuyama, "The End of History," *National Interest*, summer 1989. On liberalism and international governance, see Michael Barnett and Martha Finnemore, "The Power of Liberal International Organizations," in Michael Barnett and Raymond Duvall, eds., *Power in Global Governance* (New York: Cambridge University Press, 2005), 161–85.

8 For other statements on legitimacy and the UN, see Ian Hurd, *After Anarchy: Legitimacy and Power at the UN Security Council* (Princeton: Princeton University Press, 2007); Ian Hurd and Bruce Cronin, eds., *The UN Security Council and the Politics of International Authority* (New York: Routledge, 2008); and Ian Hurd, "Legitimacy, Power, and the Symbolic Life of the Security Council," *Global Governance*, 8, 1, 2002, 35–51.

9 Nina Tannenwald, "The Nuclear Taboo: The United States and the Normative Basis of Nuclear Non-Use," *International Organization* 53, 3, Summer 1999, 433–468.

10 R. Daniel Kelemen and Eric Sibbitt, "The Globalization of American Law," *International Organization*, 58, Winter, 1, 2004, 103–136; Beth Simmons and Zachary Elkins, "The Globalization of Liberalization: Policy Diffusion in the International Political Economy," *American Political Science Review*, 98, 1, February, 2004, 171–190; Amitav Acharya, "How Ideas Spread: Whose Norms Matter? Norm Localization and Institutional Change in Asian Integration," *International Organization*, 58, Spring 2004, 239–75; and Frank Dobbins, Geoff Garrett, and Beth Simmons, eds., Special Issue on "International Diffusion," *International Organization*, 60, 4, October 2006.

11 Shogo Suzuki, "Japan's Socialization into Janus–Faced European International Society," *European Journal of International Relations*, 11, 1, 2005, 137–164; Trine Flockhart, "Complex Socialization: A Framework for the Study of State Socialization," *European Journal of International Relations* 12, 1, 2006, 89–118; Jeff Checkel, special issue on "Socialization," *International Organization*, 59, 4, 2005; Judith Kelley, "International Actors on the Domestic Scene: Membership Conditionality and Socialization by International Institutions," *International Organization*, 58, 3, Summer 2004, 425–458.

12 For strategic social construction, see Martha Finnemore and Kathryn Sikkink, "International Norm Dynamics and Political Change," and Catherine Weaver, "Normative Tactics: The Strategic Social Construction of the World Bank's Gender Development Policy Norm," Paper presented at the annual meeting of the ISA's 50th annual convention, February 15, 2009.

13 John Ikenberry and Charles Kupchan, "Socialization and Hegemonic Power," *International Organization*, 44, 3, 1990, 283–316.

14 David Chandler, *From Kosovo to Kabul and Beyond: Human Rights and International Intervention* (London: Pluto Press, 2006); Roland Paris, "Human Security: Paradigm Shift or Hot Air?" *International Security*, 26, 2, 2001, 87–102.

15 Robert Cooper, *The Breaking of Nations: Order and Chaos in the Twenty-First Century* (London: Atlantic Books, 2003); Robert I. Rotberg, "The New Nature of Nation-State Failure," *Washington Quarterly*, 25, 3, 2002, 85–96; White House, *The National Security Strategy of the United States of America*, 2002; James Dobbins et al., *The Beginner's Guide to Nation-Building* (Santa Monica, CA: RAND, 2007); *Foreign Policy*, annual ranking of weak states.

16 Stephen Krasner and Carlos Pasqual, "Addressing State Failure," *Foreign Affairs*, 84, 4, 2005, 153–163; Jeffry Herbst, "Let Them Fail: State Failure in Theory and Practice: Implications for Policy," in R. I. Rotberg, ed., *When States Fail: Causes and Consequences* (Princeton: Princeton University Press 2003); Ashraf Ghani and Claire Lockhart, *Fixing Fragile States* (New York: Oxford University Press, 2008); F. Fukuyama, *State-Building: Governance and World Order in the Twenty-First Century* (Ithaca: Cornell University Press, 2003); Simon Chesterman, M. Ignatieff, M. and R. Thakur, eds., *Making States Work: State Failure and the Crisis of Governance* (Tokyo: United Nations University, 2005); G. B. Helman and S. R. Ratner, "Saving Failed States," *Foreign Policy*, 89, 1993, 3–21; C. Rice, "The Promise of Democratic Peace: Why Promoting Freedom is the Only Realistic Path to Security," *Washington Post*, December 11, 2005.

17 On liberal peacebuilding, see Roland Paris, *At War's End: Building Peace after Civil Conflict* (Cambridge: Cambridge University Press, 2004); Roland Paris, "International Peacebuilding and the 'Mission Civilisatrice'," *Review of International Studies*, 28, 4, October 2002, 637–656. For a slightly more optimistic assessment, see Richard Ponzio, "Transforming Political Authority: UN Democratic Peacebuilding in Afghanistan," *Global Governance*, 13, 2, 2007, 255–275.

18 The presence of all these actors can lead to considerable confusion on the ground. See Kathleen Jennings, "Unclear Ends, Unclear Means: Reintegration in Postwar Societies—The Case of Liberia," *Global Governance*, 14, 3, 2008, 327–345.

19 On peacebuilding as statebuilding, see David Chandler, *Empire in Denial: The Politics of State-Building* (London: Pluto Press, 2006); Mark Duffield, *Global Governance and the New Wars: The Merging of Development and Security* (London: Zed Books, 2001); Aidan Hehir and Neil Robinson, eds., *State-Building: Theory and Practice* (London: Routledge, 2007); Charles Call with Vanessa Wyeth, eds., *Building States to Build Peace* (Boulder: Lynne Reinner, 2008); Roland Paris and Timothy Zisk, eds., *The Dilemmas of Statebuilding: Confronting the Contradictions of Postwar Peace Operations* (New York: Routledge, 2008); Michael Wesley, "The State of the Art on the Art of State Building," *Global Governance*, 14, 3, 2008, 369–385.

20 On the relationship between sovereignty, responsibility, and intervention, see Kofi Annan, "Two Concepts of Sovereignty," *The Economist*, September 18, 1999; Francis Deng et al., *Sovereignty as Responsibility: Conflict Management in Africa* (Washington, D.C.: Brookings, 1996); William Bain, *Between Anarchy and Society: Trusteeship and the Obligations of Power* (Oxford: Oxford University Press, 2003); International Commission on Intervention and State Sovereignty, *Responsibility to Protect* (Ottawa: International Development Research Centre,

2001); International Commission on Intervention and State Sovereignty, *The Responsibility to Protect: Research, Bibliography, Background* (Ottawa: International Development Research Centre, 2001); Gareth Evans, *Responsibility to Protect* (Washington, D.C.: Brookings Press, 2008); Alex Bellamy, "Conflict Prevention and the Responsibility to Protect," *Global Governance*, 14, 2, 2008, 135–156; David Chandler, "The Responsibility to Protect: Imposing the 'Liberal Peace'?" *International Peacekeeping*, 11, 1, 2004, 59–81; Jane Krishnadas, "Rights to Govern Lives in Postdisaster Reconstruction Processes," *Global Governance*, 14, 3, 2008, 347–367.

21 John Ruggie, "Reconstituting the Global Public Domain: Issues, Actors, and Practices," *European Journal of International Relations*, 10, 4, December 2004, 499–532.

22 Dominik Zaum, *The Sovereignty Paradox: The Norms and Politics of International Statebuilding* (Oxford: Oxford University Press, 2007); James Fearon and David Laitin, "Neotrusteeship and the Problem of Weak States," *International Security*, 28, 4, 2004, 5–43; Stephen Krasner, "Sharing Sovereignty: New Institutions for Collapsing and Failing States," *International Security*, 29, 2, 2004, 5–43; Richard Caplan, *International Governance of War-Torn Territories* (Oxford: Oxford University Press, 2005).

23 See Michael Barnett and Raymond Duvall, "Power in International Relations," *International Organization*, 59, Winter 2005, 39–75.

24 Quoted from Gareth Evans, *Responsibility to Protect* (Washington, D.C.: Brookings Press, 2008), p. 175.

25 David Rieff, *A Bed for the Night: Humanitarianism in Crisis* (New York: Simon and Schuster, 2002); David Kennedy, *The Dark Side of Virtue: Humanitarianism Reassessed* (Princeton: Princeton University Press, 2004); Alex de Waal, *Famine Crimes* (Bloomington: Indiana University Press, 1998); Fiona Terry, *Condemned to Repeat?* (Ithaca: Cornell University Press, 2002); Alex Cooley and James Ron, "The NGO Scramble," *International Security* 27, 1, 2002, 5–39; and Clifford Bob, *The Marketing of Rebellion: Insurgents, Media and International Activism* (New York: Cambridge University Press, 2005).

26 Michael Barnett, *Eyewitness to a Genocide: The United Nations and Rwanda* (Ithaca: Cornell University Press, 2002).

27 I explicitly develop this argument in Michael Barnett, "Evolution Without Progress? Humanitarianism in a World of Hurt," *International Organization*, 63, 4, 2009, 621–43.

28 John Hutchinson, *Champions of Charity: War and the Rise of the Red Cross* (Boulder: Westview Press, 1997).

Section I
UN and world order

2 Bringing in the new world order

Liberalism, legitimacy, and the United Nations

Boutros Boutros-Ghali. *Agenda for Peace*, **2d ed.** New York: United Nations, 1995, 159 pp.

Commission on Global Governance. *Our Global Neighborhood*. New York: Oxford University Press, 1995, 410 pp.

Gareth Evans. *Cooperating for Peace*. St. Leonards, Australia: Unwin and Hyman, 1993, 224 pp.

Report of the Independent Working Group on the Future of the United Nations. *The United Nations in Its Second Half-Century*. New York: Ford Foundation, 1995, 53 pp.

The end of the cold war and the attendant security vacuum unleashed a flurry of intellectual activity, including numerous commissions, that reflected on the world that was being left behind and the world that should be created in its place. The reports under review in this article are among the best and most influential of the lot, and they have two defining qualities. The first is the attempt to capitalize on the post-cold war moment to escape the pessimism of realism and to envision an international order secured without the threat of force. These reports share the belief that multilateralism must supplant the security practices that defined the cold war, that the language of assurance must replace the language of deterrence, and that states should build institutions rather than militaries. Second, these reports advocate strengthening the role of the United Nations in security politics. The UN was already flexing its long-atrophying muscles at the close of the cold war as it helped many protracted regional and domestic conflicts to wind down, served as a central player during the Gulf War, and undertook numerous peacekeeping operations of tremendous complexity, scope, and size. The international body, once relegated to the back seat in security matters, had become the darling of the hour, a development these reports want to see become permanent rather than transitory. The reports discussed here wax eloquent about the transformational possibilities for global politics and about the role of the UN as the prospective global deliverer.

The reports have been overtaken by events, however. They began their inquiries during the optimistic period of the early 1990s but began publishing their findings just as the UN was suffering a series of setbacks, most notably in Somalia, Rwanda, and Bosnia. While the commissions were painting a progressive shift in global politics and advocating a central role for the UN in security affairs, many parts of the world where the UN was present were descending into chaos if not hell—and arguably with the assistance of the UN. Furthermore, states demonstrated through their pocketbook an unwillingness to see a strengthened UN. Consequently, the news conferences announcing publication of the findings of the various commissions were greeted with little enthusiasm and much cynicism. Their reception symbolized the UN's hard times.

Arguably few international relations scholars were surprised by this turn of events. The UN has long labored under theoretical obscurity because of the general view that it is a bit player, first, on the global scene and, second, in terms of the central research questions of the discipline.[1] Realists and institutionalists largely agree on the false promise of the UN. Neorealists view institutions as permissive and subservient to power politics and therefore dismiss a role for the UN in global security because it lacks enforcement mechanisms that are independent of state interests. Waltz's *Theory of International Politics*, the bible of neorealism, speaks volumes with its near silence on the UN;[2] and the UN's post-cold war activities have elicited strong reaction from prominent neorealists, but usually to bury them and not to praise them.[3] Policymakers have repeatedly demonstrated a willingness to weave grand dreams of a global order secured through institutions, but these dreams have invariably been shattered by the timeless realities of state interests.

Although these reports draw on many institutionalist insights, few neoliberal institutionalists have examined the UN's potential contribution to international security. Perhaps for good reason. The conditions under which they posit that institutions "matter"—when actors have convergent interests and desire to establish norms to overcome collective action and coordination problems—are not present when it comes to the UN and the area of security. During the cold war the great powers rarely turned to the UN as a forum for dispute settlement (except for some peacekeeping episodes), and when they did have convergent security interests they avoided the UN in favor of institutional arrangements that they could more readily control. That the major powers turned to the UN after the cold war reflects that, albeit temporarily, they had converging interests.[4] But the UN's recent decline suggests either that those converging interests have now diverged or that the major powers have found other institutional arrangements to further their security. While neoliberals have broadened their empirical scope to include security, they know better than to stake their credentials or their theories on the UN. Neorealism and neoliberal institutionalism then are in league in their dismissal of the UN, sharing as they do the general belief that international order is founded on force coupled with institutional restraints that are supported by a convergence of state interests.

But the reports under review offer an additional message—that international order is produced not only by force coupled with institutional aids but also by legitimacy. Read in this way, these commissions provide a blueprint for how the post-cold war order should be built. To be sure, these reports pay lip service to handing the UN a standing army and a central role in a collective security system, and they insist that the UN be invested with new policy instruments to strengthen its role in conflict resolution. Certainly, if one judges these commissions by whether their proposals have been implemented, then they have failed. But beyond their languishing recommendations, these commissions offer a series of discursive moves and rhetorical arguments about what constitutes legitimate state action and a legitimate international order. Because these reports were looking to the international order that would succeed the cold war, they focus on the constitutive foundations of global politics, how the new international order would be legitimated, what its specific content should be, and how the recalcitrant might come to accept these principles. On such issues, these commissions are suggesting, the UN should occupy a central position.

Three issues stand out. First, the international order valorized in these reports is a liberal order. These reports are informed by a distinctly liberal worldview and recommend a strengthened UN that can facilitate such an outcome. This raises the second issue: legitimacy in global politics. In a series of intriguing observations and hypotheses concerning the legitimation process in global politics at this historical moment, they remind international relations scholars of the potential importance of the concept of legitimacy, a concept that once found a central place in the works of the classical realists but that has fallen out of favor in recent decades.[5] The concept appears in various guises in these reports in terms of (1) how all international orders must be legitimated if they are to have any staying power; (2) how the legitimation principles of a particular order can shape state practices; and (3) how the UN can be the site for the legitimation of a particular order and for holding states accountable to its norms. The UN, they suggest, can shape state practices by establishing, articulating, and transmitting norms that define acceptable and proper state behavior. Third, these commissions understand that not all actors will find this vision attractive or attainable. Hence, they envision the UN as an agent of normative integration that can increase the number of actors who identify with and uphold the values of a liberal international order. This chapter is organized according to these three central themes.

Overview of four commissions

Some background information about the central orientations of these reports is in order. Boutros-Ghali's *Agenda for Peace* was the first to appear and is the cornerstone of the other documents under review. Undertaken at the request of a Security Council that was reeling from the growing demands placed on its agenda, *Agenda for Peace* was drafted by various longtime UN hands (including James Sutterlin, now in residence at Yale University) to fashion the role of the United Nations in the post-cold war order. *Agenda for Peace* immediately became the subject of controversy and vigorous debate. Third World states worried that Boutros-Ghali's vision handed more power to a Security Council that was controlled by the great powers, which, in turn, might threaten their sovereignty. In turn, the great powers—that is, the permanent members of the Security Council—feared that a strengthened UN might reduce their autonomy and power. Notwithstanding these reservations, the absence of any other blueprint on the security agenda guaranteed that *Agenda for Peace* would shape the debate on the post-cold war order. And indeed at the UN and in capitals throughout the world, member states debated its various proposals and its call for a revitalized UN.

Many of its specific proposals were not warmly received, notably for a standing UN army; and others that had been discussed initially, notably for a greater role in peace enforcement, have now been discarded because of recent setbacks. Nevertheless, its broad conceptualization of security and the future international order continues to inform the thinking of many policymakers. Specifically, *Agenda for Peace* suggests that (1) the threat of domestic insecurity is a legitimate concern of the UN because it has the potential to undermine regional security and any semblance of a cosmopolitan sensibility; and that (2) conflict has a life cycle, from preventive measures to peacekeeping and peace enforcement to postconflict nation building. This highly provocative and far-reaching document is testimony not only to its times and the UN's now departed secretary-general but also to a particular moment in world politics. That Boutros-Ghali's vision exceeded what member states were ready to accept was generally conceded in his *Addendum to the Agenda for Peace*: gone are the more ambitious proposals such as a standing army under the direction of the secretary-general and ever present is the notion that the UN will have to delegate tasks and responsibilities to other state and nonstate actors and learn to work with them as it attempts to fulfill its increasingly modest security agenda.

Gareth Evans's *Cooperating for Peace* represents another synthetic statement on the role of the UN and regional organizations in shaping the face of security and countering the new security threats. Evans, Australia's foreign minister, desired to weigh in on the post-cold war security debates and timed the publication of the book to coincide with the opening of the 1993 General Assembly. Written with considerable input from scholars at Australian National University, the blue book was well received and quickly viewed as a necessary companion to *Agenda for Peace*.[6] Evans is most concerned with the new security threats that emanate from domestic rather than from traditional interstate conflicts, and he offers a set of measured categories—peace building, peace maintenance, peace restoration, and peace enforcement—to meet the severity of the conflict. His proposed solution, cooperative security, reflects the attempt to find a middle ground between the concepts of common and collective security, which, in his view, are too focused on military solutions, and the concept of comprehensive security, which is, well, too comprehensive to be of much value to policymakers.[7] Attached to these concepts are a series of proposals—including a greater use of sanctions, the establishment of new peacekeeping training centers, and expanded roles for civilian police—that will better enable the United Nations to establish international regimes and engage in in-country reconstruction. According to Evans, international regimes and domestic reconstruction are the twin paths to a stable international order.

Our Global Neighborhood, the product of the Commission on Global Governance, a distinguished panel of experts and policymakers, represents a self-conscious attempt to consider the future global order by synthesizing and extending many of the central arguments of prior commissions on the future of the world economy, security, and environment.[8] It should be noted that the background papers for the commission were written by liberal-minded scholars, including Ernst Haas and Peter Haas, and nowhere in the bibliography or citations is there a submission that is identifiable as realist.[9] The report is striking for its willingness to entertain numerous proposals designed to alter how states conduct their relations and organize their security.

While many of the proposals are familiar and draw on the ideas found in *Agenda for Peace* and *Cooperating for Peace*, it goes beyond them in five respects. First, it focuses on the UN's role in economic, social, and environmental matters because an increasingly complex and integrated global polity requires similarly comprehensive international organizations. Second, it argues that traditional notions of security, defined by the state's defense of its territorial borders, do not exhaust the meaning of security in the current era; that is, since security has environmental, economic, and humanitarian components, the concept of security must be shifted away from its locus on the state and toward individuals. Third, *Our Global Neighborhood* is less constrained by or committed to the idea of state sovereignty than is Evans, who is unapologetically statist, or Boutros-Ghali, who as secretary-general of an interstate organization is also committed to sovereignty. Indeed, the vision of global governance in *Our Global Neighborhood* situates states alongside international and regional organizations, nongovernmental and intergovernmental organizations, and other transnational actors. Fourth, it is most explicit in its interest in issues of governance and seeing the UN as the most likely candidate to guide the ongoing global transformation. Fifth, the commission found it imperative to address the question of the values of global society and devotes an entire chapter to the subject.

Finally, the Report of the Independent Working Group on the Future of the United Nations, *The United Nations in Its Second Half-Century* (Independent Working Group), also examines the relationship between the future course of global politics and the potential functions of the UN. The project (funded by the Ford Foundation, supported by the Secretariat, and overseen by Paul Kennedy and Bruce Russett of Yale University) resembles *Our Global Neighborhood* in three important respects. First, it situated the

UN within a global context that is marked by a growing and deepening interdependence. Second, it offers an integrated view of global politics and invests tremendous effort in developing proposals for the UN's security instruments and increasing its economic and social functions in ways that will enable it to manage the intensifying effects of interdependence. Third, it devotes considerable discussion to the need of the international community to "save failed states."[10] This agenda item is justified on principled, political, and strategic grounds: by saving failed states, the international community will better that community and foster a more stable international order.

Each of the four reports offers a far-reaching vision of the current challenges to a stable international order, as well as numerous proposals for stabilizing that order. Even in better times, which these are not, most of these proposals would not likely see the light of day. Nonetheless, despite the inhospitable climate, some reforms continue. For instance, steps have been taken to establish effective stand-by arrangements for peacekeeping forces; there have been important developments for effecting the bureaucratic transition from peacekeeping and peace building; and in February 1997 the first informal consultations took place between the Security Council and several nongovernmental organizations on a matter of international peace and security (the Great Lakes region of Africa). These and other policy reforms receive considerable attention in these reports.[11] But an exclusive focus on how few of the proposals have been implemented risks prematurely dismissing a set of reports that provides a window into, and conceivably contributed to, the legitimation process in global politics.

A liberal international order?

The portrait painted by these reports is, not surprisingly, largely of a liberal international order; after all, many of those involved in the framing, drafting, and writing of these documents are self-described liberals—organic intellectuals (to use Gramsci's term) and epistemic communities (to use the term favored by constructivists).[12] These are intellectuals who believe in progress; the capacity of individuals to learn from the past; the construction of new political institutions to increase freedom and reduce the likelihood of physical violence; and thus the ability to improve the "moral character and material welfare of humankind."[13] But there are four other elements that define these documents as quintessentially liberal.[14]

First, these reports start from the premise that "international relations are being transformed by a process of modernization."[15] The opening pages of the reports detail how thickening economic, political, environmental, cultural, and communicative networks are revolutionizing the texture of global politics. The terms of reference for the Global Governance Commission (p. 366) stress those transformational qualities of global society that exhibit the "forces of integration and division" and thus present it with tremendous "uncertainty, challenge, and opportunity." The Independent Working Group

(p. 4) similarly proclaims: "In the context of global forces unleashed in the past 50 years, only a collective effort can give states the framework and the strength to shape their own destiny in the promising but turbulent times that lie ahead. Our Report derives from this conviction." The communications revolution, continues the Independent Working Group (p. 7), is collapsing space and bringing us into greater contact, for good and for ill. Interdependence and modernization present new opportunities and challenges, and these reports are driven by a fear that interdependence, if unchecked, will have disastrous consequences for both national and international politics.

Second, these reports support the notion that international organizations in general and the UN in particular are needed to deal with the dizzying effects of modernization in these transitional times to help ameliorate conflicts that arise from interdependence.[16] There is historical precedent for this function of the UN: it helped to manage the earlier global transformation from the era of empires and colonialism to the era of sovereignty. As a critical forum for handling the rapid decolonization that followed World War II,[17] the UN justified its intervention on grounds of principle and security and it established numerous institutional mechanisms to encourage a relatively peaceful and speedy transition.[18] Boutros-Ghali observes that the present era, too, defined as it is by globalization and disintegration, demands international organizations like the United Nations.[19] In general, these commissions hold to the liberal tradition that looks to international organizations to help states cope with interdependence.

Specifically, it is the United Nations in their view that is in a position to help the global polity through the difficult times ahead. With respect to security affairs, they endorse multilateralism and advance numerous institutional designs based on the lessons of institutionalism to foster a more stable and secure international order.[20] To this end, the UN can be a neutral forum in which states and nonstate actors can voice their grievances, communicate their preferences, and coordinate their policies. Further, it can establish confidence-building agreements and foster transparency so as to encourage states to adopt a more defensive and less militarized security posture.[21] And finally, it can create oversight and monitoring mechanisms to assure states that others will not defect from their agreements, most famously expressed by the UN's peacekeeping activities.[22] Most of these documents speak directly to the issue of enhancing the UN's ability to oversee and monitor (though not necessarily enforce) international and domestic agreements.

Third, these reports are quite unabashed in promoting the spread of democracy; the days are past when the UN dared not tread in the domestic realm because it feared violating state sovereignty. The world should be populated by democratic states, these reports uniformly claim, on principle and because of peace and security issues. Boutros-Ghali asserts that modern states possess certain constitutive foundations that revolve around democratic principles.[23] *Our Global Neighborhood* (p. 66) links democracy and legitimacy and asserts that the "democratic principle must be ascendant. The need for greater democracy arises out of the close linkage between legitimacy and effectiveness."[24]

The demand for democracy is also justified on peace and security grounds. Whereas the prevailing belief during the cold war had been that international order was premised on balances of power and some regulative norms that produced something akin to an "anarchical society,"[25] the reports under consideration here argue that domestic politics matters and that empirical sovereignty—the notion that states have some degree of legitimacy and control over their society and within their borders—enables states to uphold the norms of international society.[26] Simply stated, the rule of law at home is the foundation of the rule of law abroad.[27] Democracy, according to Boutros-Ghali, is the ultimate guarantor of peace. In the *Agenda for Peace* he writes:

> The authority of the United Nations system to act in this field [human rights] would rest on the consensus that social peace is as important as strategic or political peace. There is an obvious connection between democratic practices—such as the rule of law and transparency in decision making—and the achievement of true peace and security in any new and stable political order.

Gareth Evans (p. 53) enthusiastically seconds the sentiment. Indeed, all four reports take this assumed connection between domestic and international order to justify greater intervention in domestic affairs.

Not only will an international system populated by democratic states decrease the likelihood of interstate war, but democratic states also will reduce the likelihood that domestic tensions will become militarized and internationalized. While the reports acknowledge traditional interstate sources of violence and conflict, they nearly assume that the root causes of most conflicts reside in the domestic sphere. Thus, *Our Global Neighborhood* predicts that even though interstate war is not extinct, "in the years ahead the world is likely to be troubled primarily by eruptions of violence within countries" (p. 81), and the Independent Working Group focuses on intrastate conflict. These reports hold that the patterns of war are shifting and that the best way to minimize domestic violence (and thus the prospect of international violence) is to widen the community of democratic states.

All four reports, particularly *Our Global Neighborhood* and *The United Nations in Its Second Half-Century*, emphasize the importance of human rights as an issue of domestic and international governance. Since the mid-1980s the UN has become quite active in the area of human rights, a change from the cold war period and the era of decolonization, when the United Nations was prohibited by member states from investigating and considering issues of human rights.[28] Today, most peacekeeping operations have a human rights component, and the UN held a World Congress in Vienna in 1993 and established the position of high commissioner for human rights the following year.[29]

Human rights has emerged on the international agenda for several reasons, but one catalyst is the belief that "civilized" states should respect human rights and have some degree of domestic accountability based on democratic principles of rule, because they represent both a means to an end, for example, international order, and an end in itself. The international community increasingly treats respect for human and ethnic rights as a matter of principle and an issue of peace and security.[30] Because of the presumed relationship between domestic and international order, then, these reports look to the UN to articulate the constitutive features of the modern state.

The fourth, liberal, dimension of these reports is the shift away from the sovereign state as the principal actor in global politics and toward, first, identity-based groups such as nations, indigenous peoples, women, and ethnicities, and, second, the individual as a central actor. There has always been tension between the UN's role as representative of sovereign states and its role as representative of peoples and individuals who have universal rights and deserve the protection of the international community. For most of its history the UN has resolved that tension in favor of state sovereignty, but these reports advocate a change in the direction of greater balance. The Global Governance Commission has a chapter on the values of the global community, which states are exhorted to respect; while these values are forwarded as principled rather than liberal, few liberals would object to them. The Independent Working Group advocates the protection of the "social fabric" of societies in which the "rights of every individual are guaranteed by the rule of law, people can participate in their own governance, and disagreements over policy issues are settled peaceably" (p. 34). These reports, moreover, propose a set of institutions—including the rule of law, democracy, and markets—to promote political and economic opportunity and freedom. These reports, then, are attempting to protect individual rights by instilling liberal values within already constituted sovereign states.

Furthermore, as the documents narrate, modernization processes and interdependence are creating new networks of association that include domestic challenges to the state, a proliferation of transnational movements and organizations, and a nascent global civil society. The Global Governance Commission reviews at length the changing ways that individuals identify and locate themselves vis-à-vis other communities. Increased interdependence has created a "common neighborhood," whose members have mutual interests and also share an increasingly common culture. Thus, even if the state remains the primary actor in global politics, the results of interdependence, both positive and negative, are to create new networks and associations, many of which are attempting to guide the state's activities in the domestic and international sphere.

Although NGOs and transnational organizations are playing an increasingly important role in various international issues, they tend to be included in international organizations such as the UN only on an ad hoc basis because such international organizations usually restrict participation to states. Consequently, the Independent Working Group and the Global Governance Commission propose to establish various mechanisms at the UN and its sister organizations to include these nonstate actors more fully in all aspects of the decision-making process. They envision new councils that directly link peoples and the organs of the international community in ways that challenge the state's monopoly on decision-making authority at the global level. The hope is to give domestic groups normative leverage over states that violate the norms of the international community on issues of domestic governance.

To summarize: we can consider these documents to be liberal to the extent that their narratives are informed by a belief in progress: that modernization and interdependence are transforming the character of global politics; that institutions can be established to help manage these changes; that democracy is a principled issue and can enhance peace and security; and that the UN has an obligation to protect individuals, promote universal values, and create institutions that can encourage political and economic freedom. These assertions are more than simply a set of proposals for peace and security, they are also a blueprint for a durable, stable, and legitimate international order. Thus, a recurring theme of these reports is what constitutes legitimate state action and how the UN can gather both the resources and the authority to fulfill this new mandate. Such matters speak directly to the larger issue of legitimacy in global politics.

Legitimacy

In offering positions on what should be the rules of the game and what is considered acceptable behavior, these reports address the concept of legitimacy, both substantive and procedural. First, ends that are considered desirable and the means selected to pursue these ends should be viewed as proper by the relevant political community; and second, the decision-making process should correspond to practice that is deemed proper by the members of the community.[31] Substantive legitimacy dominates the discussion in the reports, although they also consider the importance of institutional reforms for furthering procedural legitimacy, for instance, the need to reform the Security Council and democratize other organs of the United Nations system.

Because political orders are social constructs and a product of material and normative forces, the reports focus on how these orders are produced and the struggles that are waged to establish their legitimation principles. "Politics is not merely a struggle for power," observed Inis Claude, "but also a contest over legitimacy, a competition in which the conferment or denial, the confirmation or revocation, of legitimacy is an important stake."[32] Kissinger began his classic *A World Restored* by stating that the central issue for the post-Napoleonic order was the construction of a set of socially recognized and collectively legitimated principles that determines what is permissible and what is prohibited.[33] In many respects, these reports apply Kissinger's historical concerns to the post-cold war era.

How then are international political orders legitimated? As Claude noted in his classic article, a notable phenomenon of the twentieth century is that the agents of legitimization tend to be international political organizations, and since World War II that function has been nearly monopolized by the UN.[34] These reports reinforce Claude's observation, as the debate over the goals of the international community and the acceptable means to achieve those goals arguably centered in and around the UN, because only there would any emerging arrangements obtain some moral standing and legitimacy. After all, any international political order—or any political order for that matter—needs to be legitimated if it is to have any staying power or be based on anything other than coercion. And the UN provides a forum for collective legitimation, a place where the international order is coronated.

It is impressive how many proposals and discussions about the future international order occurred through the vehicle of the United Nations. Why would major and minor powers alike turn to the United Nations? Various explanations point to material considerations, of course, but it is worth considering the UN's symbolic role in the international community. One of the first acts of an independent state, for example, is to apply for admission to the United Nations, for, as former Secretary-General Pérez de Cuéllar observed, joining the UN is the "final confirmation of independence, nationhood, and sovereignty."[35] These reports articulate both implicitly and sometimes explicitly the necessity of locating a "center" not only to provide the international community with a concrete steering mechanism but also to give it a symbolic footing and some meaning. As Gareth Evans observes, "The world needs a center, and some confidence that the center is holding: the United Nations is the only credible candidate."[36] And as *Our Global Neighborhood* affirms, it is the only international forum that has the legitimacy and stature to operate in these matters. During this period of rapid change and fluidity it can best provide the stabilizing influence needed by the international system.[37]

Following Emile Durkheim, one can ask whether the UN represents the collective beliefs of states in a way that is almost quasi religious in character. "There can be no society," Durkheim wrote, "which does not feel the need of upholding and reaffirming at regular intervals, the collective sentiments and collective ideas which make its unity and its personality."[38] The turn to the UN after the cold war becomes more plausible in light of its symbolic role vis-à-vis the international community. Indeed, the turn to the UN may even be necessitated by "dynamic density," that is, intensifying patterns of interaction that are generating new forms of social organizations and collective representations.[39] In general, even if the principles of the international community embodied in the UN Charter and in its thousands of documents and resolutions do not have the standing of social facts, the UN is still the cathedral of the international community, the organizational repository of the community's collective beliefs.[40]

What is the source of the UN's legitimacy? The UN is the only organization that approximates universality and is invested by states as having some
degree of moral authority. Most simply, it has this legitimacy and authority
by virtue of the fact that member states invest legitimacy in it.[41] To be sure,
the UN's legitimacy has varied over time and across constituencies, but no
other regional or international organization ever emerged to rival it, even
when it was at its lowest ebb.[42] Indeed, whereas neoliberal institutionalism
might view the UN's universality as a potential liability for overcoming collective action problems, these reports hold that it is its very universality that
generates its legitimacy and thus its ability to encourage states to comply with
international norms.

The reports expect the UN to legitimate the broad principles of state
action, not a new role for it. The UN embodies many of the most important
constitutive norms of the international community, norms that, in effect,
prescribe how modern, sovereign states are expected to behave. Dorothy
Jones observes that there are "nine fundamental principles that constitute a
summary of state reflection upon proper action in the international
sphere. . . . All nine can be found in the United Nations Charter but the
authors of the document did not create them."[43] These principles can be
thought of as constitutive norms, for they tell states how to enact their identity as members of the international community; and these norms emerge
from both a climate of fear, that is, a concern for what might happen if these
basic norms were not heeded, and a hope for how the international community ought to operate.[44] And while the architects of the UN did not invent
these norms, the UN gave them an institutional home and legitimacy. The
reports reiterate these principles and stress the importance of renouncing
war (except in self-defense) and unilateral intervention and of embracing a
multilateral sensibility.

States of course do violate these norms of state action, but such violations
do not tell us whether the norms shape state behavior on other occasions; that
is, do states ever alter their actions in order to be viewed as legitimate by other
states? These reports are betting on it. While recognizing that at times there
may be no substitute for the heavy hand of state power—and to this end they
discuss sanctions and multilateral military operations—these documents
posit that states also care about their legitimacy because they are part of an
international community from which they derive their rights, obligations, and
authority to act in legitimately sanctioned ways.[45] Power, these documents are
suggesting, is conferred on those who adhere to the community's values and
norms, and leadership is not only about having military power but also about
projecting moral purpose.[46] Inis Claude contends that if collective legitimization function of the UN shapes states' behavior because, simply put, state
officials have made it important by their actions and statements. The very
demand for this function is its source of power and thus its causal force.[47]

These reports offer various proposals designed to use the UN status and
moral authority to guide state action. Several of the proposals in *Our Global*

Neighborhood can operate only if states care about their reputation. One proposal to stop "grave threats to the security of people" is to develop a Council of Petitions to include a panel of distinguished, independent individuals whose task would be dedicated to safeguarding the security of peoples by making recommendations to the secretary-general and the Security Council. "It would be a Council without any power of enforcement. But the eminence of its members and the quality of its proceedings can foster a measure of respect that will give its conclusions considerable moral authority" (p. 262). The commission also asserts that the easiest and most efficient method for ensuring compliance is through direct contact, publicity, deterrence, and the "mobilization of shame" (p. 328).[48] This highlights one of the UN's most important functions (and one on which it holds a monopoly): to distribute seals of approval and disapproval. "The UN's functions in proclaiming principles and conferring legitimacy," write Roberts and Kingsbury, "remain central to the effective maintenance of international society."[49]

But does the search for legitimacy shape the behavior of the most powerful?

> If legitimate power is . . . power that is valid according to rules, and where the rules themselves are justifiable by and in conformity with the underlying beliefs, then the main way in which the powerful will maintain their legitimacy is by respecting the intrinsic limits set to their power by the rules and the underlying principles on which they are grounded. Legitimate power, that is to say, is limited power.[50]

Power and legitimacy, in short, are not conflicting concepts but rather are complementary ones.[51] The powerful, too, want their actions to be viewed as legitimate, if only to maintain their power and further their interests. Even the powerful, in this view, cannot act in an expedient and narrowly self-interested manner and must observe international society's underlying rules and norms.

Thus it is a striking feature of the post-cold war period that even the most powerful states seek the UN's stamp of approval. While there are materially based reasons for this development, these reports highlight cosmopolitanism.[52] The Global Governance Commission, for instance, suggests that increasing interdependence and a growing global civic identity is one factor in how state officials think about themselves, conceptualize their interests, organize their activities, and desire to have their actions collectively legitimated. The UN's stamp of approval, however, does not come without cost: the operation must be viewed as consistent with the goals of the member states, its very design is subject to amendment during the authorization process. The result is that the member state seeking authorization forfeits considerable autonomy. The reports uniformly celebrate this development.

Such a development may be particularly important in the area of humanitarian intervention. While these documents express tremendous support for the concept of humanitarian intervention, there is the chronic danger that states will claim that their interventions are, by definition, humanitarian, when, in fact, they are designed to further their own interests. For this reason, the reports insist that the authority to legitimate a humanitarian operation must reside with the UN; it need not be the executing agent, but at the very least it should be the authorizing forum that legitimates such actions and ensures that they really are consistent with the goals of the international community and implemented using the means accepted by that community.[53]

In general, these documents are an important contribution to the debate over the post-cold war international order. For them, the UN fulfills a legitimation function in global politics: not only does it potentially legitimate the principles upon which the future international order rests, but the legitimation of those principles carries with it the expectation that states will honor its norms. States will violate these norms to be sure, but the reports are suggesting that states do have available to them various mechanisms for stabilizing their social relations, including their ability to confer or deny approval and legitimacy.

The UN as an agent of normative integration?

As advocates of a liberal international order, these reports will be read differently by their various audiences, depending on how receptive they are to the prospect of such an order and on how they view the role they are supposed to play in bringing it about. The West is the first audience. Sometimes it is subtly chastised for being hypocritical and not abiding by the rules that it established; this is one reading of the emphasis on strengthening the role of international law and the International Court of Justice in adjudicating disputes. More often, however, the most powerful Western states are criticized for not providing the (liberal) leadership role for which they are well suited materially and ideologically. The U.S. is the primary, though unnamed, culprit. While it celebrates liberalism and speaks of enlarging the community of democratic states, it has been wont to support politically and financially the very institution that might operate effectively to this end. The international community needs leadership to accomplish collective action, and the likely leaders are liberal, Western states. These reports, then, are in part attempts to convince Western states of where their interests reside.

The Third World sits in a different place. Arguably, much of the Third World is viewed by these commissions not as a source of support for a liberal international order but rather as a potential site of resistance. Nearly all the reports are concerned with securing the compliance of those most resistant to and most distant from the liberal international order; these are actors located almost exclusively in non-Western societies. This highlights an important feature of the UN: though ostensibly a global organization, it is in fact dedicated to addressing Third World and North–South issues. As Anthony Parsons observes, the UN, far from maintaining a global jurisdiction, is generally "preoccupied with the problems of the newly independent majority, namely the dangerous disputes in the so-called Third World."[54] This focus is as true today as it was during the UN's first forty years. Boutros-Ghali's proclamation that the UN's mandate in this era of globalization-cum-disintegration is to develop markets and impart the rule of law and democracy leaves little uncertainty about the problem and its proposed solution.[55]

This raises a central issue: how do the weak come to give their consent to a political order, especially since the legitimation principles that undergird an international order usually represent the interests of the powerful and operate to their relative advantage.[56] Whether the weak accept an order from which they might not fully benefit depends on whether and how its norms and values come to be universalized and internalized, such that the values of the individual are projected to be the values of humanity.[57] The extent to which this occurs affects the degree to which coercion and selective incentives will be necessary to reproduce a particular order and enhance the prospects for social integration.[58]

These reports identify a number of theories that purport to explain how and why the weak consent to a particular order. The weak are more likely to accept the principles forwarded by the strong, in the first instance, if such principles are convincingly framed as universal rather than particularistic. The very legitimation of these principles by the UN is an important step in this direction. By contrast, resistance is likely if these values are seen as Western in orientation or as fostering the West's continued power in global politics.

Second, the UN conceivably represents a source of state identity and interests by providing the organizational space for interstate interaction. *Our Global Neighborhood* also observes that the UN's deliberative functions— generally disparaged for being all talk all the time—represent a source of new interests, practices, and conceivably identities. Chadwick Alger once observed that interaction among member states at the UN led to a socialization process, fostering new identities and interests.[59] Other scholars too have noted that international organizations represent a site of new identities, interests, and categories of action.[60]

These reports also propose the establishment of various mechanisms and institutions that might help convey norms from the North to the South.[61] If it is successful at this, the United Nations can help to create new categories of actors, new interests for actors to pursue, and new strategies that reflect new identities and interests. The Independent Working Group proposes to establish a social council that is "empowered to supervise and integrate the work of all UN activities relating to issues of social development" and grants nonstate actors access to its deliberations. The other reports, though not proposing new councils, are equally insistent on the need to establish mechanisms by which the UN can regulate those societies that are in "distress."

Indeed, the UN's post-cold war activities can be seen as an attempt to expand the number of actors who are committed to and can be counted as part of a liberal political order. Consider the UN's second-generation peace-keeping operations:[62] they have largely concerned facilitating the transition from civil war to civil society, from "failed state" to a state able to govern itself, by investing it with popular legitimacy and democratic forms of rule that nominally include new constitutions, human rights provisions, elections, and so on.[63] Several of these peacekeeping operations established and trained new civilian police forces modeled along Western lines and designed to foster democratic identities and practices. Most of these reports also advocate channeling more resources into postconflict peace-building measures aimed at resolving conflicts before they escalate.

To summarize, these reports suggest that all international political orders need some measure of legitimacy if they are to be sustained without the threat or deployment of force. At the heart of the matter is the degree to which the weak and those who might not ever or evenly benefit from that order accede to its principles. The more states disagree on fundamental rules, particularly states that view themselves as victims of this system, the more precarious the international order.[64] These reports identify the UN as a central agent for advancing this process of narrowing the number of states that object to a liberal international order and thus for achieving normative integration. In this respect, these reports were written by "sociological liberals," individuals who do not believe that liberalism is an analytic category that stands prior to society but rather believe that liberal individuals and societies emerge from social and historical processes.[65] Conceivably, the UN can contribute to international order by shaping state action through its legitimation function and the articulation and transmission of the norms of state action in domestic and international spheres. At least so these commissions predict.

Conclusion

The reports under consideration represent a debate over the post-cold war international order, the struggle to legitimate a liberal international order, and an attempt to extend the circle of believers. Despite the UN's current financial straits and the political paralysis that weakens its ability to act as an agent of legitimation and norm transmission, the UN nevertheless has symbolic standing and a legitimation function. This function may prove to be particularly important when the rules of the game are in flux, that is, when there is a transition from one order to another or when there are significant challenges to the established order. No other international organization or body has the capacity to legitimate the underlying principles and norms of the international order, so it is to the UN that states turn for legitimation and sanction. These commissions remind international relations scholars that international order is founded not only on a stable balance of power but also on a set of legitimation principles. Certainly, few political orders are ever sustained by shared norms alone, but fewer still have existed for any length of time without them. What classical realist scholars understood has been forgotten by contemporary students of global politics.

If these reports can be taken as indicative of the debate over the substance of the international order, the champions of liberalism seem to be having their day and those who feel otherwise are on the defensive. Liberal principles are accepted in the West; at issue is whether they will be accepted and internalized by non-Western states. These commissions are acting as the missionaries for the post-cold war order, preaching to the converted that the UN can be an important agent of a liberal order and hoping to widen the community of believers. Couched in this way, the discussion directs our attention toward sites of confrontation and contestation and toward the potential mechanisms that encourage the diffusion of this liberal sensibility at the global level. The UN, according to these reports, can play a critical role in both regards. Indeed, the general liberal tenor of the post-cold war order is made even more apparent if the focus is widened from the UN Secretariat to include the other organs of the United Nations system. The World Bank, the UN High Commissioner on Human Rights, the United Nations Development Program, and other organizations generally subscribe to liberal tenets. Taken as a whole, the United Nations system might be read as inextricably involved with the impressive institutional isomorphism of international politics over the last half century.[66]

Yet these reports are silent on the potential contradictions inherent in any international order in general and in liberalism in particular. Thus, they fail to acknowledge that the pursuit of some of the goals of these reports might undermine others. The reports gloss over, for instance, the disputed relationship between economic growth and democracy. They similarly fail to consider how market mechanisms, which are accepted as the proper way to organize an economy, can exacerbate tensions between identity-based groups and perhaps contribute to the disintegration of local communities in already fragile polities. Such tensions are particularly manifest in many postconflict peacebuilding situations where World Bank officials call for fiscal responsibility and structural adjustment-type policies while other parts of the UN system clamor for ethnic peace based on minimizing the costs of postconflict reconstruction. Nor do these reports consider the possible connection between liberalism and inequality.[67] Finally, they tout the construction of international organizations as the panacea for the world's problems without duly noting that while these organizations may be above power politics, they are still fraught with politics. International organizations themselves can become new sites of authority that are unaccountable to either member states or the populations they are mandated to assist, and thus might pursue policies that are at odds with the interests of either of these constituencies.[68]

But this relationship between the UN and these different strands of liberalism directs our attention to the general neglect of the UN by scholars of international relations. Whether international relations theorists consider a role for the UN in the production of international order depends on how they conceptualize international order and security. Neorealism envisions no such role for the UN because the organization does not possess coercive mechanisms or a robust collective security system. Neoliberal institutionalism generally leans toward a neorealist view in that it does not see conditions as being ripe for an effective or vibrant role for the UN. By adhering to a strict rationalism and leaning heavily on materialism, both neorealism and neoliberal institutionalism are hard-pressed to identify much of a role for the UN in the production and maintenance of international order in the ways advocated by these reports.

In contrast to neorealism, which emphasizes coercion and force, and neoliberal institutionalism, which focuses on stabilized exchange relations through norms and institutions, constructivism entertains the possibility that order is also achieved through a normative structure, an acceptance of some basic rules of the game that place normative restrictions on behavior.[69] Not all constructivists are advocates of a liberal worldview or agree that a liberal world would be a pacific world; nor would constructivists argue that coercion and stabilized exchange relations are not important factors in the reproduction of international order. But because constructivism shares with these reports a consideration of how international order is secured through normative forces, it is better able to consider, first, how international order might be produced by the articulation, legitimation, and transmission of the codes of state conduct, and second, the potential role of the UN in all the above. Few international orders are ever founded or sustained by force alone, something well understood by the policymakers who drafted these reports and wisely heeded by international relations theorists who attempt to understand their actions and the international orders that they construct and sustain.

Acknowledgments

The author would like to thank Emanuel Adler, John Boli, Marty Finnemore, Aaron Friedberg, Stephan Haggard, Bruce Russett, and Nina Tannenwald for their helpful suggestions.

Notes

1 For the rise and decline of the study of international organizations before the end of the cold war, see J. Martin Rochester, "The Rise and Fall of International Organization as a Field of Study," *International Organization* 40 (Autumn 1986); and Friedrich Kratochwil and John Ruggie, "International Organization: A State of the Art on the Art of the State," *International Organization* 40 (Autumn 1986).

2 Kenneth Waltz, *Theory of International Politics* (Reading, Mass.: Addison-Wesley, 1979), 42, 164. Waltz's one comment was to reject from consideration any possible role for the UN as a system regulator or in a collective security system because it simply reflects state interests.

3 John Mearsheimer, "The False Promise of International Institutions," *International Security* 19 (Winter 1994–95).

4 See Isabelle Desmartis, Julie Fournier, and Charles Thumerelle, "The United

Nations at Fifty: Regime Theory and Collective Security," *International Journal* 50 (Winter 1994–95); James Schear, "Global Institutions in a Cooperative Order: Does the United Nations Fit In?" in Janne Nolan, ed., *Global Engagement: Cooperation and Security in the Twenty-First Century* (Washington, D.C.: Brookings Institution, 1994); and Thomas Risse-Kappen, "Between a New World Order and Norms: Explaining the Re-Emergence of the United Nations in World Politics," in Keith Krause and Michael Williams, eds., *Critical Approaches to International Security* (Minneapolis: University of Minnesota Press, 1996).

5 See Thomas Franck, *The Power of Legitimacy among Nations* (New York: Oxford University Press, 1990). As Franck writes, "The international system's weakness . . . is its peculiar strength as a laboratory for those seeking to isolate the legitimacy factor" (p. 20). For past statements on legitimacy in international politics, see Henry Kissinger, *A World Restored* (Boston: Houghton Mifflin, 1964); and E. H. Carr, *The Twenty Years' Crisis* (New York: Harper Torchbooks, 1964). For contemporary treatments, see Mlada Bukavowsky, "American Identity and Neutral Rights from Independence to the War of 1812," *International Organization* 51 (Spring 1997); J. S. Barkins and B. Cronin, "The State and the Nation," *International Organization* 48 (Winter 1994); Kratochwil and Ruggie (fn.1); and Helen Milner, "The Assumption of Anarchy in International Relations," *Review of International Studies* 17 (January 1991), 74. The "English School" has also been attentive to the legitimacy of international orders. See Adam Watson, *The Evolution of International Society* (New York: Routledge, 1992).

6 Gareth Evans, "Cooperative Security and Instrastate Conflict," *Foreign Policy* 96 (Fall 1994). See also the related volume, Kevin Clements and Robin Ward, *Building International Community: Cooperating for Peace Case Studies* (St. Leonards and Canberra: Allen and Unwin and Peace Research Centre, Australian National University, 1994); and the interesting collection of responses to *Cooperating for Peace* in Stephanie Lawson, ed., *The New Agenda for Global Security: Cooperating for Peace and Beyond* (Canberra: Allen and Unwin, 1996).

7 Stephanie Lawson, "Introduction: Activating the Agenda," in Lawson (fn. 6), 7–8.

8 World Commission on Environment and Development, *Our Common Future* (New York: Oxford University Press, 1987); South Commission, *The Challenge to the South* (New York: Oxford University Press, 1990).

9 *Issues in Global Governance: Papers Written for the Commission on Global Governance* (Boston: Kluwer Law International, 1995).

10 See also Gerald Helman and Steven Ratner, "Saving Failed States," *Foreign Policy* 89 (Winter 1992–93); Steven Ratner, *The New UN Peacekeeping* (New York: St. Martin's Press, 1996).

11 It is impossible to determine whether these proposals led directly to these and other reforms; after all, the proposals built on both already existing "lessons learned" in recent peacekeeping operations and the recommendations of other documents and commissions. At the least these commissions lent greater credibility to these and other proposals.

12 Those scholars whose work is informed by a Gramscian approach also situate the UN system within a global, though largely economic, context and focus on its role as an agent of liberal change. See Craig Murphy, *International Organizations and Industrial Change* (New York: Oxford University Press, 1995); and Robert Cox, "The Crisis of World Order and the Problem of International Organizations," *International Journal* 35, no. 2 (1980).

13 Mark Zacher and Richard Matthews, "Liberal International Theory: Common Threads, Divergent Strands," in C. Kegley, ed., *Controversies in International Relations Theory: Realism and the NeoLiberal Challenge* (New York: St. Martin's Press, 1995), 110.

14 I derive these tenets from Robert Keohane, "International Liberalism

Reconsidered," in John Dunn, ed., *The Economic Limits to Modern Politics* (New York: Cambridge University Press, 1990); Andrew Moravcsik, "Liberalism and International Relations Theory," Center for International Affairs, Working Paper Series, no. 92–6 (Cambridge: Harvard University, 1993); Daniel Deudney and G. John Ikenberry, "Structural Liberalism: The Nature and Sources of Western Political Order" (Manuscript, 1995); Zacher and Matthews (fn. 13); and Michael Doyle, "Liberalism and World Politics," in Kegley (fn. 13).

15 Zacher and Matthews (fn. 13), 110.

16 See also James Rosenau, *The United Nations in a Turbulent World* (Boulder, Colo.: Lynne Rienner, 1992).

17 See Robert Jackson, "The Weight of Ideas in Decolonization: Normative Change in International Relations," in Judith Goldstein and Robert O. Keohane, eds., *Ideas and Foreign Policy* (Ithaca, N.Y.: Cornell University Press, 1993); Rupert Emerson, "Colonialism, Political Development, and the UN," *International Organization* 19 (Summer 1965); and Harold Jacobsen, "The United Nations and Colonialism: A Tentative Appraisal," *International Organization* 1 (Winter 1962).

18 This raises a potentially interesting, though generally unexplored, question: what role did the UN play in helping to manage the end of the cold war? As international relations theorists isolate various explanations, they tend to focus on the Soviet Union's "new thinking" and the emerging belief that the U.S. would not take advantage of its international retreat and domestic reforms. Was the easy fall of the Soviet Union facilitated by the existence of the UN? The U.S. and the Soviet Union worked jointly and multilaterally to end various regional conflicts, and they did so under the auspices of the UN. It is conceivable that by working through the UN, the Soviets (1) could rest assured that there was a forum that guaranteed them superpower status and decision-making power despite their declining stature (and perhaps caused the U.S. to give it more due than otherwise might have been the case, for example, in the negotiations preceding the Persian Gulf War in January 1991); and (2) learned through doing that the U.S. would not try to settle these and other conflicts in a manner immediately disadvantageous to the Soviets. As Roberts and Kingsbury note, Soviet premier Gorbachev increasingly and simultaneously stressed the necessity of a framework of international cooperation and the importance of the UN. See Roberts and Kingsbury, "The UN's Roles in International Society," in A. Roberts and B. Kingsbury, eds., *United Nations, Divided World* (New York: Oxford University Press, 1993), 46–47.

19 Boutros Boutros-Ghali, "Global Leadership after the Cold War," *Foreign Affairs* 75 (March–April 1996).

20 See John Ruggie, ed., *Multilateralism Matters* (New York: Columbia University Press, 1993); and Thomas Pickering, "Power and Purpose: Making Multilateralism Work," *Foreign Service Journal* (July 1992).

21 Cameron Hume, *Ending Mozambique's War* (Washington, D.C.: USIP Press, 1994); *The United Nations and Nuclear Non-Proliferation*, United Nations Book Series, vol. 3 (New York: Department of Public Information, 1995).

22 The peacekeeping literature has exploded over the past few years. For overviews and analysis, see Alan James, *Peacekeeping in International Politics* (New York: St. Martin's Press, 1990); A. B. Featherston, *Towards a Theory of United Nations Peacekeeping* (New York: St. Martin's Press, 1994); Paul Diehl, *International Peacekeeping* (Baltimore: Johns Hopkins University Press, 1993); Paul Durch, ed., *The Evolution of UN Peacekeeping* (New York: St. Martin's Press, 1993); Michael Doyle et al., eds., *Keeping the Peace: Multidimensional UN Operations in Cambodia and El Salvador* (New York: Cambridge University Press, 1997); John MacKinley and Jarat Chopra, "Second Generation Multinational Operations," *Washington Quarterly* (Summer 1992); and Thomas Weiss, ed., *The United Nations and Civil Wars* (Boulder, Colo.: Lynne Rienner, 1995). For the factual side,

see *United Nations Peacekeeping Information Notes* (New York: United Nations Press, 1995); and *Blue Helmets*, 3d ed. (New York: United Nations Press, 1996).

23 See also Boutros Boutros-Ghali, "An Agenda for Peace: One Year Later," *Orbis* 37 (Summer 1993), 329; idem, "Democracy: A Newly Recognized Imperative," *Global Governance* 1 (Winter 1995), 3–12; and the recently published *Agenda for Democratization* (New York: UN Publications, 1996).

24 See also Boutros-Ghali (fn. 23, 1995).

25 Hedley Bull, *Anarchical Society: A Study of Order in World Politics* (New York: Macmillan, 1983).

26 Robert Jackson, *Quasi-States* (New York: Cambridge University Press, 1990).

27 These reports draw on the growing literature on the "democratic peace." See Michael Doyle, "Liberalism and World Politics," *American Political Science Review* 80 (1986); and Bruce Russett, *Grasping the Democratic Peace* (Princeton: Princeton University Press, 1993).

28 Jacobsen (fn. 17), 47; and Louis Henkin, "The United Nations and Human Rights," *International Organization* 19 (Summer 1965), 512.

29 See, for instance, Philip Alston, ed., *The United Nations and Human Rights* (New York: Cambridge University Press, 1995); David Forsythe, "The United Nations and Human Rights at Fifty: An Incremental but Incomplete Revolution," *Global Governance* 1 (September–December 1995); and W. Ofuatey-Kodjoe, "The United Nations and the Protection of Individual and Group Rights," *International Social Science Journal* 144, no. 3 (1995).

30 This is not the first time that an international organization has argued that domestic politics matters for international order and is a legitimate concern of the international community. The League of Nations, too, through its mandate policies and various commissions on minority rights and plebiscites in Europe, made the case that there was an important relationship between domestic and international order. See Dorothy Jones, *Code of Peace* (Chicago: University of Chicago Press, 1991). As reflected by the League of Nations mandate system, at issue was whether or not the recognized state could maintain some semblance of order—that domestic order and the capacity to govern should be used as criteria for independence and recognition.

31 For substantive legitimacy, see Peter Berger, Brigitte Berger, and Hansfried Kellner, *The Homeless Mind* (New York: Vintage Books, 1973); W. Richard Scott, "Unpacking Institutional Arguments," in Walter Powell and Paul Dimaggio, *The New Institutionalism in Organizational Analysis* (Chicago: University of Chicago Press, 1991), 169–71; and Max Weber, *The Theory of Social and Economic Organization* (Glencoe, Ill.: Free Press, 1964), 124. For procedural legitimacy as applied to the UN, see Franck (fn. 5), 24, 25; idem, *Fairness in International Law and Institutions* (New York: Oxford University Press, 1996); and Bruce Russett, ed., *The Once and Future Security Council* (New York: St. Martin's Press, 1997).

32 Claude, "Collective Legitimization as a Political Function of the United Nations," *International Organization* 20 (Summer 1966), 368.

33 Kissinger (fn. 5).

34 Claude (fn. 32).

35 Javier Pérez de Cuéllar, "The United Nations and the United States" (Address at the fiftieth anniversary celebration, Dartmouth College, May 10, 1988). Cited from Franck (fn. 5), 9.

36 Canadian House of Commons, External Affairs Committee; quoted from Lawson (fn. 7), 3.

37 Oran Young, "The United Nations and the International System," *International Organization* 22 (Autumn 1968), 906.

38 Cited from W. Richard Scott, *Institutions and Organizations* (Thousand Oaks, Calif.: Sage Press, 1995), 10.

39 Emile Durkheim, *The Division of Labor in Society* (New York: Free Press, 1964); John Ruggie, "Continuity and Transformation in the World Polity," in Robert Keohane, ed., *Neorealism and Its Critics* (New York: Columbia University Press, 1986).

40 The importance and potential behavioral impact of the UN's symbolic role is also raised by Roberts and Kingsbury (fn. 18), 19–22.

41 Claude (fn. 32); Thomas Franck, *Nation against Nation* (New York: Oxford University Press, 1985).

42 Ernst Haas argues that a rough measure of the legitimacy of the United Nations is the degree to which "member states invoke its purposes and principles . . . to justify national policy." See Haas, *Beyond the Nation-State* (Stanford, Calif.: Stanford University Press, 1964), 133. For a good discussion of how to verify empirically whether a political order has some measure of legitimacy, see Arthur Stinchcombe, *Constructing Social Theories* (Chicago: University of Chicago Press, 1968), 162–64.

43 These principles of state action are "sovereign equality of states; territorial integrity and political independence of states; equal rights and self-determination of peoples; nonintervention in internal affairs of states; peaceful settlement of disputes between states; no threat or use of force; fulfillment in good faith of international obligations; cooperation with other states; and respect for human rights and fundamental freedoms." See Jones, "The Declaratory Tradition in Modern International Law," in T. Nardin and D. Marpel, eds., *Traditions of International Ethics* (New York: Cambridge University Press, 1992), 44–45.

44 Jones (fn. 43), 48–49. On constitutive norms and state action, see Ron Jepperson, Alexander Wendt, and Peter Katzenstein, "Identity, Norms, and Security," in Peter Katzenstein, ed., *The Culture of National Security: Norms and Identity in World Politics* (New York: Columbia University Press, 1996).

45 "Nations, or those who govern them," writes Thomas Franck, "recognize that the obligation to comply is owed by them to the community of states as the reciprocal of that community's validation of their nation's statehood." See Franck (fn. 5), 196.

46 See also Paul Schroeder, "New World Order: A Historical Perspective," *Washington Quarterly* 17, no. 2 (1994), 33; John Ruggie, "International Regimes, Transactions, and Change: Embedded Liberalism in the Postwar Economic Order," in Stephen Krasner, ed., *International Regimes* (Ithaca, N.Y.: Cornell University Press, 1983).

47 Claude (fn. 32), 374–75.

48 See also Abraham Chayes and Antonia Handler Chayes, "On Compliance," *International Organization* (Spring 1993).

49 Roberts and Kingsbury (fn. 18), 57.

50 David Beetham, *The Legitimation of Power* (Atlantic Highlands, N.J.: Humanities Press, 1991), 35.

51 Claude (fn. 32), 368.

52 For a discussion of these points, see Michael Barnett, "Spheres of Influence?" in Joseph Lepgold and Thomas Weiss, eds., *Collective Conflict Management and Changing World Politics* (Albany: State University of New York Press, 1997).

53 Gene Lyons and Michael Mastanduno tie legitimacy to the multilateral character of humanitarian operations. See Lyons and Mastanduno, "Introduction," in Lyons and Mastanduno, *Beyond Westphalia? State Sovereignty and International Intervention* (Baltimore: Johns Hopkins University Press, 1996), 12; and Martha Finnemore, "Constructing Norms of Humanitarian Intervention," in Peter Katzenstein, ed., *The Culture of National Security: Norms and Identity in World Politics* (New York: Columbia University Press, 1996).

54 Parsons, "The UN and National Interests of States," in Roberts and Kingsbury (fn. 18), 111–12.

55 Boutros-Ghali (fn. 19).
56 Robert Cox, John Ruggie, and Tom Biersteker have examined various features of how a liberal political order was established and to whose advantage it operates. See Cox, *Production, Power and World Order: Social Forces in the Making of History* (New York: Columbia University Press, 1987); Ruggie (fn. 46); and Biersteker, "The Triumph of Neoclassical Economics in the Developing World," in J. Rosenau and Ernst-Otto Cziempel, eds., *Governance without Government: Order and Change in World Politics* (New York: Cambridge University Press, 1992). See also Beetham (fn. 50), chap. 4.
57 Terry Eagleton, *Ideology* (New York: Verso Press, 1991), 56.
58 Jürgen Habermas, "Legitimation Problems in the Modern State," in *Communication and the Evolution of Society* (Boston: Beacon Press, 1979).
59 Alger, "United Nations Participation as a Learning Process," *Public Opinion Quarterly* 27, no. 3 (1963), 425. See also Claude (fn. 32), 373; Connie McNeely, *Constructing the Nation-State: International Organization and Prescriptive Action* (Westport, Conn.: Greenwood Press, 1995); and Martha Finnemore, *National Interests in International Society* (Ithaca, N.Y.: Cornell University Press, 1996).
60 John Boli and George M. Thomas, "World Culture in the World Polity: A Century of International Non-Governmental Organization," *American Sociological Review* 62 (April 1997); and McNeely (fn. 59).
61 For broader theoretical statements on the relationship between organizations and the transmission of norms and acceptable practices, see Dimaggio and Powell (fn. 31); W. Richard Scott and Soren Christensen, eds., *The Institutional Construction of Organizations: International and Longitudinal Studies* (Thousand Oaks, Calif.: Sage Publications, 1995); John Ruggie, "Territoriality and Beyond," *International Organization* 47 (Winter 1993); and Martha Finnemore, "International Organizations as Teachers of Norms," *International Organization* 47 (Autumn 1993).
62 For an expanded discussion of this argument, see Michael Barnett, "The New United Nations Politics of Peace: From Juridical Sovereignty to Empirical Sovereignty," *Global Governance* 1 (Winter 1995).
63 Amnesty International, *Peacekeeping and Human Rights* (Mimeo, January 1994); Sally Morphet, "UN Peacekeeping and Election-Monitoring," in Roberts and Kingsbury (fn. 18); Helman and Ratner (fn. 10); and David Padilla and Elizabeth Houppert, "International Election Observing: Enhancing the Principle of Free and Fair Elections," *Emory International Law Review* 7 (1993).
64 R. J. Vincent, "Order in International Politics," in J. D. B. Miller and R. J. Vincent, eds., *Order and Violence: Hedley Bull and International Relations* (New York: Oxford University Press, 1991), 54.
65 Keohane (fn. 14).
66 On institutional isomorphism, see George Thomas et al., *Institutional Structure: Constituting the State, Society, and the Individual* (Beverly Hills, Calif.: Sage Press, 1987).
67 Andrew Hurrell and Ngaire Woods, "Globalisation and Inequality," *Millennium* 24, no. 3 (1995); Marie-Cloude Smouts, "International Organizations and Inequality among States," *International Social Science Journal* 144, no. 3 (1995); Sandra Whitworth, *Feminism and International Relations: Towards a Political Economy of Gender in Interstate and Non-Governmental Institutions* (New York: St. Martin's Press, 1994).
68 See, for instance, Liisa Mallki, "Speechless Emissaries: Refugees, Humanitarianism, and Dehistoricization," *Cultural Anthropology* 11 (Fall 1996); Michael Barnett and Martha Finnemore, "The Politics, Power, and Pathologies of International Organizations" (Paper presented at the International Studies Association annual meetings, Toronto, March 20–24, 1997).

69 Alexander Wendt, "Constructing International Politics," *International Security* 20 (Summer 1995); Jepperson, Wendt, and Katzenstein (fn. 44); and Emanuel Adler "Seizing the Middle Ground: Constructivism and World Politics," *European Journal of International Relations* (forthcoming). See also Dennis Wrong, *The Problem of Order* (New York: Free Press, 1994), chap. 3; Jeffrey Alexander, *Twenty Lectures* (New York: Columbia University Press, 1987), chap. 1; and John Rhoads, *Critical Issues in Social Theory* (College Station: Penn State Press, 1991), chap. 5.

3 The new United Nations politics of peace

From juridical sovereignty to empirical sovereignty

Until a few years ago it would have been difficult to fashion a quorum of policymakers or scholars to salute the UN's role in peace and security. Notwithstanding the occasional moments that the Security Council and peacekeeping forces have offered effective mechanisms for conflict resolution, few policymakers took seriously the promise of the United Nations as envisioned in 1945. It seemed that any international peace and security issue of real significance was channeled to and handled by other forums. Scholars too were equally dismissive of the United Nations and its workings. This is particularly noticeable of realist scholarship, which viewed the UN as either unimportant, an expression of power politics, or an idealist institution that might jeopardize the state's security interests if taken seriously. Even those who saw some merit in security institutions largely overlooked the UN in favor of regional organizations such as NATO or the Conference on Security and Cooperation in Europe (CSCE). In short, there were few compelling practical or theoretical reasons to consider the UN's contribution to international security.

In retrospect, the decision by the Nobel Committee to award the 1988 Peace Prize to UN peacekeepers was prophetic. Since the end of the Cold War, the United Nations has become a principal focus for maintaining international peace and security, and there is no better symbol of the UN's resuscitation than its peacekeeping operations. Whereas there were thirteen peacekeeping operations between 1956 and 1987, there have been twenty since then. In March 1994, there were seventy thousand UN troops from seventy countries serving in sixteen operations. Not only are more serving, but more are dying: more peacekeepers have died in the past five years than in the first forty, and 22 percent of all peacekeeping fatalities occurred in the first nine months of 1993 alone. More impressive than the expanded numbers, though, are the expanded activities. Most peacekeeping operations since 1988 concern not the monitoring of, and politics between, borders but rather the politics within borders; whereas at one time peacekeepers were situated solely between two combatants that had agreed to a cease-fire, rarely if ever engaging in offensive action, now they are involved in a myriad of activities associated with nation building and peace enforcement. These "second-generation" operations have become not only one of the UN's most visible and controversial mechanisms for conflict resolution, but also one of the international community's.[1]

The United Nations, then, seems to have a greater role in maintaining international order. Yet whatever consensus there might be that the UN now has an active role in managing international security quickly yields to uncertainty as to what that role is. What is the relationship between international order, the United Nations, and this expanded peacekeeping agenda? This question can be addressed by two main observations.

First, the United Nations reflects how its member states broadly understand what maintains international order. As an institution designed to confront threats to international peace and security, its members have opinions and views concerning what constitutes a threat and how such threats might best be contained. Yet there has been an important shift in the prevailing belief among member states concerning what best fosters international order, particularly noticeable since the end of the Cold War. Whereas at one time the United Nations was concerned solely with establishing and reinforcing the principle of juridical sovereignty (that states recognize each other's existence and honor the principle of noninterference), there is increased conviction that empirical sovereignty (that states have some degree of legitimacy and control over their society and within their borders) enables states to uphold the norms of international society, juridical sovereignty, and international order. Simply put, the United Nations reflects the growing conviction that in order for states to be at peace with their neighbors they must be at peace with themselves.

Second, although the UN is ostensibly a global organization, in fact it is an organization that is dedicated to Third World and North–South issues. As Anthony Parsons observes, the UN, far from maintaining a global jurisdiction, is generally "preoccupied with the problems of the newly independent majority, namely the dangerous disputes in the so-called Third World."[2] On few occasions has the United Nations involved itself in East–West or Euro-Atlantic relations, and its primary jurisdiction has been North–South relations and the Third World, notably decolonization and development. This southerly focus is as true today as it was during the UN's first forty years; in this respect, while the end of the Cold War unleashed a new round of UN activism, that activism continues to be directed at the same locale.

These two observations form my basic argument: The United Nations and its peacekeeping operations reflect prevailing definitions of international order, and those understandings are largely directed toward the Third World. To understand the UN's role in international affairs requires viewing the organization and its activities as an expression of how its member states understand what underpins international order, and that the primary threats to that order emanate from the Third World.

To understand better the UN's role in international security requires drawing on a different theoretical tradition: the society-of-states school.

First, I briefly discuss this approach and how it offers an alternative conception of what constitutes and maintains order in interstate politics. I then argue that decolonization was an international security issue because it concerned globalizing the principle of sovereignty. The United Nations facilitated this transition from the era of empires to the era of juridical sovereignty and reflected the view that international order was premised on the collective acceptance of juridical sovereignty. Peacekeeping operations were invented to deal with problems emerging from decolonization and the globalization of sovereignty and, in this respect, reflected the understanding that juridical sovereignty and territorial integrity further international order. I then posit that there has been an important cognitive shift among many policymakers concerning what best maintains international order—a shift from juridical sovereignty to empirical sovereignty, which in turn has altered the UN's peacekeeping duties. In this view, the UN's peacekeeping operations are an expression of the increased sentiment that empirical sovereignty underpins international order. I conclude by reflecting on the implications of this discussion for the future of these second-generation peacekeeping activities as well as international relations theory.

The problem of international order

International society represents a common set of norms and institutions that bind state actors to form a community of interests. Although states might have a myriad of interests and goals, survival and security are primary and elementary. In contrast to the realist focus on alliances, hegemonies, and balances of power for maintaining state survival, a society-of-states approach elevates how state survival is maintained and how behavior is constrained by the acceptance of certain norms and institutions. Conflicts persist, wars occasionally occur, and states will balance the power of others, but by and large states have found it mutually advantageous to establish institutions and norms to further their collective interest in security and survival.[3] The main function of these norms and institutions is not to banish war and conflict but rather to minimize their frequency and magnitude.

While there exist numerous international institutions that enable states to pursue their common interests, none is more important than sovereignty. Sovereignty has both external and internal dimensions. The external side—juridical sovereignty—holds that the state is subject to no other authority and has full and exclusive powers within its territory. In this respect, sovereignty assumes that there is mutual restraint, a "live and let live" policy, embodied in the principle of noninterference. The internal side—empirical sovereignty—asserts that the state maintains order within its borders, and ideally such order is generated not only through coercive mechanisms but also with some degree of consent and legitimacy from society. Having empirical sovereignty does not mean that the state is able to ensure complete compliance with its laws, but that it has the capacity to govern society and to maintain domestic order.[4]

How does sovereignty relate to order? Hedley Bull defines international order as a "pattern of activity that sustains the elementary or primary goals of the society of states, or international society."[5] A primary goal is the sovereignty of the state in both its external (independence from outside forces) and internal (control over domestic constituents) dimensions. In other words, international or regional order is premised on the survival of the state, and "there should be a sense of *common interests* in the elementary goals of social life."[6] By converging around the principle of sovereignty and recognizing each other's right to exist, and by constructing a variety of international institutions that are based on this principle, states are able to promote both order and security. By recognizing each other's sovereignty, the authority of each to act in international affairs and to control its domestic space, states have placed limitations on their actions and created an "anarchical society."

Those working within the society-of-states approach have forwarded two ways that empirical sovereignty relates to juridical sovereignty. First, the community of sovereign states frequently employs domestic characteristics and qualities to determine whether or not to confer sovereignty on a state. A variety of criteria frequently revolving around culture, identity, and religion are combined to form a "standard of civilization."[7] In other words, certain domestic qualities and characteristics are frequently used to determine whether a state is qualified to participate in, and likely to uphold the norms of, international society. This standard was particularly pronounced through the early twentieth century but faded after World War II. Also occasionally present in debates over recognition was not the kind of government but rather its degree. As reflected by the League of Nations' mandate system, at issue were whether the recognized state could maintain some semblance of order and whether domestic order and the capacity to govern should be used as markers for recognition. A third view, prominent during the post-World War II rush to decolonization, was that the recognition would be determined by whether the state had the capacity to uphold juridical sovereignty rather than whether or not it contained empirical sovereignty. In general, the criteria for who is qualified and recognized to play the "sovereignty game" have varied historically.[8]

This fluctuating standard relates to the second way that empirical sovereignty is associated with juridical sovereignty: domestic configurations and characteristics are related to foreign policy disposition and, in turn, to international order. Simply put, domestic governance is an international governance issue. The enthusiasm with which policymakers or theorists make that connection has varied historically: sometimes they argue that there is a tight fit between empirical sovereignty and juridical sovereignty and that the former logically precedes the latter; at other times they forward a belief that mutual recognition, regardless of internal characteristics, is what matters for international order. For instance, whether empirical sovereignty was associated with international order was debated during the drive for decolonization: Would newly recognized sovereign states that lacked empirical sovereignty reject or have a difficult time abiding by the norms of international society? More recent discussions concerning whether to extend recognition to the successor states of Yugoslavia revolved around their potential behavior in international affairs.

My observation is that over the length of the Cold War the belief that empirical sovereignty logically precedes juridical sovereignty eventually yielded to the view that empirical sovereignty matters little and that juridical sovereignty alone can produce international order. The workings of the United Nations and its peacekeeping operations reflected this view. Progressively noticeable since the end of the Cold War, however, is a renewed belief among policymakers and theorists alike that empirical sovereignty underpins juridical sovereignty—and hence international order—and that greater attention should be given to advancing empirical sovereignty in those states that are deficient. The UN's activities and peacekeeping operations reflect that disposition.

The United Nations and international order after World War II

The charter of the United Nations is quite clear that sovereignty is the cornerstone of interstate relations. Article 2(1) declares that "the Organization is based on the principle of the sovereign equality of all its Members," and Article 2(7) announces that the United Nations will not intervene or interfere in the domestic affairs of states (except in the case of a Chapter VII peace-enforcement operation). Yet the UN Charter also recognized something of a division in world affairs: while sovereignty is the foundation for the community of states, in fact most states were not sovereign but rather were colonial appendages. Seizing on this inequality, the charter proclaims that this inconsistency in world affairs should be eliminated and that a principal function of the United Nations is to assist this transformation in global politics. The UN Charter, then, reflected the growing belief that decolonization was a matter of some priority and that newly decolonizing states should accept the norm of juridical sovereignty.

Three issues stand out concerning the relationship between the United Nations, decolonization, juridical sovereignty, and peacekeeping operations. First, a principal purpose of the United Nations was to facilitate the transition from the era of empires to the era of sovereignty—to globalize and universalize sovereignty as the basis of relations between states. From the beginning, the United Nations indicated that it would be actively concerned with decolonization because of its normative imperatives and security implications. Articles 11, 12, and 13, which explicitly recognize that a major reason for the UN's involvement in decolonization was its implications for international security, provided an important reason for the UN's involvement. Indeed, over time the "conviction ... spread that the continued existence of any dependency by itself created a threat to peace and security."[9]

As might be expected of an issue that had normative and security dimensions, decolonization dominated the UN's agenda for its first twenty years, and the organization established numerous institutional mechanisms to ensure that it was carried out in a peaceful manner. The Security Council, which is charged with overseeing international security issues, was not actively involved in this issue because it was increasingly paralyzed by the Cold War, and its members included two colonial powers with veto rights. Accordingly, Articles 11, 12, and 13 of the Charter became the early focal point for the decolonization movement. The defining moments came in 1960 with the passage of the United Nations Declaration on the Granting of Independence to Colonial Countries and Peoples, and then with the establishment of the Special Committee on Colonialism in 1961, which had a strong anti-colonial composition. The United Nations was actively involved in facilitating a global transformation, which represents nothing less than an issue of international order.

Second, while a pronounced view during the early debates over decolonization was that there was a close relationship between domestic and international order, that view became less visible over time and was overtaken by an alternative belief that there was no necessary connection. At the outset of the debate over decolonization, there was considerable opinion that it would be decades, if not the next century, before it was completed. Although some of the hesitations were driven by an unwillingness of the colonial powers to forgo the symbolic, strategic, and economic benefits associated with colonialism, also evident was the belief that it would be irresponsible to grant independence until the territory had achieved the capacity for self-rule. Articles 11 and 12 of the Charter are the clearest and earliest indicators of that sentiment, which reminded the administrators of the colonial or trusteeship territory of their responsibility to ready the territory for independence by investing it with the state structures and economic infrastructure required for self-government. In other words, one reason why not all were in a hurry to see rapid decolonization was that there was still considerable sentiment that colonial states had to contain some level of empirical sovereignty before being given independence.

Achieving the capacity for self-government was not only a domestic governance issue, but also an international governance issue. The idea that empirical sovereignty preceded juridical sovereignty, and that domestic order and international order were related, was particularly visible prior to World War II and lingered through the 1960 United Nations Declaration on the Granting of Independence to Colonial Countries and Peoples.[10] Governments of the period, then, evidenced some concern that rapid and hasty decolonization would produce disorder in international affairs because the affected states lacked any attributes of stateness. There was tremendous sympathy with the view that a rule of law in international society was contingent on a rule of law in domestic society.

Yet over time, the debate on decolonization contained fewer references to the relationship between empirical sovereignty and international order. Although there are many reasons why decolonization became detached from empirical sovereignty—the exigencies of decolonization, superpower conflict, and the beliefs that such concerns were simply a delaying tactic by decolonization's opponents and that independence would create a better environment for promoting human rights and economic development—the result was that there were fewer inquiries into the nature of the "self" that was prime for self-determination. The self came to be equated with the colonial territory and was generally assumed to be ripe for independence. In fact, in contrast to the League of Nations, which explicitly attended to questions of minority and ethnic rights, the United Nations paid little heed to such concerns, and the General Assembly prohibited the secretary-general from even investigating such issues.[11] In short, the fact that human rights became equated with self-determination and anticolonialism was a clear signal that the timing of independence should not be unduly affected by the lack of empirical sovereignty.[12]

Once the principle of self-determination was largely accepted and the decolonization movement was proceeding apace, the United Nations, with Third World states taking the lead, shifted attention to the importance of territorial integrity and sovereignty.[13] There is little question that many Third World leaders had a strong self-interest in accepting sovereignty. The UN also provided friendly, and sometimes not-so-friendly, reminders that independence should not be used to challenge the legitimacy of colonial borders. The United Nations was quite concerned that because these territories that were achieving self-determination were "multiple selves," their governments might attempt to create a "whole personality" through territorial adjustment. In fact, many of those newly decolonized states feared much the same possibility and used the UN to discourage such tendencies. Perhaps the most famous statement was the 1960 United Nations Declaration on the Granting of Independence to Colonial Countries and Peoples. Article 6 states:

> Any attempt aimed at the partial or whole disruption of the national unity and the territorial integrity of a country is incompatible with the purposes and principles of the Charter of the United Nations.

It is significant that many of the UN's most visible and important actions and pronouncements were concerned that decolonization would not lead to state disintegration. The United Nations increasingly echoed the position that considerations of empirical sovereignty should not be used to delay decolonization, that decolonization should not lead to territorial adjustments, and that decolonized states must accept juridical sovereignty.

What happened to the concern that international disorder would follow if a community of states were absent empirical sovereignty? Two points are worth noting. First, the decreased concern for empirical sovereignty and for decolonization sit comfortably together: each argues that discussions of the self are nonessential, constitute an unwarranted interference in domestic affairs, and are an obstacle to decolonization and international stability. Second, the norm of juridical sovereignty is quite consistent with the realist paradigm and balance-of-power perspectives that dominated the thinking of Western policymakers: both juridical sovereignty and balance-of-power formulations largely bracket considerations of empirical sovereignty and internal politics. When considering the requirements of a stable international order, both realism and an emphasis on juridical sovereignty converge around the importance of territorial restraint and of turning a blind eye to domestic politics. In general, realists, advocates of decolonization, and those interested in building institutions founded on the norm of sovereignty supported the view that some semblance of international order could be fostered through territorial restraint and ignoring the domestic political realm.

Peacekeeping forces and military observer missions were designed with an eye to the politics of territorial restraint and juridical sovereignty. Although peacekeeping is seen as an invention of the Cold War and superpower conflict, it was originally designed to ensure that decolonization and juridical sovereignty move in tandem. According to Brian Urquhart:

> Peacekeeping, not mentioned in the United Nations Charter, was originally developed during the post-war decolonization period as a means of filling the power vacuums caused by decolonization, and of reducing the friction and temperature, so that an effort could be made to negotiate a permanent settlement of post-colonial conflict situations.[14]

The first military observer missions were deployed to Kashmir and Jerusalem in 1947; in both cases the United Nations intended to reduce the likelihood of severe territorial challenges that emerged from the decolonization process and the establishment of juridical sovereignty.

It was inevitable that the Cold War would become injected into the politics of decolonization, and peacekeeping forces became a highly useful instrument to encourage juridical sovereignty and territorial integrity and to defuse potential superpower conflict. How peacekeeping forces worked to assuage decolonization issues and defuse superpower conflict is evident at the very invention of "Blue Helmets" during the 1956 Suez War. Although it quickly became a superpower flashpoint, the war erupted from a struggle over decolonization and juridical sovereignty. For Nasser, at issue was Egypt's right to exercise full sovereignty and control over its territory, including the Suez Canal and its operations. In other words, it was Egypt's view that despite its nominal independence from Britain in 1922, it remained a colony so long as Britain continued to circumscribe Egypt's independence with various extraterritorial rights revolving around the defense and control of the Suez Canal. Therefore, Nasser's decision to nationalize the canal in July 1956 was received by many Egyptians as a symbol of Egypt's reclamation of its sovereignty after centuries of occupation. Britain, however, treated it as a symbol of a different kind: one of its remaining souvenirs of empire had just been expropriated. The October 1956 invasion by Britain and France (and Israel) therefore represented an attempt by the colonial powers to maintain some vestige of colonial rights and limit Egypt's juridical sovereignty. Despite (or because of) Britain's and France's status as permanent members of the Security Council, the UN's General Assembly and Secretariat combined to extricate Britain and France from the canal and to defuse what had become a major superpower confrontation; the UN Emergency Force (UNEF) was approved, and "Blue Helmets" were invented and quickly dispatched to replace the British and French forces.

The other famous peacekeeping operation of the period was the United Nations Operations in the Congo (UNOC). Secretary-General Dag Hammarskjöld evoked Article 99 and seized the attention of the Security Council because of Belgium's decision to ignore the Congo's refusal to allow it to intervene in the Congo to protect Belgian citizens, and the subsequent chaos that followed the arrival of Belgian forces. The Security Council approved Hammarskjöld's proposal that the United Nations immediately dispatch peacekeeping troops to replace the Belgian forces. In other words, the UNOC and the UNEF shared similar roots: a former colonial power attempting to retain the rights of empire and to limit the juridical sovereignty of the newly independent state. The UNOC soon had a second life, however, as it actively and militarily opposed Tshombe's move to secede with the riches of the Katanga Province. The United Nations, in this respect, was enforcing Article 6 of the Declaration on the Granting of Independence to Colonial Countries and Peoples, which declared that decolonization should not lead to territorial dismemberment.

In sum, while most identify East–West conflict as the fundamental threat to international stability after World War II and therefore downplay the UN's contribution to peace and security, a major challenge was the transition from an era of empires to an era of sovereignty, with the possibility that such a transition might produce both instability and an attempt by the newly independent states to challenge the norms of international society. Part of this fear was informed by a belief that premature independence—that is, juridical sovereignty without empirical sovereignty—would have alarming consequences for global order. If this was something of a dominant view (of at least the great powers) before World War II, it bowed to another line of thought that gave independence with the expectation that empirical sovereignty was not required for this goal. The United Nations reflected this changed understanding of international order and played an important role in institutionalizing and regulating the process and pace of decolonization; and peacekeeping operations reflected the emphasis on juridical sovereignty and territorial integrity. With the exception of the United Nations operation in Cyprus (UNFICYP), all peacekeeping operations occurred in the South, and most concerned both ensuring the connection between decolonization and juridical sovereignty and maintaining territorial integrity.

The UN and Third World security after the Cold War

There are probably numerous factors driving the UN's second-generation peacekeeping agenda that involve ethnic conflict and nation building. Heading most lists is the decline and demise of the Cold War, which relaxed the constraints on the United Nations and allowed it to become actively engaged in solving many of the same conflicts that were either instigated or maintained by superpower competition. If the end of the Cold War helps explain the UN's resurgence, it does not account for why the United Nations has departed from its traditional concern with interstate dispute resolution to involve itself in nation building. To understand what is driving this emphasis on "comprehensive security"—where peacekeeping meets peace building— requires looking beyond material forces and incorporating how many policymakers understand what fosters international order. Specifically, whereas during the Cold War many officials embraced the notion that juridical sovereignty underpinned international order, there is greater attention both to empirical sovereignty and domestic threats to the state and to how the domestic realm affects international order.

Part of this increased interest in empirical sovereignty is driven by the growing awareness that Third World states face greater threats from their own societies than they do from their neighbors. Although policymakers were not oblivious to those domestic challenges during the Cold War, there was a decided tendency to downplay them because of either a realist imagery that assumed that external threats were primary, the tendency to assume that foreign elements frequently were the origin of domestic instability, or the fear that promoting political reconciliation might undermine a strategic ally. Although there were disintegrating and failing states throughout the Cold War, the lack of empirical sovereignty that has haunted many Third World states since independence has become particularly daunting and overwhelming in the last few years.

As these Third World (internal) security dilemmas become more numerous and visible, and with greater consequences for local populations and regional stability, there is increased pressure on the international community to intervene and to stop the hemorrhaging. In other words, internal conflicts challenge not only a cosmopolitan sensibility but regional stability as well: witness how a coup attempt can produce a humanitarian nightmare and mass exodus, which in turn can cause instability in a neighboring country. For instance, the explosion of ethnic violence and genocide in Rwanda in April 1994 led to a massive refugee flow that threatened to destabilize the region. Opponents of the state will frequently establish military bases and take refuge over the border, which increases the prospect of interstate conflict; the civil war in Liberia has produced that very outcome, threatened regional stability, and therefore attracted international attention and concern.

The recognition that internal rather than interstate conflict is becoming more dramatic and alarming parallels a cognitive shift among many policymakers concerning how to build a peace system. Abandoning the well-worn models of security politics that dominated their textbooks and the Cold War, perhaps the most striking feature of the post-Cold War security dialogue is that few policymakers or scholars are openly advocating a return to the balance-of-power and alliance politics of past years and are instead struggling with new arrangements to govern the peace and maintain the security order.[15] One distinct approach focuses on multilateral and institutional arrangements. Multilateralism (at least in one view) is the understanding that states have common interests—largely driven by increasing interdependence—that require joint action to obtain their common goals. This multilateral impulse also suggests that institutional arrangements can reduce uncertainty and fear and offer confidence-building measures and other devices that are designed to cultivate trust. In short, multilateralism observes that genuine and long-lasting security cannot be achieved through unilateral action.

An alternative approach to building a nonrealist security system rests squarely on empirical sovereignty. Many leaders are openly stating that they feel most secure when associated with those states that share similar identities, values, and orientations. In other words, the shift from deterrence to assurance begins by emphasizing the institutional arrangements that might be constructed to minimize uncertainty and ends with the idea that the best assurance is for states to have similar personalities and identities.

That view represents a return to the ideas of international order that dominated the pre-1945 period, but with a twist. While still holding that juridical sovereignty represents a cornerstone of international politics, many policymakers and scholars are also suggesting that empirical sovereignty is integrally related to juridical sovereignty and international order but adding that it is a particular domestic configuration and personality that generates pacific tendencies: a community of democratic states. This "pacific thesis," the subject of much attention in the political science literature over the past few years, is increasingly echoed by government officials from the West and the Third World alike, as they assert that a community of democratic states represents the best guarantor of international order.[16] This understanding is reflected in the Partnership for Peace and in the Organization of American States' Santiago Agreement of June 1991, both of which envision a mutual aid society of democratic states. After being overshadowed by juridical sovereignty through much of the Cold War, domestic and international order are now more tightly coupled in the minds of government officials.[17]

The United Nations reflects, and is a principal vehicle for defining, this emerging view that empirical sovereignty is consequential for international order. A few examples will suffice. Whereas during the 1988 plenary session of the UN General Assembly few states advanced the view that empirical sovereignty was an issue of international peace and security, many of the 1993 speeches made this connection. It was not a Western-led or Western-dominated position, for many Third World states were equally active in making this claim. Also visible is an expanded definition of security. If once the Security Council limited its definition of "threats to international peace and security" to interstate conflict, it is now adopting a more expansive conception that includes internal conflict that can generate humanitarian crises and regional instability. This expanded definition in turn creates the justification for the international community to intervene in domestic space. In fact, the Security Council's expanded definition has caused alarm in the General Assembly that the Security Council is encroaching on its jurisdiction. The Security Council is signaling that it is difficult to differentiate between domestic and international space and that empirical sovereignty is related to international order.

Finally, early in and repeatedly throughout Boutros Boutros-Ghali's *Agenda for Peace*, juridical sovereignty is elevated as the constitutive principle of international relations. Yet Boutros-Ghali also writes that the United Nations should have the authority to intervene in domestic space and participate in nation-building activities; in doing so, he is arguing for an expanded definition of security and forwarding that empirical sovereignty affects international order. Although some might read the *Agenda for Peace* as containing the contradictory propositions that the United Nations must simultaneously honor juridical sovereignty and have the authority to intervene in domestic space, perhaps a more profitable interpretation is that it reflects the view that states are able to uphold juridical sovereignty only after they achieve empirical sovereignty. Boutros-Ghali's *Agenda for Peace*, as well as his essay in this issue, testifies to a renewed understanding of the relationship between domestic and international order.

Peacekeeping operations are a direct extension of the renewed concern for empirical sovereignty on the part of the international community. I want to comment on two aspects of these second-generation operations. First, these operations attend to internal security and domestic order. If most peacekeeping operations prior to 1988 concerned the transition from decolonization to juridical sovereignty and maintenance of territorial integrity, nearly all since then concern the transition from civil war to civil society. In many respects, operations in Namibia (UNTAG) were the turning point between those two phases: while UNTAG oversaw Namibia's independence, and therefore was quite consistent with the first phase of peacekeeping operations that facilitated decolonization and globalized sovereignty, it also presaged the upcoming second-generation operations as it ran the elections that signaled Namibia's independence. The operation in Cambodia (UNTAC) was monumental in its size, complexity, and length and provided the United Nations with a forum to implement a peace agreement, to oversee the establishment of a transnational government, and to engineer an election. The UN operation in El Salvador (ONUSAL) represents the first time that the United Nations was directly involved in all phases of domestic conflict resolution: from brokering and negotiating the agreement, to overseeing demilitarization, to reconstituting the police force, to running the election.

Actions in Somalia (UNOSOM) and Bosnia (UNPROFOR) are noteworthy because they are Chapter VII operations that provide the United Nations with peace enforcement capacities to take offensive action against those who attempt to obstruct the implementation of the mandate's objectives. In general, nearly all the post-1988 operations concern nation building and peacemaking.

Second, many of the proposals for reforming peacekeeping operations pertain to strengthening the capacity to facilitate the transition from civil war to civil society. One proposal is to increase the UN's ability to offer electoral assistance and administer elections. The UN's first involvement came with UNTAG, and soon thereafter the organization was providing electoral assistance throughout the Third World. Indeed, the demand was so great that the United Nations established the Electoral Assistance Unit in 1992, and its offices and capabilities have expanded rapidly over the last few years to keep pace with growing demand. The UN's electoral assistance to South Africa represented something of a departure, and perhaps a sign of things to come, for it was the first time that the United Nations had administered an election that was not part of a peacekeeping operation.

The United Nations is also considering ways to strengthen the relationship between peacekeeping operations and human rights. Peacekeeping operations reflect a growing concern for human rights and humanitarian intervention, and many operations contain human rights components, monitor and enforce locally brokered human rights agreements, observe human rights conditions on the ground, and attempt to instill greater respect for basic human rights. Here the significant departure was ONUSAL, which included a specific human rights component with a clear framework for UN verification. Subsequently, ONUSAL established a human rights division within its peacekeeping headquarters, the first of its kind, and that division played a key role in enforcing human rights, monitoring violations, establishing an atmosphere of greater trust and reconciliation among the population, and attempting to instill greater respect for human rights through various mechanisms, including human dignity courses in the new police academy that trains the new national police. Since then, many peacekeeping operations have had human rights divisions that investigate charges of human rights violations and actually teach human rights. The Vienna Declaration from the 1993 World Conference on Human Rights recognized the importance of peacekeeping operations in promoting human rights and championed this involvement:

> The World Conference on Human Rights, recognizing the important role of the human rights components in specific arrangements concerning some peace-keeping operations by the United Nations, recommends that the Secretary-General take into account the reporting, experience and capabilities of the Centre for Human Rights and human rights mechanisms, in conformity with the Charter of the United Nations.[18]

Two points are worth highlighting here. First, the demand for the United Nations to become more actively involved in human rights derives from pressures from international and domestic groups; not only are the UN and the international community interested in transmitting a greater respect for basic human rights, but many domestic groups that are the targets of human rights violations are hoping to use the United Nations and other international agencies to deter further violations. Second, the UN's active and growing involvement in that area represents a radical departure from both its first-generation peacekeeping operations and its past stance toward human rights. Throughout the Cold War, the UN was generally prohibited from venturing into that terrain; United Nations involvement in human rights was limited to development and decolonization, and any expression for the rights of minorities and ethnic groups was spurned as a violation of sovereignty and as a distraction from the core issue of global political and economic inequality. Accordingly, the UN's involvement in human rights represents both a radical change from its past stance and a reflection of a changing definition of security.

Another indication that the United Nations and its peacekeeping operations are becoming more involved in peace building is that there are growing pressures to reform the bureaucracy within both the Secretariat and the United Nations system. The UN system is a complex of autonomous and semiautonomous institutions that concern various political, cultural, social, and economic aspects of domestic and international life. While each unit was established to handle a distinct functional area, the growing recognition that security is multidimensional and multifaceted is forcing those organizations to widen their policy domain, to come into daily contact with other UN agencies, and to coordinate their activities (or at least to recognize that they should if they are to attain their common objectives). For instance, many peacekeeping operations include not just a military operation but also police, human rights, demining, demobilization, and economic components; this means that the Secretariat must now negotiate and coordinate with UNDP, UNHCR, the World Bank, and other UN agencies during a peacekeeping operation. How to create the institutional linkages between these various UN agencies has become a major issue in peacekeeping reform, and there is wide recognition that the success of these second-generation operations depends mightily on their coordination; one possible response offered by Boutros-Ghali is to establish integrated field offices within each peacekeeping operation.[19]

Perhaps more noteworthy, yet far more neglected, has been the expansion of UN Civilian Police (uncivpols). Once used sparingly, they have become the workhorse in many second-generation operations. There were nearly 3,600 uncivpols in UNTAC alone, and as of June 1994 there were 2,200 uncivpols from thirty-seven countries, including 1,144 in Mozambique. The numbers belie their importance. First used in UNTAG to monitor the withdrawal of South African and guerrilla forces, the decolonization process, and the elections, uncivpols have become a critical component of most operations. They have become involved in a wide range of activities in many operations, including monitoring the activities of local police; handling prisoners; accompanying local police on patrol; conducting parallel investigations with local police and then comparing their results and findings; conducting independent patrols and maintaining law and order; observing the exchange of refugees, displaced persons, returnees, and prisoners of war; monitoring political gatherings, rallies, and demonstrations and acting as surrogate bodyguards for political candidates; visiting prisons to observe the treatment of prisoners and minority groups; monitoring trials of those arrested from minority groups; assisting humanitarian aid agencies such as the UNHCR and the ICRC; and recording and investigating human rights violations.

Another responsibility of uncivpols is worth highlighting: training and retraining local police forces. The United Nations is attempting to restore civil order and stability, which ultimately means that state institutions have some degree of legitimacy, and doing so begins with law and order. Underlying much ethnic conflict is the knowledge that those in charge of maintaining order—the military and the police—are politicized and represent the primary threats to people's lives. Therefore, uncivpols have been charged with the critical task of retraining and depoliticizing new national police forces in Haiti, Somalia, and El Salvador, and this activity is likely to be a real growth area for peacekeeping operations. In general, uncivpols are enmeshed in the peace-building process as they consciously attempt to foster a greater respect for human rights, instill the police with some degree of legitimacy, encourage the democratization process, and facilitate the transition from civil war to civil society.

In sum, these second-generation peacekeeping operations are a direct reflection of the emerging view that empirical sovereignty and the domestic characteristics of states are related to international order. Policymakers and scholars alike are advocating a departure from balance-of-power and realist frameworks for keeping the peace, and advocating that a more stable international order rests on the assurance that states do not have the motivation to go to war; that motivation, or lack thereof, is frequently located within the domestic realm. Peacekeeping forces are a direct reflection of this emerging view. To understand better the UN's current role in international order requires a fuller consideration of how policymakers define security and understand what produces a stable international order.

Conclusion

During the Cold War, the United Nations received little credit for its role in maintaining international peace and security because it was not a player in East–West matters and not directly involved in those events that consumed U.S. and Soviet policymakers. Yet viewing the UN's activities as a reflection of dominant understandings of international order illuminates its past and present roles in maintaining international order. If the UN's first period pertained to decolonization and reflected the belief that juridical sovereignty and territorial integrity provided the basis of international order, thus far this second-generation agenda symbolizes the view that the lack of empirical sovereignty and state legitimacy can be a threat to international peace and security, that domestic governance is associated with international governance. The United Nation's peacekeeping activities mirror prevailing and competing sentiments concerning what generates international order.

If there has been a shift in how policymakers understand what makes for a stable international system, there has been relatively little change in the belief that the Third World represents the primary threat to that stability. Throughout its history, the United Nations has maintained a vigilant focus on the Third World and North–South relations. During the UN's first phase it was actively involved in decolonization and the globalization of juridical sovereignty, and during this second phase it is seemingly engaged in globalizing empirical sovereignty. This does not imply that the United Nations will go wherever it detects a Third World state beset by domestic instability —for whether the UN actually authorizes a peacekeeping operation depends on a host of factors—but that when it does approve an operation it is highly likely to be in the Third World. If the West is the source of, and has generally accepted, the principles and norms of international society, the Third World has either opposed or had a more difficult time adhering to them because of international, transnational, and domestic pressures. Accordingly, the international community contains numerous mechanisms and instruments that have implicitly and explicitly attempted to increase the prospect that Third World states will conform to those norms of international society. The United Nations and its peacekeeping operations can be understood as part of this larger process. The UN, then, attempts to establish international order not only by establishing constraints and incentives to state action but also, more important, by encouraging states to adopt new characteristics and configurations that are understood to correspond to the requirements of a stable international order.

Whether the United Nations maintains this expanded peacekeeping agenda depends on material and cognitive factors. To be sure, without the material resources and diplomatic support from key countries, it is highly unlikely that the UN will continue to involve itself in nation-building activities; at present the UN is having a difficult time obtaining the money, staff, and material required to perform its various missions. A state's decision to contribute the required resources depends, at a very basic level, on whether it views those operations as furthering its interests. To the extent that policymakers embrace the view that security is interdependent and multidimensional, and that domestic and international order are integrally connected, then it is more likely that the UN will obtain the resources it requires to perform those activities. In other words, a core issue for understanding the future of these second-generation activities is whether Third World and Western states find them to be consistent with their security interests. This is a matter of some debate in many capitals throughout the world, which in turn leads to a larger issue of what are the state's security interests and what are the best means to pursue them. At a very basic level, then, the debate over the United Nations and its peacekeeping operations is also a debate over the definition of national interest and state security, as well as what creates a stable international order.

Acknowledgments

This research was completed while the author was a Council on Foreign Relations International Affairs Fellow at the U.S. Mission to the United Nations.

The author wishes to thank the Department of Political Science at the University of Wisconsin and the U.S. Mission to the United Nations for their support. He also benefited from comments offered by Paul Diehl and Nina Tannenwald. The views expressed in this essay are solely those of the author.

Notes

1 Paul Lewis, "The Peacekeeper in Chief Needs More Soldiers," *New York Times*, 4 March 1994, p. 2. See John MacKinley and Jarat Chopra, "Second Generation Multinational Operations," *Washington Quarterly* (Summer 1992): 113–131, for an extended discussion of this definition.
2 "The UN and National Interests of States," in A. Roberts and B. Kingsbury, eds., *United Nations, Divided World* (New York: Oxford University Press, 1993), pp. 111–112.
3 Hedley Bull's *Anarchical Society* (New York: Columbia University Press, 1977) offers the defining statement of this approach.
4 This distinction draws directly from Robert H. Jackson, *Quasi-States: Sovereignty, International Relations and the Third World* (New York: Cambridge University Press, 1990).
5 Bull, *Anarchical Society*, p. 8.
6 Ibid., p. 53, emphasis in original.
7 See Gerrit Gong, *The Standard of "Civilization" in International Society* (New York: Oxford University Press, 1984).
8 Jackson, *Quasi-States*, p. 36.
9 Rupert Emerson, "Colonialism, Political Development, and the UN," *International Organization* 19 (Summer 1965): 486.
10 David Kay, "The Politics of Decolonization," *International Organization* 21 (Autumn 1967): 786–811.
11 Harold Jacobson, "The United Nations and Colonialism: A Tentative Appraisal," *International Organization* 16 (Winter 1962): 47.
12 Louis Henkin, "The United Nations and Human Rights," *International Organization* 19 (Summer 1965): 512. In *Quasi-States*, p. 95, Jackson notes that only after it became apparent that decolonization would proceed before "self-government" was achieved that the "unquestionable assumption that the transfer of sovereignty must be contingent on empirical conditions began to be undermined."
13 John Spencer, "Africa at the UN: Some Observations," *International Organization* 16 (Spring 1962): 381.

14 "The UN and International Security After the Cold War," in Roberts and Kingsbury, *United Nations, Divided World*, pp. 91–92.
15 Boutros Boutros-Ghali, *Agenda for Peace* (New York: United Nations, 1992).
16 Michael Doyle, "Liberalism and World Politics," *American Political Science Review* 80 (1986): 1151–1169; and Bruce Russett, *Grasping the Democratic Peace* (Princeton: Princeton University Press, 1993).
17 Clinton's policy of enlargement is perhaps the clearest policy statement of the relationship between the two. See Anthony Lake, "From Containment to Enlargement," *Dispatch* 4, no. 39 (1993). Also recognize that the office in the Pentagon that was to oversee peacekeeping operations was called the "Office of Democracy of Peacekeeping," which signals how the two elements are linked in the American mind. See Morton Halperin, "Guaranteeing Democracy," *Foreign Policy* 91 (Summer 1993): 105–122, for a related discussion.
18 *Vienna Declaration and Programme of Action*, adopted 25 June 1993 (UN Document A/CONF.157/23).
19 Amnesty International, *Peacekeeping and Human Rights*, January 1994, fn. 110. Mimeo.

4 The United Nations and global security*

The norm is mightier than the sword

It is ironic that, at the same moment that the international community seems to have discovered that international security might be fostered through cooperative security measures, the United Nations has used its post-Cold War freedoms to exercise its enforcement capacities and to entertain their further development. The beginning of superpower cooperation and the experience of the Gulf War stirred a discussion of the meaning and merits of collective security, and the drift of peacekeeping into peace enforcement created a gray zone called "Chapter VI-1/2" operations.[1] Such developments reflect an underlying sentiment that as a security organization the United Nations should possess robust enforcement mechanisms. Simply put, it is not enough to be a forum for considering threats to international peace and security; the United Nations must possess the mechanisms to combat them as well.

Recent events, however, have demonstrated that neither the United Nations nor its member states are quite ready for this day.[2] A lesson of Somalia and Bosnia is that the Security Council took relatively lightly the idea of peace enforcement and operating without obtaining the consent of the parties, not fully considering the strategic, political, and ethical issues involved. Consequently, there seems to be a growing belief that peace enforcement might be better left to states and peacekeeping to the United Nations.[3] There is evidence, moreover, that the Security Council is learning that peacekeepers should be used not as symbols of the international community's concern but only when the conditions are ripe for them on the ground. Initially, the Security Council was so quick to authorize any proposed mission that many quipped that "the UN never met an operation it did not like." By the fall of 1993, however, many state and UN officials were grumbling that such automatic authorizations had left the United Nations stretched thin and unable to operate effectively. The Security Council responded by adopting a set of criteria for determining whether or not to approve or to extend a peacekeeping operation. This set of criteria focused on the issue of consent of the parties and how best to enhance the United Nations' ability to monitor compliance with agreements and encourage trust between combatants.[4]

Such developments redirect attention to how international institutions can foster interstate cooperation without enforcement mechanisms. By establishing a set of normative arrangements and expectations to govern the behavior of their members, and monitoring mechanisms to encourage compliance with those norms, international institutions can encourage trust and cooperation. The following discussion will employ these institutional insights to demonstrate their consistency with the United Nations' distinctive contribution to international security as a builder rather than enforcer of norms. Not only does the United Nations provide a set of norms that indicate how states should behave in the international community, but it frequently monitors the compliance of states with these norms. This view of the United Nations is both pragmatic and principled; it is consistent with what member states are willing to support and it reclaims the United Nations' distinctive and principal role as a mechanism to encourage global security through noncoercive means.

The United Nations, norms, and security

There is an increasing recognition by the Security Council and others that the United Nations can best contribute to international peace and security through noncoercive mechanisms. In this important respect, the Security Council's view is consistent with that of many international relations theorists who argue that international institutions can foster interstate cooperation without robust enforcement mechanisms.[5] Specifically, institutions can facilitate cooperation by clarifying norms, rules, and principles that guide state behavior, by defining a range of acceptable behavior, and by creating greater certainty of compliance with these norms by others through the establishment of monitoring mechanisms. Institutions, in short, contain normative arrangements that suggest what behavior is acceptable and monitoring devices to encourage states to adhere to those norms.

This view of how international institutions can foster cooperation offers important guidance in thinking about how the United Nations might contribute to international security. As an international institution the United Nations both articulates various norms, codified in the Charter and numerous other international documents and resolutions, and monitors the compliance of states with these norms. That the United Nations and other international institutions signal how states are to behave and provide mechanisms to regulate that behavior suggests two types of norms—constitutive and regulative, respectively—when considering how institutions such as the United Nations can encourage cooperation among states.[6] The following discussion, therefore, suggests how the United Nations, by operating on the principle of the consent of the parties, can encourage the development of a more stable and cooperative security architecture through the articulation and transmission of norms and the establishment of mechanisms to encourage transparency in interstate and internal matters.[7]

Regulative norms

Most intuitive is that institutions establish regulative norms that help states overcome collective action problems associated with interdependent choice. Even when they desire to cooperate to further their self-interest, states still need to negotiate explicit rules to encourage compliance and reciprocity, that is, to ensure that cooperation begets cooperation. A striking feature of the post-Cold War security dialogue is that policymakers are not advocating a return to alliances and balances of power to maintain the peace but rather are exploring how multilateral mechanisms and security institutions can reduce uncertainty and fear and offer confidence-building measures and other devices that might cultivate trust. The understanding that states have common interests, largely driven by increasing interdependence, that require joint action to obtain their common goals is the heart of a multilateral view.[8]

The United Nations has at its core a multilateral sensibility, and since the Cold War member states have been more supportive and cognizant of its contribution in this area. For instance, the United Nations is presently debating various ways to establish confidence-building agreements, transparency in arms accumulation, and other sorts of arrangements that will encourage states to adopt a more defensive and less militarized security posture. The United Nations' good offices are frequently used for mediation activities, and the organization played a critical role in negotiating the peace agreements in Mozambique and El Salvador and between Iran and Iraq.[9] In general, the United Nations, whether in New York or elsewhere, provides an important forum for both state and nonstate actors to discuss their points of disagreement and to resolve conflicts.

International institutions provide not only the forum for negotiating such cooperative arrangements but also the monitoring mechanisms that give states the assurance that others will not defect from their agreements. Because states generally do not trust that others will keep their word or abide by their agreements, they desire mechanisms to monitor compliance; in short, they operate according to Reagan's dictum of "trust but verify." The United Nations, because of its neutrality, is well-suited to this role and is being used in imaginative ways to encourage transparency: the United Nations Angola Verification Mission monitored the withdrawal of Cuban troops from Angola; the United Nations Special Commission oversees Iraq's weapons program; and the Electoral Assistance Unit (established in 1992) provides technical support and election monitoring for fledgling democracies.

The most famous UN oversight mechanism, of course, is peacekeeping—the deployment of UN troops to observe a cease-fire arrangement or to implement a peace agreement between two or more parties. Although the explosion of peacekeeping has jeopardized its very future, most member states remain highly committed to improving the effectiveness of UN peacekeeping; the Clinton administration's Presidential Decision Directive (PDD) 25 on multilateral peacekeeping operations and the UN "Contact Group of

34 on Peacekeeping" highlight a sustained understanding that peacekeeping represents a valuable tool for dispute settlement.[10] Accordingly, member states continue to contemplate various ways to make peacekeeping more effective, for instance, by establishing Article 43 stand-by agreements, improving the bureaucratic capacity of the Department of Peacekeeping Operations, and augmenting the UN's civilian police capacity for monitoring local police forces. These and other proposals seek to enhance the United Nations' ability to oversee (although not to enforce) international and domestic agreements. In general, the United Nations' role is consistent with that of other international institutions: its purpose is to establish verification mechanisms to allow states and nonstate actors to trust one another.

Demand for UN peacekeeping, however, outstrips its capacity. As the United Nations runs short of resources and finds itself unable to serve this monitoring function, it is exploring other arrangements, most notably by literally joining forces with major powers and regional organizations that are frequently dominated by a regional power. Simply put, the decision to rely more fully on those states that have the capability and willingness to partake in security operations (and monitoring functions) is a direct result of the unwillingness of member states to support operations unless they have a stake in the outcome. These developments have led many to fear creeping spheres of influence, the overshadowing of any independent or effective role for the UN by the great powers, and a failure of UN stand-ins to observe the organization's strict standard of neutrality.[11]

To overcome these concerns the United Nations is establishing a generalized set of principles and norms that are intended to guide the behavior of those who receive its stamp of legitimacy. Significant in this respect were the authorized U.S. action in Haiti and the Russian operation in Georgia. Many U.S. policymakers fear that Russia might attempt to reestablish military control over the post-Soviet states, and by seeking UN approval for its invasion of Haiti the United States sought to exact some measure of influence over future Russian military activities in its near abroad.[12] Pointedly, the Russian permanent representative to the United Nations stated that "the Russian Federation attaches great importance to the total transparency of the operation authorized by the Security Council for a multinational force in Haiti. Such transparency is essential to ensure complete confidence in the actions of the multinational force by the international community and support by the international community for that operation."[13] As U.S. officials saw it, the same rule would apply to Russian military activities outside its borders.

The Security Council approved the Russian operation in Georgia on the condition of the simultaneous deployment of 136 UN monitors to ensure that Russia adhered to UN standards of behavior and observed strict neutrality.[14] As most saw it, the UN monitors represented an important mechanism to encourage Russia to be on its best behavior. France, for one, welcomed the decision by Russia to seek authorization from the United Nations and observed that "this operation thus becomes a part of the process of a political settlement that is under the auspices of the United Nations. . . . It emphasizes the regulatory functions that the Security Council has now shouldered for peacekeeping activities carried out by powers or by regional forums."[15] In general, as the United Nations searches for major powers and regional organizations to help with its rather expansive security agenda, it is articulating a set of norms and principles that are intended to guide the behavior of those states and organizations that act with its approval.

Major powers and others who receive the blessing of the United Nations, therefore, are being held accountable for their actions in some fundamentally new ways. This represents a critical role for the United Nations. In her provocative book on the relationship between hegemony and morality, Lea Brilmayer intimates the difficulty of delineating mechanisms to hold the world's most powerful states accountable to other states.[16] I am suggesting that these norms, which are directed at those who operate with the United Nations' authorization, are desired by the major powers, other Security Council members, and the Secretariat staff; all, so it seems, have a strong interest in ensuring that there is no purely instrumental use of the United Nations and that even major powers are held accountable for their actions. Because of scarce resources and (something of) a division of labor, there will sometimes be a cop on the beat, sometimes community patrols (regional organizations) and sometimes an outside security service (the United Nations), but in all instances there is a strong interest in making sure that all cops operate according to the same standards.

The growing trend of delegating responsibility for implementing the Security Council's decisions highlights another potentially important role for the United Nations: to coordinate and contract the peacekeeping contributions of state and nonstate actors. The prevailing assumption is that because the United Nations administers the decisions of the Security Council it must be involved in all aspects of the actual implementation. This assumption overlooks the important implementation role other state and nonstate actors might play, with the United Nations performing a coordinating and contracting function. There are various precedents here. A critical feature of many peacekeeping operations is the retraining of local police forces and removing land mines; both represent important developments for facilitating the transition from civil war to civil society. Yet because the United Nations does not have expertise or the resources to undertake such activities on its own, it identifies various member states and nonstate actors that can contribute to this end and then helps to organize their actions. By becoming more active in coordinating contributions from a myriad of public and private agencies the United Nations will better realize its mandated responsibilities, improve cost-effectiveness, and give member states a greater interest in, and knowledge of, peacekeeping operations.[17] That the United Nations should consider ways to coordinate the activities of its member states rather than duplicate or supplant them is becoming a dominant theme of many peacekeeping reform proposals; this coordination function is comparable to the role played by many international institutions.

Constitutive norms

Less intuitive, but no less important for encouraging cooperation than regulative norms, are constitutive norms, which can be understood as norms that directly express the actor's identity. Individuals frequently behave in certain ways and not others because of the relationship between such behavior and the individual's identity. This is also true for states. Certain state behavior is considered inappropriate because, for instance, it is inconsistent with what it means to be a "civilized" or "modern" or "sovereign" state; modern, civilized states do not possess colonies, they do not settle their differences through war, they do not violate basic human rights, and so on. In these and other cases, certain classes of behavior are viewed as reflective of the state's identity; these norms, then, essentially signify how a state is or is not to enact a particular identity.

Many of the most important constitutive norms of the international community are embodied in the United Nations. These norms, in effect, model appropriate behavior for modern, sovereign states. Dorothy Jones observes that there are "nine fundamental principles that constitute a summary of state reflection upon proper action in the international sphere. . . . All nine can be found in the United Nations Charter but the authors of the document did not create them." These principles of state action are: "sovereign equality of states; territorial integrity and political independence of states; equal rights and self-determination of peoples; nonintervention in internal affairs of states; peaceful settlement of disputes between states; no threat or use of force; fulfillment in good faith of international obligations; cooperation with other states; and respect for human rights and fundamental freedoms."[18] These principles can be thought of as constitutive norms, for they tell states how to enact their identity as states of the international community.

Although it is impossible to detail the origins of these norms, two points are worth emphasizing. First, these norms can emerge from fear of what might happen if they are not heeded—that is, because of self-interest and a survival instinct. Therefore, although these norms might have originated in the West, they have been utilized and defended throughout the world by the weak against the strong as a normative armor against their actions. So while these norms are frequently used by the powerful and the West against the weak and the Third World, the weak and the Third World have also used those very global norms to constrain the powerful and the West. For instance, although the principle of noninterference is violated on a daily basis, the Third World is most active in attempting to maintain the principle as a normative defense against the intrusions of the powerful. Second, these norms also emerge from a climate of hope, a generalized (though by no means uniform) sense of how the international community ought to operate. For instance, those pressing for decolonization were able to use the Western-inspired norms of national self-determination to compel the colonial powers to expedite the decolonization process. Those arguing for the importance of universal human rights, nondiscrimination toward women, and so on, operate not only out of fear but also out of a vision of the ideal international community they desire.[19] These constitutive norms, in short, can originate from the desire for security and progress.

The United Nations, therefore, plays an important role in articulating norms of state behavior, and these norms are desirable because they represent a better and (hopefully) more stable international order. Consider the decolonization movement. The UN Charter and its articulation of the norm of self-determination signaled that one of its key objectives was to facilitate the transition from the era of empires to the era of sovereignty—to globalize and universalize sovereignty as the basis of relations among states. That the United Nations played an important role in this issue cannot be attributed solely to the strategic and material interests of the major powers; it was also due to the efforts of many who made principled arguments for decolonization and had them codified in the Charter. The fact that decolonization had a prominent place on the United Nations' agenda virtually guaranteed that those states that attempted to retain their colonial privileges would be increasingly viewed as acting in an illegitimate manner by the international community. Moreover, the United Nations also indicated that independence meant honoring the norms of the society of states and the principle of sovereignty; to become a state meant becoming a sovereign state and recognizing its basic responsibilities. For instance, Article 6 of the 1960 UN Declaration on the Granting of Independence to Colonial Countries and Peoples stated that "any attempt aimed at the partial or whole disruption of the national unity and the territorial integrity of a country is incompatible with the purposes and principles of the Charter of the UN." Although there are various self-interested and materially based reasons why the colonial states began the process of decolonization and the newly independent Third World states largely honored juridical sovereignty, in both cases the United Nations played an important role in demarcating the expected behavior of modern states.

The case for decolonization was made not only on principled grounds but was also framed as an issue of international peace and security. Articles 11, 12, and 13 of the UN Charter explicitly recognized that a major reason for the United Nations' involvement in decolonization was international security. Indeed, over time the "conviction . . . spread that the continued existence of any dependency by itself created a threat to peace and security."[20] At a fundamental level, then, the United Nations was involved in an elementary issue of international order and should be credited with assisting the relatively peaceful transformation of the relationship between the North and the South. Not only did the United Nations codify some basic constitutive norms—the principles of self-determination and sovereignty—but it also established numerous institutional mechanisms designed to regulate the decolonization process and encourage a peaceful transition. The United Nations played an important role in the history of decolonization by articulating and expressing the norms that should govern interstate behavior.

Over the past decade, a striking feature of UN activities has been its increasingly active involvement in articulating and transmitting the constitutive norms of domestic behavior in order to foster a more stable and desirable international order. If the prevailing belief was once that international order was premised on balancing power and discounting domestic politics, there is now an increased conviction that domestic politics matters and that empirical statehood—the idea that states have some degree of legitimacy and control over their society and within their borders—should enable states to uphold the norms of international society.[21] By emphasizing the strong relationship between domestic and international order, member states are moving from the language of deterrence to that of assurance and recognizing that the assurance that states will not act aggressively is furthered when states do not have the motivation to go to war. This motivation, in turn, is best minimized by preventing conflicts from arising in the first place, a prevention that is due in no small measure to some level of domestic stability.[22] Although domestic stability can be effected through democratic or authoritarian means, many member states and the UN Secretariat believe that there is a strong relationship between democratization and peaceful change. For instance, at the 1993 United Nations General Assembly member states from the Third World and the West alike affirmed their belief in a strong relationship between democracy and international peace. Boutros Boutros-Ghali has made countless statements that the UN should be more actively involved in promoting democracy across the globe.[23] Simply put, not just any domestic order creates the foundations for international order—the rule of law at home creates the rule of law abroad.[24]

The understanding that there is a strong relationship between domestic and international order is evident in these second-generation peacekeeping operations.[25] This can be seen most vividly in the area of human rights. Although the UN Charter specifically mentions its importance, it is only in the recent past that the United Nations has pressed the issue. There is growing acceptance, for instance, that "civilized" states should respect human rights and have some degree of the domestic accountability that is associated with democratic principles of rule, both because this accountability is a means to an end (for example, international order) and because it is an end in itself. It is increasingly the case that respect for human and ethnic rights is treated as both a principle and a peace and security issue.[26]

Peacekeeping operations reflect a growing concern for human rights, and many operations contain human rights components: monitoring and enforcing locally brokered human rights agreements, observing human rights conditions on the ground, and attempting to instill greater respect for basic human rights. Here the significant departure was the United Nations Observer Mission in El Salvador (ONUSAL), which included a specific human rights component with a clear framework for UN verification. Subsequently, ONUSAL established a human rights division in its peacekeeping headquarters. The first of its kind, this division has played a key role in enforcing human rights, monitoring violations, establishing an atmosphere of greater trust and reconciliation among the population, and instilling greater respect for human rights through various mechanisms, including human dignity courses in the police academy that trains the new national police. Many peacekeeping operations now have a human rights division that both investigates charges of human rights violations and teaches human rights. The Vienna Declaration from the 1993 World Conference on Human Rights recognized the importance of peacekeeping operations in promoting human rights:

> The World Conference on Human Rights, recognizing the important role of the human rights components in specific arrangements concerning some peacekeeping operations by the United Nations, recommends that the Secretary-General take into account the reporting, experience, and capabilities of the Centre for Human Rights and human rights mechanisms, in conformity with the Charter of the United Nations.[27]

Related to this, the UN Human Rights Office in Vienna created a "human dignity" course for all 1,100 UN civilian police serving in Mozambique; the intent, according to one UN official, was to find a mechanism to transfer certain human rights standards to the local Mozambican police and to the UN civilian police who would take this knowledge with them when they returned home.

Three points are worth highlighting here. First, the demand for the United Nations to become more actively involved in human rights derives from pressures from international and domestic groups; not only are the United Nations and the international community interested in transmitting a greater respect for basic human rights, but many domestic groups that are the targets of human rights violations hope to use the United Nations and other international agencies to deter further violations. Second, the United Nations' active and growing involvement in this area represents a radical departure from both its first-generation peacekeeping operations and its past stance toward human rights. Throughout the Cold War the United Nations was generally prohibited from venturing into this terrain; UN involvement in human rights was limited to development and decolonization, and any expression for the rights of minorities and ethnic groups was spurned as a violation of sovereignty and a distraction from the core issue of global political and economic inequality. Accordingly, the United Nations' involvement in human rights both represents a radical change from its past stance and reflects a changing definition of security. Third, by encouraging recognition of human rights and democratic systems of rule, the United Nations is establishing a particular vision of how member states should organize their domestic relations. This highlights an important but little recognized feature of international institutions: they not only help to coordinate state interests but also shape the very identity and interests of the state.

Part of the reason that the United Nations serves this function as a transmitter and articulator of constitutive norms is because it is endowed with tremendous legitimacy by the community of states. Thomas Franck and Inis Claude help us to understand why this is the case. Franck highlights that states seek to be viewed as legitimate by other states and to be understood as acting with a degree of moral authority and sanctioned purpose.[28] States, Franck claims, not only represent the political communities contained within their borders, but are also embedded in a larger international community from which they derive their rights, obligations, and authority to act in legitimately sanctioned ways. "Nations, or those who govern them," writes Franck, "recognize that the obligation to comply is owed by them to the community of states as the reciprocal of that community's validation of their nation's statehood."[29] Legitimacy, therefore, is conferred by others when the state convincingly demonstrates that it abides by the community's norms. Claude nicely supplements Franck's argument by pointing out that the United Nations is the only organization that approximates universality and has the authority to distribute seals of approval and disapproval. No other organization rivals the United Nations in these crucial respects.[30]

A striking feature of the post-Cold War period is that even the most powerful states appear to be seeking the United Nations' seal of approval with greater frequency. Although there are many possible explanations for this development, perhaps the most provocative is that a growing cosmopolitanism is causing major powers to seek the United Nations' authorization. Power is increasingly conferred on those who demonstrate adherence to the community's values and norms, and leadership is not only about having military power but also about projecting a moral purpose. Power and influence, in this respect, are not a function solely of military might and economic wealth, but also of perception. The United States' power in the international system derives not only from its military might but also from its relationship to the international community's dominant norms. Canada and the Scandinavian states wield greater influence in world affairs than might be expected from their military power because of their close association with the values espoused by the international community and embodied in the United Nations. Power and influence, in short, derive not only from brute military power and the capacity to dominate but also from an association with the dominant norms of the community and the capacity to persuade. If a state's influence and power is shaped by its ability to abide by and be identified with these norms, then the norms will have a powerful effect on state behavior.

The state, which derives its authority and legitimacy not only from its citizens but also from the community of states, is embedded in an increasingly dense normative web that constrains its foreign policy in general and its use of military force in particular. While states will continue to act unilaterally when their national interests are at stake, changing definitions of security, growing interdependence, and expanded community boundaries are causing the military actions of many states to be legitimated not only by their citizens but also by the international community. As suggested earlier, prominent in this regard is that U.S. officials are increasingly seeking the United Nations' authority and stamp of legitimacy.[31] In a series of interviews, many senior foreign policy officials of the Clinton administration spoke of the United States' need to have the United Nations legitimate its military activities and stressed that the domestic and international forces that are causing this development operate with nonpartisan effect on Democratic and Republican administrations alike. In fact, the first significant post-Cold War instance of this phenomenon was Bush's decision in the fall of 1990 to turn to the United Nations to legitimate his forthcoming war against Iraq. While many in the United States criticized him for asking the United Nations to approve an action that they viewed as a prerogative of a great power and a sovereign state (including Kuwait's right to request assistance in its self-defense), without the United Nations' "stamp of approval" it is highly debatable whether Congress would have supported Bush's decision to initiate war against Iraq. In general, major powers want to be viewed as acting on behalf, and in a manner that is consistent with the norms, of the international community—a perception that is increasingly based on UN approval.

This search for legitimacy and UN accreditation is also driven by financial and political considerations. Most prominent here is the greater interest in burden-sharing. Because of increasing budgetary pressures at home, major powers are looking to the United Nations and other multilateral mechanisms for financial and security assistance. Prospective coalition partners, however, are increasingly demanding that the United Nations approve the multilateral operation before they will join. In other words, even when the most powerful states search for coalition partners, they are discovering that such partners are demanding that the operation receive accreditation from the United Nations because of its legitimation function. For instance, as the United States attempted to assemble a multinational operation for post-invasion Haiti, a chief concern was finding a civilian police force that was to retrain and monitor the Haitian security forces; the United States discovered that many of the likely contributors, most notably Canada, were willing to participate under a UN flag but not under the "banner of a U.S. led invasion force."[32] The UN stamp of approval does not come cost-free; the operation must be viewed as consistent with the goals of the member states, and its very design is subject to amendment during the authorization process. Regardless of whether the motor force is domestic, strategic, or economic, states are increasingly seeking UN approval because of the organization's status as an agent of collective legitimization; the outcome is the imprint of global and normative forces on the state's foreign policy.[33]

It would be a mistake, therefore, to discount the power of these norms in shaping the behavior of even the most powerful states. Many realists suggest that the United Nations is little more than a "rubber stamp" for the great powers and that neither it nor its norms have much effect on state actions. This view can be countered in three ways. First, the very decision to seek Security Council approval provides major and minor powers alike with an important opportunity to alter the actions of, and to hold accountable, even the largest members. While the most powerful have the greatest influence, even the less powerful have some say over the outcome (which, of course, gives the organization its collective legitimacy).[34] Second, the ability to participate in, and accrue benefits from, the group frequently depends on abiding by the group's norms and standards of behavior,[35] and these norms increasingly involve not only the state's foreign policy but also its domestic behavior. Many states are attempting to exhibit, for instance, a commitment to such values as democracy and human rights in order to receive the benefits of fellowship with the West, and they are demonstrating their adherence to such values through their activities at the United Nations. A final way of countering the realist claim that the United Nations and the search for legitimacy has no effect on the state behavior is to pose a simple counterfactual scenario: would the state's foreign policy behavior change if the United Nations and the desire for legitimacy were imagined out of existence? I doubt that even the most stalwart critic of the United Nations or the most loyal disciple of realism would desire to dismantle the United Nations or defend the idea of a world in which norms do not affect outcomes.[36] The United Nations can be judged effective to the extent that states change their behavior as a consequence of its existence; "it is not an all-or-nothing proposition."[37] In short, norms matter for producing a more stable security order, and the United Nations, as an articulator and transmitter of these norms, contributes to peace and security.

Conclusion

After the Cold War many entertained the possibility that the United Nations might increase its involvement in security affairs and become a muscular security organization. Such visions, however, outstripped either what the United Nations was immediately capable of accomplishing or what the member states were willing to support. These developments demand a more pragmatic assessment of the United Nations to learn what it can do well, what it cannot do well, and how it can become more effective.

The tendency to use the United Nations as an agent of peace enforcement, and without the proper conditions on the ground, did immense harm to both the organization and the very people it was supposed to help. As Thomas Weiss argued here last year, the willingness of the member states to use the United Nations in Bosnia arguably made a bad situation worse by heightening problems on the ground and making a long-term solution that much more elusive.[38] Recent peacekeeping episodes, most notably in Somalia, have also caused grave damage to the United Nations' reputation and, hence, to its legitimacy. Indeed, the United Nations' involvement in enforcement activities has dangerously eroded its reputation and legitimacy, the prime sources of its ability to encourage states to abide by its norms.[39] By shying away from enforcement actions and ceasing to use peacekeepers as symbols, the Security Council can do much to solidify the United Nations' legitimacy and therefore its ability to compel states to abide by its decisions. There is growing recognition that the United Nations cannot always help others at all times and that to do so can make matters worse and undermine the organization's distinct contribution to international security.

The Clinton administration's policy toward peacekeeping exemplifies a growing awareness of its limitations and potential contributions. Candidate Clinton spoke approvingly of a UN standing army, and U.S. ambassador to the UN Madeline Albright advocated assertive multilateralism and saving failed states. Such talk quickly disappeared after the events in Haiti and Somalia in October 1993, and there was much concern that such setbacks would cause the United States to withdraw its support from the United Nations. Notwithstanding its diminished zeal, the United States returns time and again to the United Nations and, in doing so, has developed a keen interest in seeing that when the United Nations is "selected it is effective." What is particularly instructive here is: a diminishing interest in seeing the United Nations involved in peace enforcement; a continuing interest in using the United Nations as a forum for establishing cooperative security arrangements; the attempt to further develop the mechanisms of transparency, including peacekeeping, that encourage states to resolve their conflicts and adopt more cooperative arrangements; a greater recognition that peacekeepers should not be used as symbols but only when the conditions are ripe and the UN obtains the consent of the parties; and a growing awareness that the United Nations represents a highly valuable forum for articulating the norms of acceptable behavior in the community of states. The United Nations, therefore, can make an important contribution to security even if it never develops robust enforcement capacities. "Much of what the UN can do in the area of international security regime building," James Schear observes, "does not require rigid adherence to the ideal of collective security."[40]

There is, then, an important convergence between the pragmatic and the principled. That member states are recognizing that the United Nations is presently neither well-designed nor well-equipped to engage in enforcement activities is consistent with the view that the United Nations makes its distinctive contribution to peace and security when operating with the consent of the parties and through noncoercive means. Although there will be future episodes in which member states cannot wait for consent (such as during humanitarian operations), it is important that the decision to operate without consent be treated as the exception rather than the rule and be taken seriously rather than lightly.[41] Consent has been the foundation for, and the source of legitimacy of, UN activities, and its value will be tarnished, if not lost, if it becomes another coercive instrument. The international community already has more coercive mechanisms than it needs, but few organizations have the reputation and capacity to foster security through peaceful means.

Notes

* The author gratefully acknowledges support from the United States Institute of Peace, which funded the research for this article, as well as Martha Finnemore for her comments on an earlier draft.

1 Barry Blechman, "The Military Dimensions of Collective Security," in R. Coate, ed., *U.S. Policy and the Future of the United Nations* (New York: Twentieth Century Fund Press, 1994), 67–88; and Jeffrey Laurenti, *Directions and Dilemmas in Collective Security: Reflections from a Global Roundtable* (United Nations Association of America, 1994).

2 See, for instance, Bruce Clark, "Idealism Gives Way to Disenchantment," *Financial Times*, April 19, 1994, 15; Paul Lewis, "Reluctant Peacekeepers," *New York Times*, December 12, 1993, 22; Julia Preston, "Vision of a More Aggressive UN Now Dims," *Washington Post*, January 5, 1994, 24; and Brian Hall, "The World's Cops, Kicked Around," *New York Times Magazine*, January 2, 1994.

3 Responding to President Clinton's suggestion that the United Nations become more active in peace enforcement and battling the Bosnian Serbs, Michael Rose, commander of the UN Protection Force (UNPROFOR) said, "If someone wants to fight a war here on moral or political grounds, fine, great, but count [the United Nations] out. Hitting one tank is peacekeeping. Hitting infrastructure command and control, logistics, that *is* war, and I'm not going to fight a war with painted tanks." Roger Cohen, "UN General Opposes More Bosnia Force," *New York Times*, September 29, 1994, 7.

4 S/PRST/1994/22, May 3, 1994.

5 See, for instance, Oran Young, *International Cooperation* (Ithaca: Cornell University Press, 1989), and Robert Keohane, *International Institutions and State Power* (Boulder: Westview Press, 1989).

6 See Martin Hollis, *The Cunning of Reason* (New York: Cambridge University Press, 1988), 137–41. Norman Fain, in *Normative Politics and the International Community* (Philadelphia: Temple University Press, 1987), 206–8, offers a comparable argument by drawing on Terry Nardin's distinction between purposive and practical associations in *Law, Morality, and the Relations of States* (Princeton: Princeton University Press, 1983).

7 See Lea Brilmayer, *American Hegemony: Political Morality in a One-Superpower World* (New Haven: Yale University Press, 1994), for a detailed discussion of the concept of consent.

8 See John Ruggie, ed., *Multilateralism Matters* (New York: Columbia University Press, 1993), and Thomas Pickering, "Power and Purpose: Making Multilateralism Work," *Foreign Service Journal*, July 1992, 31–34.

9 Stephen Baranyi and Liisa North, *Stretching the Limits of the Possible: United Nations Peacekeeping in Central America* (Ottawa: Canadian Centre for Global Security, 1992). See Saadia Touval, "Why the UN Fails," and Giandomenico Picco, "The UN and the Use of Force," *Foreign Affairs* 73 (September/October 1994), 14–18 and 44–57, respectively, for contrasting views on the effectiveness of the United Nations as a mediator.

10 Report of the Special Committee on Peacekeeping Operations, "Comprehensive Review of the Whole Question of Peacekeeping Operations in All Their Aspects," A/49/136, May 2, 1994.

11 "Spheres of Influence," *Financial Times*, August 8, 1994, 12; James Boone, "US and Russia Broker Haiti Invasion Deal," *London Times*, August 8, 1994, 9.

12 Author interview with top-ranking U.S. official, June 8, 1994, Washington, D.C.

13 S/PV.3413, July 31, 1994, 23.

14 "UN Endorses Russian Troops for Peacekeeping," *New York Times*, July 22, 1994, 3.

15 S/PV.3407, July 21, 1994, 4. Also see Douglas Hurd and Andre Kozyrev, "Challenge of Peacekeeping," *Financial Times*, December 14, 1993, 14, in which they write that any Russian peacekeeping force must abide by basic CSCE and UN principles of consent of the parties and political neutrality. Also see John Thornhill, "U.S. Approves Role of Russian Troops within CIS States," *Financial Times*, September 7, 1994, 16.

16 *American Hegemony*, 220–21.

17 The coordination task concerns not only organizing the participants once they arrive on the scene but also establishing general standard operating procedures and guidelines to facilitate interoperability. This is a particularly visible feature of many proposals for peacekeeping training. A major drawback of the fact that the United Nations must rely on the contributions of its member states is that national contingents are frequently trained according to different peacekeeping manuals and procedures. This severely undermines the effectiveness and efficiency of the operation. Various proposals have been designed to overcome such problems and to further the interoperability of different national contingents; prominent is the idea of the United Nations as either a coordinator, actively encouraging states to increase their level of specialized training and providing some multilateral coordination of their activities, or a contractor, concentrating on training national units at existing national training centers. See Barry Blechman and J. Matthew Vaccaro, *Training for Peacekeeping: The United Nations' Role* (Washington: Stimson Center, 1994).

18 "The Declaratory Tradition in Modern International Law," in Terry Nardin and David Marpel, eds., *Traditions of International Ethics* (New York: Cambridge University Press, 1992), 44–45.

19 Ibid, 48–49.

20 Rupert Emerson, "Colonialism, Political Development, and the UN," *International Organization* 19 (Summer 1965), 486.

21 The term empirical statehood derives from Robert Jackson, *Quasi-States* (New York: Cambridge University Press, 1990).

22 Part of this increased interest in the domestic sphere is driven by the growing awareness that Third World states face greater threats from their own societies than they do from their neighbors. Although policymakers were not oblivious to these domestic challenges during the Cold War, there was a decided tendency to downplay them because of (1) a realist assumption that external threats were primary, (2) the tendency to assume that foreign elements caused domestic instability, or (3) the fear that promoting political reconciliation might undermine a strategic ally. As these Third World internal security dilemmas become more numerous and visible, and of greater potential consequence for local populations and regional stability, there is increased pressure on the international community to intervene.

23 See, for instance, Boutros Boutros-Ghali, "An Agenda for Peace: One Year Later," *Orbis 37* (Summer 1993), 329, and "The Democratization of International Relations," *Global Governance* 1 (January 1995).

24 The claim that there is a relationship between domestic and international order is not novel. From Kant's *Perpetual Peace*, which provides the founding statement on the relationship between democracies and pacific relations, to colonial discourse on the timing of decolonization, which frequently argued that the colony could achieve independence only after it had achieved a level of political development that demonstrated its ability to abide by the norms of international society,

theorists and policymakers have frequently argued that there is a strong relationship between democracy and peace in general and domestic order and international order in particular.

25 See Michael Barnett, "The New UN Politics of Peace," *Global Governance* 1 (January 1995), for an expanded discussion of this argument. Boutros-Ghali's An *Agenda for Peace* (New York: United Nations Press, 1992) can be read as making a claim for the relationship between domestic and international order.

26 The increased importance of these human rights norms underscores how different constitutive norms can conflict; specifically, the respect for human rights and the principle of noninterference clash in the area of humanitarian intervention. That the norms of society, whether domestic or international, might occasionally conflict is not surprising. Moreover, it is expected that there will be greater tension between the interstate and domestic constitutive norms with a growing interdependence and a blurring of the distinction between the domestic and the international. See James Rosenau, *Turbulence in World Politics* (Princeton: Princeton University Press, 1990), 211–16.

27 Vienna Declaration and Programme of Action, adopted on June 25, 1993 (UN Document a/conf.157/23).

28 Franck, *The Power of Legitimacy Among Nations* (New York: Oxford University Press, 1990).

29 Ibid., 196.

30 Claude, "Collective Legitimization as a Political Function of the United Nations," *International Organization* 20 (Summer 1966), 367–79.

31 Ernst Haas argues that a rough measure of the legitimacy of the United Nations is the degree to which "member states invoke its purposes and principles ... to justify national policy." *Beyond the Nation-State* (Stanford: Stanford University Press, 1964), 133.

32 Eric Schmitt with Michael Gordon, "Looking Beyond an Invasion, U.S. Plans Haiti Police Force," *New York Times*, September 11, 1994, 12.

33 One implication of this growing cosmopolitanism is that states are likely to maintain a continued interest in responding in some fashion to humanitarian crises (notwithstanding the much heralded "donor fatigue"). However, when states contribute, they want to do so in a multilateral rather than unilateral fashion. According to one State Department official who was involved in the drafting of PDD-25, the interagency review on multinational peacekeeping operations, it was critical to strengthen the United Nations' peacekeeping abilities for humanitarian operations, otherwise the United States would have to become more fully involved; the United States will continue to feel compelled to contribute to humanitarian operations, he said, and it is better to act multilaterally through the United Nations than unilaterally.

34 Another indication that the decision to go the United Nations concedes some measure of decision-making autonomy is the fact that many actively oppose the United States' increased tendency to seek UN approval. Congressman Doug Bereuter, for one, remarked: "One of the growing perceptions in this post-Cold War era seems to be that we need some sort of multilateral approval, usually the UN, in order to take action, even though it is clearly in our national interests, and I am, frankly, concerned about that." Committee on Foreign Affairs, House of Representatives, *U.S. Participation in United Nations Peacekeeping Activities* (Washington: U.S. Government Printing House, 1994), 50.

35 Paul Schroeder, "New World Order: A Historical Perspective," *Washington Quarterly* 17 (February 1994), 33.

36 There is a critical body of research that demonstrates how both regulative and constitutive norms alter state behavior. See, for example, the series of recent

workshops sponsored by the Social Science Research Council (New York) under the project title of "Norms and National Security."

37 Oran Young, "Effectiveness of International Institutions," in J. Rosenau and E. Cziempel, eds., *Governance Without Governments* (New York: Cambridge University Press, 1992), 163.

38 "UN Responses in the Former Yugoslavia: Moral and Operational Choices," *Ethics & International Affairs*, 8 (1994), 20. Also see Richard Betts, "The Delusion of Impartial Intervention," *Foreign Affairs* 73 (November/December 1994), 20–33.

39 This is one conclusion from the United Nations Transition Authority in Cambodia (UNTAC). When local parties refused to heed its directives, the United Nations chose to negotiate rather than fight, thereby conserving its legitimacy.

40 Schear, "Global Institutions in a Cooperative Order: Does the United Nations Fit In?" in Janne Nolan, ed., *Global Engagement* (Washington: Brookings Press, 1994), 246.

41 See Martha Finnemore, "Constructing Humanitarian Norms of Intervention." Paper delivered at the SSRC-sponsored conference, "Norms and National Security," Stanford University, October 16–18, 1994; also see Laura Reed and Karl Kayson, eds., *Emerging Norms of Justified Intervention* (Cambridge: American Academy of Arts and Sciences, 1993).

5 Humanitarianism with a sovereign face

UNHCR in the global undertow

During the Cold War, UN organizations routinely presented themselves as "apolitical" and "humanitarian" as a signal to states that they understood their place and recognized sovereignty's canon of noninterference. Beginning in the mid-1980s and accelerating after the end of the Cold War, however, UN organizations became more deeply involved in the domestic affairs of states. The United Nations has increased its activities in the areas of women's rights and human rights. UN peacekeeping began trying to save "failed states" and help with the difficult transition from civil war to civil peace. And UNHCR became increasingly active in the area of refugee reintegration and erasing the "root causes" of refugee flight. UN organizations that once knew their place in the sovereign system of states and bundled their humanitarianism to the principle of noninterference were now venturing beyond the border's edge and proclaiming that their standing as humanitarian organizations permitted them to tread on once sacred ground.

This development represents both a remarkable shift in the UN's role in global and domestic politics and a transformation of "actually living humanitarianism" (de Wall, 1998). Since the beginning of the last century, states have constructed a spectacular skyline of multilateral organizations, most of which were intended to further their shared interests and some of which were designed to promote their shared values. States cautiously evoked the language of humanitarianism for fear that such transcendental concerns might swamp their core interests and undermine their sovereignty. As a consequence, when states did create humanitarian international organizations they made sure that they were highly circumscribed in scope and mindful of state sovereignty.

Yet a defining feature of world politics over the last two decades is the highly significant and reinforcing transformation in the character of sovereignty and the meaning of humanitarianism. Because of a confluence of developments, episodic events, and a view that domestic conflict undermined international security, the understanding that sovereignty is defined by its core principle of noninterference has yielded to the emerging legitimation principle of popular sovereignty—that sovereignty resides in peoples and not in states and that states should possess some attributes that are largely liberal in order to honor individual liberties and rights. One effect of this transform-ation in the meaning of sovereignty is that UN agencies are at greater liberty to intervene in the domestic affairs of states, nowhere more evident than in the practice of humanitarianism. Whereas once humanitarianism meant helping individuals after they had managed to crawl across an international border, now UN agencies can parade their humanitarian credentials in order to bring relief and protection to people regardless of their geographic circumstances. The changing character of sovereignty has transformed the meaning and practice of humanitarianism, allowing once shy UN agencies to strut into new domains.

Is this expanding humanitarianism a good thing? We almost instinctually applaud whenever state officials feel the need to behave decently and with civility toward their populations, and if the growing complex of humanitar-ian organizations is partially responsible for that outcome, terrific. But the demurs are growing. Humanitarian organizations are increasingly accused of becoming bureaucratized, acting like an industry, becoming overly pragmatic and forgetting their principles, protecting their own interests and sacrificing their humanitarian ideals (*see, e.g.,* Rieff, 1997; Barnett and Finnemore, 1999; Maren, 1997). Humanitarian organizations are not immune to the iron law of bureaucratization. As humanitarian organizations have become better estab-lished and more deeply involved in politics, they have become more deeply political.

Such developments are relevant to any discussion of UNHCR's past, present, and future role in global and domestic politics. States established UNHCR to help them carry out their responsibilities to refugees, but they carefully limited their obligations and made sure that UNHCR's working definition of humanitarianism included the principle of noninterference. Beginning in the late 1970s, however, UNHCR became more deeply involved in the affairs of refugee-producing countries because states wanted the refu-gees to go home as soon as possible, and the growing ethos of popular sover-eignty made it possible and desirable to think about the prevention and the root causes of refugee flows. As a consequence, UNHCR's humanitarianism no longer stops at the border's edge. This is a positive development to the extent that the international community is now concerned with the causes and remedies of displaced peoples regardless of whether an individual has crossed an international border.

Yet the combination of state pressures and normative developments that have permitted UNHCR to become more involved in the domestic affairs of states contains its own dangers. Specifically, UNHCR is encouraged to look inward because states have tired of their obligations under refugee law and the principle of popular sovereignty. This has two dire implications. One is that the meaning and practice of humanitarianism is altered, not always for the better. As UNHCR's humanitarianism has extended, its "pragmatism" has deepened. The challenge for UNHCR is to encourage a humanitarianism that does not widen the humanitarian space with one hand and constrict it with the other so that humanitarianism would become the enemy of refugee rights. The other related danger is that UNHCR might become complicit with a strategy of "containment." This strategy is not bereft of ethical under-pinnings or normative redemption, for if states are unreceptive to individuals seeking asylum and if the best prospect of long-term protection is "home," then UNHCR can pragmatically make this devil's compact. This strategy, moreover, is linked to the broader global project of "rebuilding" states and societies along a liberal model. The extent to which UNHCR wants to find itself attempting to save failed states is a matter of debate, but there is every reason to believe that an agency that is busily trying to construct new states might not be very good at the equally strenuous task of protecting the rights of the displaced.

This essay first reviews the changing relationship between multilateralism, sovereignty, and humanitarianism and links that conceptual discussion to the emergence of the international refugee regime. It then examines the combin-ation of state pressures and the normative principle of popular sovereignty that enabled a more political and pragmatic UNHCR to widen its activities under the humanitarian banner and to concern itself with the circumstances in the refugee-producing country. Next the article suggests that the expanding humanitarian umbrella might be a stealth agent for a policy of containment and a threat to refugee rights. To illustrate this possibility, the article briefly examines the concern that the decided preference for repatriation is brushing up against the principle of voluntary repatriation, how UNHCR's reintegra-tion activities might unintentionally hinder flight, and the debate over the definition of category of internally displaced peoples and the concern that the concept makes it more likely that states will deny asylum. The totality of these developments generate the worrisome possibility that a more pragmatic UNHCR is potentially (though unwittingly) implicated in a system of con-tainment. I conclude by reflecting on UNHCR's role in global politics and the dangers of a sovereignty-led humanitarianism.

Sovereignty and humanitarianism

States have had an increasingly intense, century-long romance with the idea of establishing institutional means to help them coordinate their relations in more cooperative and less conflictive ways. While the concepts and catch-phrases that describe this development change with the times—international institutions, regimes, multilateralism, and global governance are often times used interchangeably—the basic goals remain largely the same: states con-struct multilateral institutions to capture gains from exchange, coordinate shared interests, manage various externalities associated with growing inter-dependence, and settle disputes in a conflict-free manner (Ruggie, 1993). States have been primarily responsible for the steady march of global bureaucratiza-tion, a campaign guided by a statist beat.

Sovereignty has never been far from the minds of states as they have created these global institutions. This is a testimony to the simple but primeval survival impulse. Hedley Bull (1977) famously observed that survival is a state's primary goal, that survival is maintained by international order, that juridical sovereignty enables states to further their mutually reinforcing goals of survival and international order, and that states establish various international institutions that are designed to regulate their relations in a more cooperative manner and protect their sovereignty. At base, sovereignty holds that there is no authority above the state and there exists mutual restraint, a "live and let live" policy, which is embodied in the principle of noninterference. Sovereignty, in this important respect, is a security institution, and security-sensitive states are unlikely to relinquish the normative shield that provides some measure of security, maintains their autonomy, and provides an obstacle to the ambitious and intrusive designs of more powerful and aggressive states.

Yet the meaning and practice of sovereignty is more complicated and multivocal than is suggested by the pat claim that sovereignty is defined by the principle of noninterference. At issue is not only who is sovereign but what practices are associated with sovereignty. While sovereignty might have begun as a Hobbesian compact among monarchs who were interested in avoiding a religious world war, it is increasingly assigned not to monarchs and heads of state but rather to peoples. Beginning with the French and American revolutions, continuing with the liberal revolutions of the nineteenth century, spreading with the principle of national and self-determination during the early twentieth century, and increasingly evident in the growing standing of human rights principles over the last half-century, states recognize the sovereignty of peoples and their representative institutions. This is "popular sovereignty." Along with a change in the conceptual modifiers and location of sovereignty is a shift in the practices expected of modern, sovereign states. Whereas juridical sovereignty admonishes states to demonstrate self-restraint vis-à-vis one another and honor the principle of noninterference, popular sovereignty concerns the domestic practices of states, expecting them to adhere to certain domestic principles that we now define as the rule of law (liberalism) and representative institutions (democracy) (Reisman, 1990; Franck, 1992).

States have been reluctant to permit the principle of popular sovereignty to guide their foreign policy practices and shape the tenor of international politics for the obvious reason that it would challenge the principle of noninterference and, therefore, have potentially destabilizing effects. Later, this ordering principle was invested with greater legitimacy when it became attached to the principles of national self-determination and cultural autonomy. The result is that there are powerful security and normative forces behind the principle of noninterference and juridical sovereignty. For these reasons, states have appealed to sovereignty's noninterference principle to deter investigations and intrusions into domestic politics. That said, the discourse of popular sovereignty is an increasingly visible feature of international politics, imprinting diplomatic discourse, introducing "fundamentalist" international documents and treaties, and signaling which states are "legitimate" members of the international community and which ones have standing simply because they possess the rudimentary features of sovereignty.

The willingness by states to elevate the legitimation principle of popular sovereignty is strongly associated with the belief that there is a direct relationship between international order and domestic order. For instance, whether the internal character of the state is related to international order was debated during the drive for decolonization: would newly recognized sovereign states that lacked the attributes of stateness have a difficult time abiding by the norms of international society? This worry was rejected in favor of popular sovereignty defined as national self-determination (Jacobson, 1962; Jackson, 1993). But a defining feature of post-Cold War politics is the belief that domestic governance is an international governance issue. This connection is made not only on normative grounds but also because of "international peace and security." An article of strategic faith during the Cold War was that international order was premised on balances of power and some regulative norms that revolved around the principle of noninterference. But this view has yielded to the claim that because international order is best secured through domestic order, and because domestic order is best secured through democratic practices, the rule of law at home provides for the foundation of the rule of law abroad (Barnett, 1995). Democracy is increasingly treated as a principle of international order (*see*, for instance, Boutros-Ghali, 1995 and Doyle, 1986).

These shifts in the character and practice of sovereignty have shaped the character of institution-building. Most of the international institutions established by states have been mindful of juridical sovereignty and have been intended to further their functional interests (Boli and Thomas, 1999). Yet because states have increasingly espoused humanitarian values, they have increasingly permitted old organizations to introduce concerns that were once considered to be "humanitarian" and part of domestic politics, and they have established new international agencies to further and protect the international community's transcendental values. The growing willingness by states to discuss humanitarian concerns in multilateral forums was not driven by a sudden sentimentality. More important, states were now considering how to shield and protect peoples and minorities from maltreatment because of a confluence of considerations, including the belief that: 1) humanitarian issues reflect "standards of civilization"; 2) humanitarian issues could threaten domestic and international order; 3) multilateral forums were the legitimate means to handle these issues; and 4) multilateral organizations provided burden-sharing mechanisms (*see* Jones, 1991).

Because states were sensitive to the possible danger that humanitarianism might violate the principle of noninterference and hijack core national security interests, they made sure that these multilateral mechanisms were limited in scope and honored the principle of noninterference. This had several implications. First, states refused to delegate broad powers and authorities to new international bodies. Second, states placed severe restrictions on their humanitarian obligations. In almost all cases, humanitarianism could insinuate open-ended commitments that could easily violate norms of noninterference. Third, while states wrapped the principle of burden-sharing in various moral claims, including that all states should have the privilege and duty of contributing to a less cruel world, states wanted to make sure that no state was saddled with the burden (*see* Suhrke, 1998 for a discussion of burden-sharing in refugee emergencies). Fourth, international organizations like the League of Nations could involve themselves in these domestic issues only if they were invited by the member state. The principles of consent, neutrality, and impartiality now become part of the grammar of action, clearly tied to principles of noninterference.

The practice of humanitarianism and the politics of humanitarian international organizations formed in direct relationship to the practice of sovereignty and the politics of a states system organized around sovereignty. The relationship between state sovereignty and humanitarianism reveals a logocentric quality, which Jacques Derrida observes is in play whenever "one privileged term (logos) provides the orientation for interpreting the meaning of the subordinate term" (Nyers, 1999:21). States and sovereign practices shape the discourse and practices of humanitarianism. States are understood to protect "national interests" while humanitarianism refers to transcendental values and the international community's interests. States defend their citizens and have a territorial imperative, while humanitarianism involves the attempt to reduce human suffering regardless of spatial, political, or cultural boundaries. "Politics" concerns activities between states, whereas humanitarian action is apolitical and distinct from politics. "Politics" involves activities within and between states, whereas humanitarian assistance should be palliative and not preventive. States are partial, biased, and presumptive, whereas humanitarian organizations operate on the principles of impartiality, neutrality, and consent. "Politics" is dirty and pejorative, whereas humanitarian activities are pure and noble (Nyers, 1999:21; Cutts, 1998:3; Malkki, 1995). A state-centric logic shaped the issues, organizations, and practices of humanitarianism.

Humanitarianism and refugee issues

How a sovereign state system shaped the meaning and practice of humanitarianism is evident in the genesis and development of the international refugee regime. Beginning slowly after World War I and continuing with a burst of energy after World War II, states cobbled together the elements of an international refugee regime that was purposefully designed to safeguard their sovereignty while modestly coordinating their new-found but highly defensive desire to protect refugees. The very fact that there was a post-World War I refugee problem that demanded their attention was a complex by-product of many factors. Only a world of sovereign states that had categories of peoples called "citizens" and were intent on regulating population flows could produce a legal category of "refugees." The collapse of multinational empires and the creation of new, ethnically-defined states forced minorities to flee—but with few destinations available given the increasingly restrictive immigration laws. World War I and the Russian Revolution produced a huge movement of orphaned individuals, thousands of whom could neither go home nor gain legal entry into another country and thus needed a temporary haven. In response to this dramatic development and the persistent lobbying efforts of private philanthropic organizations, states established the High Commissioner for Refugees (HCR) in 1921. Reflective of their shallow humanitarianism, states gave HCR a very limited mandate and resource base and a definition of refugee that had severe geographical restrictions (Melander, 1987:7). Their less-than-charitable attitude toward refugees would be repeated in countless crises over the next two decades, most tragically in their response to the attempted Jewish flight from Nazism.

World War II provided the backdrop for the next effort to administer refugee flows. As the Allies marched toward Germany, they confronted the immediate necessity of reducing the suffering of refugees and displaced peoples, and so constructed a string of make-shift multilateral arrangements. This immediate experience and the prospect that refugees might be a permanent fixture of world politics caused member states to consider the desirability of a permanent international institution and accompanying legal norms. Thus was born the refugee convention and the UNHCR. During their debates, however, they made sure that they did not let themselves get carried away by their noble thoughts.

The general view among states was that a convention was necessary in order to provide legal protection and rights for refugees, an act not only of charity but also of survival, because of their anomalous status in international law and their invisibility in national law (Holborn, 1975:158). Still, their humanitarianism carried them only so far, quickly halted by their desire to limit their obligations and defend their sovereignty. This halting humanitarianism and defensive sovereignty was clearly present in the accepted definitions of "refugee," "protection" and "solution." Member states recognized that while there are many displaced peoples, only those who have managed to fall on the other side of the territorial divide were legally entitled to be called refugees. This served to limit their obligations and honor their sovereignty, restricting the numbers that might ask for international assistance and prohibiting the international body from intruding on domestic affairs. Member states recognized that people flee their countries for a host of reasons, but only those who are "persecuted" by the national governments are entitled to refugee status. Once again, this capped their obligations, for it omitted large numbers who might flee because of economic hardship, political events such as international and internal wars, famines, and authoritarian practices by their government. In addition, the convention did not make a direct reference to the responsibilities of the refugee producing country (Chimni, 1998:360).

States did not let their humanitarian sentiments get the better of them when they established the UNHCR either, as sovereignty provided the sketchlines for the new organization. Statism and sovereignty shaped the concept of protection. To begin, states substituted the terms "legal and political protection" that had been part of the League of Nations and IRO language with "international protection." Why? "Political" was viewed as too divisive and controversial, too closely associated with a prior meaning of "political" that implied relations between states and thus had a "partisan" and "factious" character given contemporary circumstances. Moreover, instead of "political" states began emphasizing the concept of "humanitarian." As a humanitarian and apolitical organization, UNHCR was charged with helping to coordinate the operational activities of states and NGOs and to provide legal assistance for refugees. Stated negatively, UNHCR was not expected to be an operational agency or to address ways to eliminate refugee problems which, by definition, were political matters and potentially infringed on sovereignty (Kennedy, 1986:14–15; Skran, 1992:25, 28; Holborn, 1975:89–90). Furthermore, "protection" became legal protection, that is, UNHCR was to assist refugees by "identifying them, issuing travel documents, assisting in obtaining recognition of their various legal statuses, and advocating ever more precise guidelines for handling recognized refugees" (Kennedy, 1986:5; *see also* Coles, 1989:79–80; Sztucki, 1989:290–92; Holborn, 1975:chap. 4). Reflecting on the meaning of international protection during the Cold War, Sadako Ogata (1996) said:

> UNHCR essentially waited on the other side of an international border to receive and to protect refugees fleeing conflicts. This approach was determined by the very concept of international protection of refugees which would come into play if, and only if, victims of persecution or violent conflict fled their homeland. It was also dictated by the concept of state sovereignty and the consequent reluctance of intergovernmental organizations, such as UNHCR, to be seen as being too involved in the internal conditions of countries of origin that might give rise to refugee movements.

In general, UNHCR could present itself as apolitical and humanitarian by emphasizing legal protection and using the discourse of "international protection."

States' concerns over sovereignty also shaped the discussion on the permanent solutions to refugee problems. States outlined three solutions—integration into the asylum country, resettlement to a third country, and voluntary repatriation—and the third was widely dismissed as a viable possibility. Although the central reason for its dismissal was because it was ideologically and politically unthinkable to promote refugee repatriation to communist states, another factor was the sense that repatriation could quickly involve UNHCR in political matters (Holborn, 1975:325–327). In general, state sovereignty shaped the character of the refugee law and the newly established refugee organization (Goodwin-Gill, 1996; Hathaway, 1991; Skran, 1992: 15–16).

Although the most powerful states hoped to handcuff UNHCR, over the next two decades its humanitarian profile expanded considerably. There are many reasons why its protection mission expanded from legal assistance to include other forms of assistance and why it began to provide assistance to nonstatutory refugees, including the simple fact that states sanctioned an organizational expansion that was in their (momentary) interests. It is worth noting that UNHCR was not a passive beneficiary of this process but also strove to establish precedents at permissive moments, most famously when it invented new mechanisms such as the "good offices" (Khan, 1976:56). The good offices concept allowed UNHCR to extend protection and assistance to new groups and to transform what might have been a deeply politicized issue into a humanitarian and apolitical matter (Schnyder, 1965:7, 16–17). This depoliticization benefited not only refugees but also UNHCR, for the concept alerted governments that the agency was "not guided by any political intentions or considerations" (Schnyder, 1965:8). As a consequence, humanitarianism was not only part of UNHCR's identity, it also proved to be instrumentally useful, a stealth weapon in the service of organizational expansion. States might have tagged UNHCR with a humanitarian mandate as a way of limiting its activities, but UNHCR also demonstrated the capacity to use that same label as a way to insinuate itself into new areas.

All politics is local: state pressures and normative inducements

Beginning in the late 1970s and a defining feature of international politics since the late 1980s, slowly but impressively the fulcrum of the system shifted "from the protection of sovereigns to the protection of peoples" (Reisman, 1990:872; *see also* Barkin, 1998; Dacyl, 1996). Although still respectful of the principle of noninterference, the injection of human rights norms and popular sovereignty as a legitimating principle meant that governments could no longer behave monstrously to their populations without fear of sanction by the international community. As discussed earlier, this was a centuries-long development, though events surrounding the demise and end of the Cold War rejuvenated the claim that domestic governance is related to international governance and, therefore, the international community has a legitimate right to consider domestic issues. Specifically, the end of the Cold War shifted the security agenda and the ideological fault lines, and there was growing acceptance of the claim that most wars are internal wars, that internal wars almost exclusively occur within illiberal states, and that these internal wars can represent "threats to international peace and security." This increasingly accepted causal logic and discourse gave international organizations opportunity and motive to become more thoroughly involved in domestic politics (Barnett, 1995; Mertus, 1998:334).

UNHCR was not immune to these global developments as it quickly became more deeply involved in domestic affairs and increasingly noted that internal conflicts led to massive refugee flows and that refugee flows could trigger regional instability and challenge "human security" (Ogata, 1999a, 1996b). But the factors driving UNHCR's evident interest in the circumstances of the refugee-producing country was driven not only by charitable motives. Beginning in the late 1970s, states began demonstrating "refugee fatigue" and demanding that refugees go home as soon as possible. This strongly encouraged UNHCR to emphasize repatriation as the preferred durable solution, which triggered a growing interest in the factors that prohibited repatriation and were the root causes of refugee flows (*see also* Mooney, 1999:204).

State pressures

By the late 1970s, Western and Third World states were growing weary of the heavy burdens placed on them by the refugee regime and demanded a change. Western states were disturbed by the ever-expanding number of asylum requests (Skran, 1992:8). Moreover, the profile of the typical refugee had changed. Whereas once he or she was from an Eastern bloc country attempting to escape to the West, now he or she was from the Third World and frequently attempting to gain entry to Western states for what these states viewed as illegitimate reasons. In response, they instituted their own brand of racial profiling and began denying asylum to more individuals and demanding a reform in asylum and refugee law in ways that restricted access (Hathaway, 1991:115). Third World states also were becoming increasingly intolerant of refugee flows and demands. In many respects, the reasons were highly understandable. After all, refugees impose tremendous financial, environmental, and political costs, often times entangling the host country into an unwanted conflict with the refugees' national government. As a consequence, many Third World governments were now rolling up the welcome mat, often times stating that their ability to carry out their international legal obligations depended on assistance from UNHCR, wealthy states, and NGOs ("Note on International Protection," August 27, 1990:6). There were an increasing number of refugees whose presence was barely tolerated, if at all, by states, and states were more actively engaged in what the High Commissioner referred to as a policy of "deterrence" (Executive Committee of the High Commissioner's Programme, "Note on International Protection," August 31, 1983:3).

Western and Third World governments now shifted decisively their preferences regarding the three durable solutions—away from resettlement and third country asylum and toward repatriation. And they expected an understanding UNHCR to play ball, which it did for a variety of reasons (Loescher,

1989:10). First, the growing number of refugees was creating a financial crisis for UNHCR who, in turn, became quite interested in reducing the increasingly expensive and numerous refugee camps (Pitterman, 1985:51–54; *see also* Gordeneker, 1981:78; Harrell-Bond, 1989:50–51; Stein, 1986: 279). Second, because fewer countries were willing to integrate and resettle the growing number of refugees, UNHCR had very little choice but to consider repatriation (*see* Hathaway, 1991:115; Harrell-Bond, 1989:45). To make matters worse, the reality was that states were refusing to honor asylum law and were forcibly repatriating refugees. UNHCR could sit on the sidelines with its principles, but a principle-bound UNHCR was no help to refugees who were in immediate danger. Only a thick-skinned or self-destructive organization would have been dismissive of powerful patrons and upon those whom it was dependent for resources and permission to act.

UNHCR officials admit that states were pushing them toward repatriation measures, but they also insist that there were desirable reasons for UNHCR to revise its "exilic" bias (interviews with UNHCR officials, Washington, DC and Geneva). Indeed, they assert that the "environment" of the Cold War and the circumstances of the refugees precluded them from considering repatriation, and, accordingly, when the environment and circumstances changed they rushed through the open door in order to do what refugees wanted. Moreover, UNHCR not only was influenced by state demands but also was persuaded by new developments in refugee law, refugee activities, and ethical understandings. The Cold War context had substantially shaped refugee law and the assumed desirability of asylum and resettlement. But now most refugees were from and in the Third World, who largely viewed their exile as temporary and who wanted to go home sooner rather than later. This development stimulated greater interest in new features of refugee law, including issues of repatriation, *nonrefoulement* and cessation clauses (Hathaway, 1991; Goodwin-Gill, 1996). Moreover, refugees were "spontaneously repatriating," returning voluntarily to their home countries without the assistance of UNHCR or other relief organizations. As such, UNHCR began initiating activities to hasten and ease their reintegration and debating when it was safe for refugees to return (Cuny and Stein, 1989). Finally, whereas once it was believed that asylum was the most humane solution to the plight of the refugee, an increasingly popular view was that repatriation was the most desirable and humane alternative given that it helps the individual return "home" (Frelick, 1990; Warner, 1994). The legal, institutional, and ethical climate was more oriented toward repatriation. The growing emphasis on repatriation led to considerable interest in the conditions in the refugee-producing country that represented an obstacle to repatriation and that caused refugee flight. UNHCR began slowly, simply escorting refugees back home to ensure that they had a "safe and dignified" return. Then it introduced "quick impact projects," which were designed to make it economically attractive to return and desirable to stay. After that UNHCR began to insinuate itself into the political situation of the refugees, becoming a more forceful spokesperson for the rights of minorities and peoples. As one UNHCR official reflected, "We used to give them seeds and supplies and a handshake at the border, but now we are increasingly involved in the economic, political, and human rights situation of the home country" (interview with UNHCR official, January 28, 2000).

Furthermore, the newly formed conceptual marriage between repatriation as a durable solution and repatriation as a form of protection encouraged greater interest in preventing refugee flows, getting at their root causes, and lobbying for state responsibility (on prevention, *see* Chimni, 1993:444 and Frelick, 1993; on root causes, *see* Coles, 1989:203 and Executive Committee of the High Commissioner's Programme, "Note on International Protection," August 31, 1983:2; on state responsibility, *see* "Note on International Protection," August 27, 1990:8). Although these concepts attended to different facets of refugee flows and solutions, they shared an interest in: 1) reducing the causes of refugee flows, which were frequently attributed to "violations of human rights and, increasingly, by military or armed activities" (Executive Committee of the High Commissioner's Programme, "Note on International Protection," August 31, 1983:2); and 2) making sure that those refugees that were repatriated stayed at home. In general, UNHCR began to supplement "activities related to traditional forms of protection . . . with increased activities within countries of origin. These have a dual purpose: to ensure the durability of the solution of voluntary repatriation through respect for fundamental human rights and the restoration of national protection for returnees; and to seek to prevent arising conditions which could leave people no choice but to flee" ("UNHCR's Protection Role in Countries of Origin," March 18, 1996, EC/46/SC/CRP.17, p. 1; *see also* Executive Committee of the High Commissioner's Programme. "Annual Theme: The Pursuit and Implementation of Durable Solutions," August 30, 1996, p. 2. A/AC.96/872).

By 1990, UNHCR began to legitimate its involvement in the circumstances of refugee-producing countries because of the apparent link between refugee flight and threats to international peace and security ("Note on International Protection," August 27, 1990:7). This was not mere conjecture. In an age where internal conflict was leading to massive refugee flows that caused regional instability, and where the displacement of populations was not simply a tragic by-product of war but rather was its intended effect, there were good reasons to see refugee flows as a cause and consequence of domestic and regional turmoil. Largely because there were more refugees fleeing due to civil wars and more individuals who were being denied the right of asylum, beginning with the 1991 Iraq War and then blossoming with Bosnia UNHCR began to bring relief to displaced peoples instead of waiting for displaced peoples to step over an international border.

One debate within UNHCR was whether it could maintain its humanitarian and apolitical standing given its growing involvement in the affairs of refugee-producing countries (Coles, 1989:211). UNHCR was long aware that measures might and should be taken to reduce the factors that caused refugee movements, but its humanitarian and nonpolitical character prohibited it from becoming too intrusive. Now there seemed no turning back. According to the High Commissioner, while some championed this activist role others feared that it would compromise its humanitarian work and enmesh it in political disputes. The High Commissioner preferred to find a middle ground, one that defined as humanitarian any action that increased the well being of the individual while avoiding those controversies that were highly political and best handled by states (Coles, 1989:244–45). As a consequence, humanitarian assistance could include prevention, which was always preferable to the cure, and the attempt to foster respect for human rights, for this would help reduce refugee flows.

This response might have caused a political uproar before the 1990s, but not afterwards. UNHCR suddenly found itself carrying out new humanitarian tasks in highly unstable domestic environments, forcing justificatory action to catch up with emerging practice. In 1991, UNHCR's Working Group on International Protection considered whether it could maintain its apolitical credentials alongside its growing involvement in the refugee-producing country. It offered four observations and conclusions. First, "the evolution of UNHCR's role over the last forty years has demonstrated that the mandate is resilient enough to allow, or indeed require, adaptation by UNHCR to new, unprecedented challenges through new approaches, including in the areas of prevention and in-country protection." Refugee rights, the document noted, are part and parcel of human rights; thus, UNHCR's role as protector of refugee law legitimates its growing concern for the violations of human rights that lead to refugee flows. Second, UNHCR's humanitarian expertise and experience has been recognized by the General Assembly as an appropriate basis for undertaking a range of activities not normally viewed as being within the Office's mandate" ("Note on International Protection." August 25, 1992:4). Third, "the High Commissioner's non-political mandate requires neutrality;" but "neutrality must be coupled with a thorough understanding of prevailing political and other realities." Fourth, whereas once humanitarianism meant avoiding the political circumstances within the home country and honoring the principle of noninterference, it soon began to include aspects of the state's internal affairs. UNHCR properly noted that it was not violating state sovereignty because it was operating with the consent of the state (except in those circumstances where there was no state to give consent), but there was little doubt that what was permissible under the humanitarian label had significantly expanded (*see also* Gilbert, 1998:356).

Humanitarianism as containment

Because of pragmatic and principled forces by the early 1990s UNHCR was quickly becoming more deeply enmeshed in the internal affairs of states. Pragmatic forces were pushing UNHCR to consider repatriation as the durable solution if only because states were less willing to harbor refugees.

Principled arguments were now more warmly received because of the emerging legitimation principle of popular sovereignty. But a humanitarianism that was imprinted by pragmatic and principled considerations could become a disfigured humanitarianism if it meant that states were willing to expand the humanitarian agenda because of their unwillingness to shoulder their traditional obligations under refugee law. The desire to get refugees get back home, a fine impulse by most accounts, could lead to *nonrefoulement* and involuntary repatriation. The desire to help displaced peoples of all kinds, regardless of whether they were on one side or the other of an international border, could mean that states were willing to help the internally-displaced because they were not giving individuals the opportunity to flee across a border and seek asylum. The desire to eliminate the root causes of refugee flows, a noble sentiment without doubt, could mean that individuals would be discouraged from fleeing a country that was improving and safe. This expanding humanitarian agenda, in short, could erode the traditional protection guarantees and rights given to refugees and become part of a system of containment. If so, humanitarianism could become the foe of refugee rights.

Repatriation, voluntary and involuntary

A twenty year long debate in refugee protection concerns how to balance the impulse for repatriation with refugee rights. The Executive Committee (EXCOM) of the UNHCR increasingly espoused a positive view of repatriation, encouraged UNHCR to create the conditions that enabled repatriation, claimed that refugee rights had to be balanced against the rights of states and peacebuilding initiatives (Executive Committee of the UNHCR, Conclusion 18, XXXI, 1980), and then, in 1997, declared that "any increased incidence of voluntary repatriation is a positive development" (UN doc. A/AC.96/887, September 9, 1997). Although these discussions tried to balance the desire for repatriation with the principle of *nonrefoulement* and voluntary repatriation, these discussions incrementally but decisively led to a relaxation of the safeguards before repatriation and a changed meaning of voluntary repatriation (Goodwin-Gill, 1989:263–65; Harrell-Bond, 1989:44–45; LCHR, 1991:61).

UNHCR also wrestled with how to reconcile its newfound preference for repatriation with its longstanding protection and assistance mission and how to ensure that repatriation did not undermine the principles of voluntary repatriation and *nonrefoulement* (LCHR, 1991:3). This debate began in earnest in the 1980s, but became more pressing during the 1990s when UNHCR had to consider refugee repatriation to post-conflict situations that were far from the ideal conditions usually prescribed. The divisions over how to balance the pressure to repatriate with the principle of voluntary repatriation are typically portrayed as comprising of fundamentalist and pragmatist camps. Fundamentalists maintained a more legalistic approach that suggested a human rights orientation toward refugee rights and decried moderating moves toward repatriation as coming at the expense of the UNHCR's unique role as the agent of the refugees and compromising its independence vis-à-vis governments. Pragmatists argued the case for allying with governments, held a more expedient, political and pragmatic view of refugee law if only because they feared that ignoring systemic trends and pressures might compromise UNHCR's overall effectiveness, and believed that the organizational and doctrinal shift in favor of repatriation righted a defect in the system that tended to privilege protection officers who were legally oriented and lacked detailed knowledge of the region over those who had area expertise (LCHR, 1991:18, 117–119; Coles, 1989:399; Weiner, 1998:442–43).

Steadily and ultimately, UNHCR became much more favorably disposed toward repatriation, that return will and should happen under less than ideal circumstances, and that UNHCR must and should actively promote repatriation as soon as possible (Stein and Cuny, 1993, cited in Chimni, 1993:448; *see also* Zieck, 1997:438–39; Takahashi, 1997:594, 602; Barnett, 2000). Repatriation was no longer a permanent solution but was now the durable solution. Repatriation now became tantamount to protection. UNHCR's organizational chart was restructured so that regional offices that held more pragmatic views no longer had to report directly to a Protection Division that saw itself as the "priest of principles." UNHCR began to develop new norms and rules that made desirable and proper repatriating under less demanding conditions and to introduce new terminology and categories of safe return that clearly differentiated repatriation under ideal conditions from repatriation under less than ideal conditions.

Most important, what voluntary meant in voluntary repatriation began to alter. Voluntary repatriation demanded that the refugee consent to return to a country that in his or her view no longer represented a threat to his or her safety. But UNHCR officials began introducing new concepts like "voluntariness" that meant that refugee consent was no longer necessary and that the home situation need only have appreciably improved or held out the promise of improving. This development was partially driven by pressing circumstances as UNHCR officials increasingly found that it was nearly impossible to ascertain consent from thousands of people and that post-conflict situations provided the possibility for safe repatriation under less than ideal conditions.

However understandable, the emergence of voluntariness meant that refugee assessment of the situation or consent to repatriation was no longer necessary, leading to the possibility that UNHCR officials might violate traditional refugee rights in two important respects. First, there was no longer the requirement that the home situation had improved appreciably and no longer represented a threat to the safety of refugees. Less than ideal conditions can be a euphemism for the simple fact that refugees are being asked to return to a situation that remains highly volatile and the pathogens of threat remain in the environment. There are any number of reasons to justify return under less fortunate circumstances. In a world where ultimate protection is bound up with the preferred durable solution of repatriation, repatriation and protection become kissing cousins. Such discursive coupling is facilitated by the stark recognition that exile and camp life represents no safe haven. Camp life is almost always unstable and insecure and contains no hope for the future; repatriation is almost by definition a more desirable outcome assuming that the situation at home has marginally and steadily improved. Also, knowing that other durable solutions are unavailable and that the only solution is return, UNHCR officials are poised to think about the minimal conditions that are required before repatriation can proceed and encouraged to create those conditions if they do not presently exist. The result is that repatriation can occur under less exacting standards, and refugees can be encouraged to return to a situation that resembles the one that triggered their flight.

Second, refugees are no longer required to provide informed consent before UNHCR authorizes a repatriation exercise. As UNHCR officials concede, its determination to promote repatriation is based not only on the refugees' preference but more fundamentally on UNCHR's objective assessment of whether life was better at home relative to life in the camps. Refugees, in this view, cannot objectively assess the situation, that is, take into account first the short- and long-term prospects of the situation at home relative to the situation in the camps and second for how long UNHCR officials might be present and able to maintain some necessary safety features (Chimni, 1999). But where protection increasingly becomes tantamount to repatriation, UNHCR officials are increasingly of the view that getting refugees home, even to highly unstable situations, is preferred and legitimate. The moral benchmark is no longer whether the totality of rights available to refugees are defended and honored but rather whether one course of action is more likely to provide better protection to refugees—according to UNHCR's assessment.

UNHCR might well be correct that refugees should repatriate under less than ideal conditions because their circumstances will become even less ideal if they remain in exile. But the issue at hand is whose voice counts and what calculations are used to determine the efficacy of repatriation. The shift away from absolute standards regarding the desire by refugees to repatriate given their assessment of the situation in the home country toward a comparative evaluation by agency officials regarding whether refugees would be more secure at home or in the camps has the direct implication of privileging the agency's knowledge claims over those offered by refugees. A consequence of these changes is that the principle of voluntary repatriation has been stretched to its finite limits. As one high-ranking UNHCR official confessed, "Defin-ition of voluntariness has been stretched to the point that it violated refugee rights and informed consent. . . . That is a statement of fact" (interview in Geneva, January 28, 2000).

While state pressures have certainly encouraged this development and might very well force UNHCR to choose between the "least bad" alternatives, UNHCR also bends principles even in the absence of compelling pressures. This was clearly evident in the case of the Burmese Rohingyas in 1994–95, and it is noted in other instances over the years (*see, e.g.*, Stein, 1986; Zieck,

1997:434; Cuny and Stein, 1989:306; Goodwin-Gill, 1989:274; Crisp, 1984; Human Rights Watch, 1997:5–12). UNHCR's repatriation culture, in short, creates more permissive conditions for any single exercise. The result is that it is more likely that the principle of voluntary repatriation will be stretched to the point that it violates traditional refugee rights—yet retains an ethical and proper quality because it enables UNHCR to give refugees the ultimate form of protection, repatriation.[1]

In-country protection and reintegration

UNHCR's emerging concern with the causes of refugee flows and willingness to become more involved in the lives of the returnees is a positive development in many respects. But the growing involvement in in-country protection contains several dangers that revolve around whether individuals might be discouraged from fleeing and thus exercising their right to seek asylum (Frelick, 1993; Barutciski, 1996; Weiss and Pasic, 1996; Cunliffe and Pugh, 1999:191). Such a possibility was readily acknowledged by the High Commissioner, who observed, "In-country protection, *e.g.*, through the establishment of internationally guaranteed safe zones, however, needs to be weighed against the rights of individuals to leave their own country, to seek and enjoy asylum or return on a voluntary basis, and not be compelled to remain in a territory where life, liberty, or physical integrity is threatened" ("Note on International Protection," September 9, 1991:10). While this might be a legitimate fear, the High Commissioner reassured that "the object of prevention is not to obstruct escape from danger or from an intolerable situation, but to make flight unnecessary by removing or alleviating the conditions that force people to flee" ("Note on International Protection," August 31, 1993:10). For many observers this danger is not simply latent, it also is manifest.

There is another danger that derives from UNHCR's increasingly common situation where it stands on one side of the border advocating a repatriation under less than ideal circumstances and on the other side of the border determining whether the conditions at home are improving or safe. Simply put, UNHCR has a possible conflict of interest. UNHCR claims that repatriation represents a key way to protect refugees in the long run, is the most desirable solution to refugee problems, and can occur under less than ideal conditions. The result is that repatriation is highly dependent on a (marginally) improved situation in the refugee-producing country. Yet if the assessment given by refugees is no longer the most important factor, then whose voice counts? UNHCR increasingly claims that it can objectively survey the situation, a capacity that is enhanced by its presence on the other side of the border. The result is that UNHCR might be tempted to oversell its capacity to monitor the return and the overall political situation at home in order to encourage repatriation under less than ideal conditions.

This very development occurred in the case of the Rohingyas of Burma. In the early 1990s, nearly 250,000 Burmese Rohingyans fled for Bangladesh, who quickly demanded their immediate repatriation. UNHCR signed a Memorandum of Understanding (MoU) with Bangladesh that stipulated that the refugees could be repatriated under less than ideal conditions and as soon as possible and another MoU with Burma that allowed UNHCR to monitor the return and reintegration. UNHCR then proceeded to authorize a repatriation exercise on the grounds that Burma was better than it was and that because it now had a presence in Burma it had a rare opportunity to help reintegrate and protect the returnees.

UNHCR claimed that Burma was better. But was it, and who was to say? There were two disturbing features associated with its claim. First, UNHCR's ability to judge accurately the situation was highly suspect given its limited knowledge. When in June 1994 it was asserting that the human rights situation had improved, UNHCR had few staff in the field, a difficult time monitoring all of the remote villages and towns, and was nearly always accompanied by SLORC on its rounds. In addition, UNHCR offered its appraisal of the situation in Arakan without a more comprehensive assessment of the situation in Burma or incorporating the damning reports by the UN Human Rights Commission (Petrasek, 1999:8; MSF/H, 1997:21). As a consequence, UNHCR potentially held a distorted picture of the human rights situation, a distortion that made the Burmese regime seem less brutal than it was because it based its evaluation on the limited observations of its field officers. Still, the mere presence of UNHCR put it in a very powerful position to judge whether the information regarding abuses was accurate or not (HRW, 1996:15). The moral of the story is that an agency that advocates repatriation under less favorable circumstances might not be the best judge of the human rights situation in the refugee producing country (*see also* Cunliffe and Pugh, 1999:198; Goodwin-Gill, 1999:243).

Once the refugees returned, UNHCR is rumored not only to have encouraged them to stay but discouraged new flight, to the point that it potentially violated their right to seek asylum. This had several dimensions. UNHCR officials reportedly refused to give bona fide displaced peoples refugee status. Although UNHCR was on record as saying that life had improved in Burma, Rohingyas were continuing to flee, often times including those who had recently repatriated. UNHCR officials explained this continued flight by pointing to push and pull factors: these were very poor people who also tended to migrate during the dry season, and they were attracted to the welfare provisions provided by refugee camps. UNHCR officials were reluctant to classify these people as refugees because their desire to leave was primarily motivated by economic factors, and UNHCR feared that classifying them as refugees and giving them the assistance that comes with some classification would only encourage more flight (Petrasek, 1999; interviews with UNHCR officials; USCR, 1996:3, 7; Amnesty International, March 5, 1997). NGOs and local populations rebut this explanation on two grounds: while economic factors certainly played a role in the decision to flee, the Rohingyans' deteriorating economic condition is connected to their standing as a persecuted minority and to human rights violations (USCR, 1996:7; MSF/H, 1997:10); moreover, UNHCR officials failed to actively seek out new asylum seekers, thus making it less likely that they would receive refugee status. In these and other ways, UNHCR reportedly encouraged individuals to stay at home by making it more likely that those who fled would not receive a fair asylum hearing or gain refugee standing.

The case of the Rohingyans is related to an increasingly common situation where UNHCR's provision of in-country protection might inadvertently discourage individuals from exercising their right to seek asylum. There are now a host of concepts, including preventive protection and internal flight alternatives, that are essentially designed to discourage flight and to bring safety to people rather than people to safety. This logic operated in Bosnia in 1992 and with the Rohingyas in Burma 1994 (Barnett, 2000; Landgren, 1998:427). While these conceptual and operational innovations can be defended on the grounds that they represent pragmatic responses to an environment that increasingly forces UNHCR to choose between the "least bad" of alternatives, they also can have the (unintended?) effect of discouraging flight because they are intended to provide an alternative to exit (Mertus, 1998; Goodwin-Gill, 1999).

Such a possibility is more probable when UNHCR becomes involved in peacebuilding activities (Ogata, 1999b; *see also* Gilbert, 1998:165; McRae, 1999). UNHCR is on record as believing that repatriation can occur under less than ideal conditions, and a logical extension of this claim is that the conditions that can reasonably justify the decision to flee have been tightened. A consequence is that UNHCR might be tempted to discourage individuals from seeking asylum if it, along with other agencies, is actively involved in trying to improve the domestic political situation—a tendency reinforced by the knowledge that relief can be provided to those still within their country. The result is that UNHCR might find itself compromising its protection role as it provides in-country assistance and delivers humanitarian aid; principles yield to pragmatism and political expediency (Gilbert, 1998:365–66). Although UNHCR might still be able to provide in-country protection without necessarily sacrificing refugee rights, even its defenders recognize this danger (Mooney, 1999:216).

Who is a refugee?

Before the 1990s, displaced peoples would have to cross an international border before they could expect UNHCR assistance and protection. Many within the agency and various private aid agencies argued that this was an arbitrary distinction; after all, they should be in the business of helping displaced populations because of similar circumstances and not only those who somehow passed a territorial marker. UNHCR intermittently looked after IDPs during the pre-1990 period (though it refused to categorize them as refugees) because of exceptional circumstances and in those instances when refugees intermingled with IDPs. But any whisper that UNHCR should take on the mandate for IDPs was quickly and roundly muzzled by a supramajority of UNHCR officials who worried about becoming more entangled with domestic politics, diluting their protection mandate, and giving states another opportunity to backtrack from refugee rights, and of state officials who balked at sanctioning an open-ended commitment that threatened state sovereignty (Goodwin-Gill, 1996:11, 14; LCHR, 1991:55; *see also* Gilbert, 1998:362–64).

States began to soften their stance because of two factors (*see* Cohen and Deng, 1998:3–6, for a list of factors). One was a humanitarian ethos. Events surrounding the end of the Cold War, notably the end of empires and outbreak of civil wars, led to the mass movements of populations, some of whom crossed an international frontier and many of whom had not and could not. In terms of gross numbers, nonconvention "refugees" were dwarfing conventional refugees after the 1980s, but they were not deemed as legally and administratively part of the international community's protection mission. These displaced peoples were now making front page news, and the "CNN effect" was seemingly pulling the international community directly to their side (Cohen and Deng, 1998:3–6).

State interests were the other factor. Specifically, states were insisting on repatriation as the durable solution and on a more restrictive definition of refugee (back to the 1951 definition) at the very same moment that the end of the Cold War had triggered a dramatic increase in the numbers of displaced peoples. The question was: how were states going to reconcile their desire to narrow the doorway without completely turning their backs on their humanitarian commitments? Comparable to the self-interest singed by humanitarianism that led to the initial establishment of the category of refugee, many states decided to sanction IDPs because they wanted to be released from other obligations under international refugee law (Hathaway, 1991:115–16). The turning point came with the Gulf and Yugoslavian Wars. In the first instance, Turkey refused to give comfort to a Kurdish population that it viewed as a potential fifth column, and so UNHCR and other member states assisted the displaced in the mountains of northwestern Iraq. The wars in Yugoslavia created several waves of refugees, many of whom sought shelter from European countries. The European countries, however, limited the numbers. Denied the exit option, these victims of war were at immediate risk. Not wanting to appear completely heartless, the European states encouraged UNHCR to provide relief to these internally-displaced populations (Weiss and Pasic, 1996; Barutciski, 1996; Cohen and Deng, 1998:55). In short, states slowly approved the concept of IDPs not because of an abundance of humanitarianism but because of its very absence.

UNHCR officials have had mixed reactions to these developments. In stylized terms, pragmatists favored an expanded definition and wanted to help the displaced based upon their circumstances and not their locations, and fundamentalists feared that an expanded definition would make it easier for states to avoid their obligations under refugee law and would dilute UNHCR's core mission. The debate within UNHCR continues today, most recently triggered by U.S. Ambassador Richard Holbrooke's off-the-cuff remark that UNHCR should be given the mandate for all displaced peoples and the response by UNHCR that it would continue to help IDPs on a case-by-case basis but had little interest in expanding its bureaucratic reach.

The debate over the development of the category of the IDP and its implications for UNHCR highlights that such developments precipitate reconsideration of the meaning of sovereignty and raise potentially troubling concerns for traditional refugee rights. Many have observed that it is impossible to consider IDPs without taking up the question of sovereignty. For instance, in their report from a recent workshop on IDPs in Africa, Crisp and Mooney (1999:474) write that the conference "agreed on the need to reconceptualize the traditional notion of sovereignty. Rather than being used as a means of resisting internal or external scrutiny, sovereignty should be perceived in terms of the duties of all states to protect and respect the rights of their citizens and promote international peace and security."

Although UNHCR might be encouraging states to take more responsibility for their citizens as it becomes more deeply involved in tending to the internally-displaced,UNHCR also is in danger of hollowing out refugee rights. This is possible in at least two related respects. Now that there is an internationally recognized category of IDPs, the expectation by many states is that individuals seeking safety have alternatives to exodus and should be encouraged to stay at home. UNHCR is rumored to oblige state desires. Moreover, when UNHCR tends to IDPs it typically provides assistance—and not protection. The result is that it is accused of failing to speak out on protection matters for fear of jeopardizing its assistance capacity (Cohen and Deng, 1998:165, 256–57). In this way, the concept of IDP joins with other categories that are essentially designed to limit the possibility for flight, to build a general system of containment. For instance, at the 1993 Excom meeting, Ogata stated that the UNHCR should become involved in internally-displaced only when specifically requested by the UN, when IDPs are intertwined with refugees, and when involvement might help to prevent a refugee flow (Cohen and Deng, 1998:130, 170). While the former claim links up to a humanitarian ethos, the latter links to a system of containment.

In general, UNHCR's shifting humanitarian mandate is potentially checkered with advances and setbacks for refugees and their rights. UNHCR's developing involvement in the internal affairs of states, the desire to eliminate the root causes of refugee flows, the desire to give refugees an alternative to fleeing their homes, and the interest in getting them home as quickly as possible can all be seen as progressive shifts in the humanitarian agenda. But these developments also join up with a sovereignty-driven humanitarianism that can curtail the rights and numbers of refugees. The result is that humanitarianism can become implicated in a system of deterrence and containment.

The future

The circumstances surrounding UNHCR's birth and the environment in which it developed have clearly influenced its personality and practices. States schooled UNHCR so that it would know its place in the sovereign system of states and the limits of states' humanitarian sentiments. But environmental changes, including the increasing legitimation principle of popular sovereignty, have expanded considerably UNHCR's humanitarian space. This represents both good news and bad news. The good news is that UNHCR's field of humanitarian vision has widened to the extent that it can now extend protection inside the border's edge, bring safety to people, and consider how to eliminate the root causes of displacement. The bad news is that UNHCR has been given this license to look inward because states are less willing to give asylum to and harbor refugees. "Actual living humanitarian" can be Janus-faced, and UNHCR is discovering that sometimes being a humanitarian agency means selling short protection principles (*see also* Goodwin-Gill, 1999:242–43).

UNHCR and other international organizations are shaped by their environment. Global governance, to the extent that we are interested in governance, is always about power backed (ideally) by legitimacy, and Northern states retain the economic, political, and cultural power in world politics. In this formulation, UNHCR's role is bound up with a global governance that is designed to maintain and reproduce an international order defined by a states system (sovereignty), whose principal beneficiaries are Western states (contain the refugees), and that contains a cultural hegemony (liberalism and individual rights). Within reason, UNHCR's activities (and the activities of any international organizations, for that matter) can be traced to these global features. UNHCR's practices have always been mindful of sovereignty, though the prevailing understanding of sovereignty has shifted over the years. UNHCR has been understandably sensitive to the needs of the powerful states, and such matters have duly shaped its "pragmatic" character. The global, secular religion is liberalism, and as UNHCR seeks ways to eliminate the root causes of refugee flows it nearly always reaches for a liberal solvent. We should not be surprised, therefore, that UNHCR's pragmatism and principles have led it develop a profile of humanitarianism laced with containment.

The claim that UNHCR's activities reflect its environment does not mean that UNHCR has no autonomy, for it does. It has autonomy deriving in part from the fact that there is always slack between the agent and the principals, from its role as protector of refugee law and individuals who fall between the protection of national states, and from its standing as a bureaucratic organization that is increasingly viewed as an authority and lead agency over refugee matters (Chimni, 1998; Barnett and Finnemore, 1999). The new humanitarianism, moreover, has concentrated more power and authority into the hands of humanitarian agencies in general and the UNHCR in particular. As the lead agency in refugee matters and as the world's foremost expert on refugees and displaced peoples, UNHCR is conferred authority. As an agency that is increasingly involved on both sides of the border, UNHCR is serving as the executor of repatriation programs, the *de facto* human rights monitor, and as a humanitarian trustee. This implies the centralization of power and authority in the hands of UNHCR. This can all be for the good. After all, UNHCR has repeatedly demonstrated a willingness to stand up to powerful states when, in its view, they violate refugee law and endanger refugee lives. It takes seriously its role as the guardian of refugee law and the displaced.

Yet over the last decade we have become more savvy (and some would say cynical) about the practices and effects of humanitarianism. We are now disabused of the grand conceit that humanitarianism is apolitical, and we recognize that it is deeply political and therefore can be associated with good and bad (Cutts, 1998:5). Humanitarian international organizations are increasingly aware that their noble actions can be exploited by local actors for ulterior and malevolent purposes, that principles like neutrality and impartiality which justify passivity and in action are forms of intervention can contribute to unwanted outcomes, and how the very process of choosing between moral dilemmas is a political act that privileges one set of values and outcomes over another.

But the unsavory features of the new humanitarianism go beyond these observations to include a consideration of the various roles played by these organizations in global politics, how they are containers of centralized power and authority, and whose "pragmatism" can be disturbingly disconnected from those in whose name it acts. Whereas once we likened humanitarian agencies to white knights on muscled steeds charging to rescue the powerless and weak, we are more aware that these knights also are interested in mundane activities such as career advancement, protecting the agency's reputation, and cultivating the largess of patrons, and are likely to use political and pragmatic considerations to navigate the moral dilemmas that populate complex emergencies. We are less willing to take the rhetoric of and presentation of self by humanitarian international organizations at face value and more likely to wonder whose interests are being served by any set of policies. We now recognize that states can be humanitarians and that humanitarians can be cunning politicians. None of this means that we need to be saved from our saviors. But it does suggest that asking more about the activities of those who are expected to carry out our principles is not only good politics, it also is sound humanitarianism.

Note

1 Further evidence of this repatriation culture is UNHCR's claim that repatriation is in and of itself a "success," and that repatriation is presumed to be the best way to protect refugees even though there have been few studies that have evaluated what

has happened to those who have repatriated, (*see* Chimni, 1998:364; Bascom, 1994; Rogge, 1994).

References

Amnesty International (1997) "In Search of Safety: The Forcibly Displaced and Human Rights in Africa," AI Index: AFR. January 5.

Anonymous (1997) "The UNHCR Note on International Protection You Won't See," *International Journal of Refugee Law*, 9(2):267–273.

Barbero, J. (1993) "Refugee Protection during Conflict: A New Conventional Wisdom," *Refuge*, 12(8):7–12.

Barkin, J. S. (1998) "The Evolution of the Constitution of Sovereignty and the Emergence of Human Rights Norms," *Millennium*, 27(2):229–252.

Barnett, M. (2000) "UNHCR and Involuntary Repatriation: Environmental Developments, the Repatriation Culture, and the Rohingya Refugees." Paper delivered at the International Studies Association annual meetings, Los Angeles, March 16–20.

—— (1995) "The New U.N. Politics of Peace: From Juridical Sovereignty to Empirical Sovereignty," *Global Governance*, 1(1):79–97. Winter.

Barnett, M. and M. Finnemore (1999) "The Politics, Power, and Pathologies of International Organizations," *International Organization*, 53(4):699–732. Fall.

Barutciski, M. (1998) "Involuntary Repatriation when Refugee Protection Is No Longer Necessary," *International Journal of Refugee Law*, 10:236–255.

—— (1996) "The Reinforcement of Non-Admission Policies and the Subversion of UNHCR: Displacement and Internal Assistance in Bosnia-Herzegovina," *International journal of Refugee Law*, 8(1):49–110. January/April.

Bascom, J. (1994) "The Dynamics of Refugee Repatriation: The Case of Eritreans in Eastern Sudan." In *Population Migration and the Changing World Order*. Ed. W. Gould and A. Findley. New York: John Wiley and Sons.

Boli, J. and G. Thomas (1999) "INGOs and the Organization of World Culture." In *Constructing World Culture*. Ed. J. Boli and G. Thomas. Stanford: Stanford University Press. Pp. 13–49.

Boutros-Ghali, B. (1995) "Democracy: A Newly Recognized Imperative," *Global Governance*, 1(1):312. Winter.

Bull, H. (1977) *Anarchical Society*. New York: Columbia University Press.

Chimni, B. S. (1999) "From Resettlement to Repatriation: Towards a Critical History of Durable Solutions to Refugee Problems," *New Issues in Refugee Research*. Working Paper No. 2. Geneva: UNHCR.

—— (1998) "The Geopolitics of Refugee Studies: A View from the South," *Journal of Refugee Studies*, 11(4):350–374.

—— (1993) "The Meaning of Words and the Role of UNHCR in Voluntary Repatriation," *International Journal of Refugee Law*, 5(3):442–460.

—— (1991) "Perspectives on Voluntary Repatriation: A Critical Note," *International Journal of Refugee Law*, 3(3):541–546.

Cohen, R. and F. Deng (1998) *Masses in Flight*. Washington, DC: Brookings Press.

Coles, G. (1989) "Approaching the Refugee Problem Today." In *The Question of Refugees and International Relations*. Ed. G. Loescher and L. Monahan. New York: Oxford University Press. Pp. 373–410.

—— (1985) *Voluntary Repatriation*. Geneva: UNHCR.

Crisp, J. F. (1984a) "The Politics of Repatriation: Ethiopian Refugees in Djibouti," *Review of African Political Economy*, 30:73–82.
—— (1984b) "Voluntary Repatriation Programs for African Refugees: A Critical Assessment," *Refugee Issues*, 1(2):23.
Crisp, J. and E. Mooney (1999) "Report on the Workshop on Internal Displacement in Africa, Addis Ababa, October 19–20, 1998," *International Migration Review*, 33(2):468–483.
Cunliffe, S. A. and M. Pugh (1999) "UNHCR as Leader in Humanitarianism: A Triumph of Politics over Law?" In *Refugee Rights and Realities: Evolving International Concepts and Regimes*. Ed. F. Nicholson and P. Twomey. New York: Cambridge University Press.
Cuny, F. and B. Stein (1989) "Prospects for and Promotion of Spontaneous Repatriation." In *The Question of Refugees and International Relations*. Ed. G. Loescher and L. Monahan. New York: Oxford University Press.
Cutts, M. (1998) "Politics and Humanitarianism," *Refugee Survey Quarterly*, 17(1):1–15.
Dacyl, J. (1996) "Sovereignty Versus Human Rights: From Past Discourses to Contemporary Dilemmas," *Journal of Refugee Studies*, 9(2):136–165.
Demusz, K. (1998) "From Relief to Development: Negotiating the Continuum on the Thai-Burmese Border," *Journal of Refugee Studies*, 11(3):231–249.
Deng, F. (1995) "Dealing with the Displaced: A Challenge to the International Community," *Global Governance*, 1. Winter.
de Wall, A. (1998) *Famine Crimes*. Bloomington: Indiana University Press.
Doyle, M. (1986) "Liberalism and World Politics," *American Political Science Review*, 80:1151–1169.
Feller, E. (1990) UNHCR and the International Protection of Refugees—Current Problems and Future Prospects," *International Journal of Refugee Law*, 2:335–346. September.
Franck, T. (1992) "The Emerging Right to Democratic Governance," *American Journal of International Law*, 86(1):46–91. January.
Frelick, B. (1993) "Preventing Refugee Flows: Protection or Peril," *World Refugee Survey*. Pp. 5–13.
—— (1990) "The Right to Return," *International Journal of Refugee Law*, 2:442–448.
Gilbert, G. (1998) "Rights, Legitimate Expectations, Needs, and Responsibilities: UNHCR and the New World Order," *International Journal of Refugee Law*, 10(3):349–388.
Goodwin-Gill, G. (1999) "Refugee Identity and Protection's Fading Prospect." In *Refugee Rights and Realities: Evolving International Concepts and Regimes*. Ed. F. Nicholson and P. Twomey. New York: Cambridge University Press. Pp. 220–252.
—— (1996) *The Refugee in International Law*, 2nd Edition. New York: Oxford University Press.
Gordenker, L. (1981) "Organizational Expansion and Limits in International Services for Refugees," *International Migration Review*, 15(1):74–87.
Harrell-Bond, B. (1989) "Repatriation: Under What Conditions Is it the Most Desirable Solution for Refugees?" *African Studies Review*, 32:41–69.
Hathaway, J. (1997) "The Meaning of Repatriation," *International Journal of Refugee Law*, 9(4):551–558.
—— (1991) "Reconceiving Refugee Law as Human Rights Protection," *Journal of Refugee Studies*, 4(2):113–131.

Holborn, L. (1975) *Refugees: Problem of Our Time: The Work of the United Nations High Commissioner for Refugees*, 2 volumes. Metuchen, NJ: Scarecrow Press.

Human Rights Watch (1997) *Uncertain Refugee: International Failures to Protect Refugees*, 9:1. April.

—— (1996) "Burma: The Rohingyan Muslims Ending a Cycle of Violence?" 8:0. September.

Human Rights Watch/Asia and Refugees International (1997) "Rohingya Refugees in Bangladesh: The Search for a Lasting Solution," 9:7. August.

Jackson, R. (1993) "The Weight of Ideas in Decolonization: Normative Change in International Relations." In *Ideas and Foreign Policy: Beliefs, Institutions, and Political Change*. Ed. J. Goldstein and R. Keohane. Ithaca: Cornell University Press. Pp. 111–138.

Jacobsen, H. (1962) "The United Nations and Colonialism: A Tentative Appraisal," *International Organization*, 1:37–56. Winter.

Jones, D. (1991) *Code of Peace: Ethics and Security in the World of the Warlord States*. Chicago: University of Chicago Press.

Kennedy, D. (1986) "International Refugee Protection," *Human Rights Quarterly*, 8:1–69.

Kourula, P. (1998) *Broadening the Edges: Refugee Definition and International Protection Revisited*. The Hague: Martinus Nijhoff Publishers.

Landgren, K. (1998) "The Future of Refugee Protection," *Journal of Refugee Studies*, 11(4):416–432.

Lawyers Committee for Human Rights (LCHR) (1991) *UNHCR at 40: Refugee Protection at the Crossroads*. New York: LCHR.

Loescher, G. (1994) "The United Nations, the UN High Commissioner for Refugees, and the Global Refugee Problem." In *U.S. Policy and the Future of the United Nations*. Ed. R. Coate. New York: Twentieth Century Fund.

—— (1989) "Introduction: Refugee Issues in International Relations." In *Refugees and International Relations*. Ed. G. Loescher and L. Monahan. New York: Oxford University Press. Pp. 1–33.

Loescher, G. and L. Monahan, eds. (1989) *The Question of Refugees and International Relations*. New York: Oxford University Press.

Malkki, L. (1995) "Refugees and Exile: From 'Refugee Studies' to the National Order of Things," *Annual Review of Anthropology*, 24:495–523.

Maren, M. (1997) *The Road to Hell*. New York: Free Press.

McRae, J. (1999) "Aiding Peace . . . and War: UNHCR, Returnee Reintegration, and the Relief–Development Debate," *New Issues in Refugee Research*, Working Paper No. 14. Geneva: Center for Documentation and Research, UNHCR.

MSF/Holland (1997) "Better off in Burma? The Plight of the Burmese Rohingyas." November.

—— (1995a) "MSF's Concerns on the Repatriation of Rohingyan Refugees from Bangladesh to Burma." May 1.

—— (1995b) "Awareness Survey of Rohingyan Refugee Camps," March 15.

Melander, G. (1987) "The Two Refugee Definitions," Raoul Wallenberg Institute of Human Rights and Humanitarian Law, Report No. 4, Lund, Sweden.

Mertus, J. (1998) "The State and the Post-Cold War Refugee Regime: New Models, New Questions," *International Journal of Refugee Law*, 10(3):320–347.

Mooney, E. (1999) "In-Country Protection: Out of Bounds for UNHCR?" In

Refugee Rights and Realities: Evolving International Concepts and Regimes. Ed. F. Nicholson and P. Twomey. New York: Cambridge University Press. Pp. 200–219.

Moore, J. (1998) *Hard Choices: Moral Dilemmas in Humanitarian Intervention*. Lanham, MD: Rowman & Littlefield Publishers.

Morris, N. (1997) "Protection Dilemmas and UNHCR's Response: A Personal View from within UNHCR," *International Journal of Refugee Law*, 9((3):492–499.

—— (1990) "Refugees: Facing Crisis in the 1990s—A Personal View from within UNHCR," *International Journal of Refugee Law*, 2:38–57.

Nyers, P. (1999) "Emergency or Emerging Identities? Refugees and Transformations in World Order," *Millennium*, 28(1):1–26.

Ogata, S. (1999a) "Half a Century on the Humanitarian Frontlines." Lecture delivered at Graduate Institute for International Studies, Geneva, November 25.

—— (1999b) "On the Humanitarian Frontlines: New Challenges to Refugee Work." Lecture delivered at Harvard University, November 8.

—— (1996) "World Order, Internal Conflict, and Refugees." Lecture delivered at Harvard University, October 28.

Petrasek, D. (1999) "Through Rose-Coloured Glasses: UNHCR's Role in Monitoring the Safety of the Rohningya Refugees Returning to Burma." Unpublished paper.

Pitterman, S. (1985) "International Responses to Refugee Situations: The United Nations High Commissioner for Refugees." In *Refugees in World Politics*. Ed. E. Ferris. Praeger Press. Pp. 43–81.

Reiff, D. (1997) "Charity on the Rampage," *Foreign Affairs*, 76(1):132–139. January/February.

Reisman, W. M. (1990) "Sovereignty and Human Rights in International Law," *American Journal of International Law*, 84(4):866–876.

Rogge, J. (1994) "Repatriation of Refugees." In *When Refugees Go Home: African Experiences*. Ed. T. Allen and H. Morsink. Geneva: UNRISD.

Ruggie, J., ed. (1993) *Multilateralism Matters*. New York: Columbia University Press.

Schnyder, F. (1965) "Extracts from Lectures at the Hague Academy of International Law." HCR/RS/32, October 26.

Skran, C. (1992) "The International Refugee Regime: The Historical and Contemporary Context of International Responses to Asylum Problems." In *Refugees: The Asylum Dilemma in the West*. Ed. G. Loescher. College Station: Pennsylvania State University Press. Pp. 8–34.

Stein, B. (1986) "Durable Solutions for Developing Country Refugees," *International Migration Review*, 20(2):264–282.

Stein, B. and F. Cuny (1994) "Refugee Repatriation during Conflict: Protection and Post-Return Assistance," *Development in Practice*, 4:1.

—— (1993) "Repatriation in a Civil War/Conflict Situation." Paper presented at Roundtable Consultation on Voluntary Repatriation and UNHCR, Geneva, Switzerland. June 2–3.

—— (1991) "Repatriation under Conflict," *World Refugee Survey*.

Suhrke, A. (1998) "Burden-Sharing during Refugee Emergencies: The Logic of Collective Versus National Action," *Journal of Refugee Studies*, 11(4):396–415.

Sztucki, J. (1989) "The Conclusions on the International Protection of Refugees Adopted by the Executive Committee of the UNHCR Programme," *International Journal of Refugee Law*, 1(3):285–318.

Takahashi, S. (1997) "The UNHCR Handbook on Voluntary Repatriation: The

Emphasis of Return over Protection," *International Journal of Refugee Law*, 9(4):592–612.

UNHCR (1995) *State of the World's Refugees: In Search of Solutions*. New York: Oxford University Press.

U.S. Committee for Refugees (1996) "USCR Site Visit to Bangladesh, June 20–July 1." Issue Brief.

—— (1995) *The Return of the Rohingyan Refugees to Burma: Voluntary Repatriation or Refoulement?* Washington, DC: U.S. Committee on Refugees.

Warner, D. (1994) "Voluntary Repatriation and the Meaning of Return to Home: A Critique of Liberal Mathematics," *Journal of Refugee Studies*, 7(2/3):160–174.

Weiner, M. (1998) "The Clash of Norms: Dilemmas in Refugee Policies," *Journal of Refugee Studies*, 11(4):433–453.

Weiss, T. and A. Pasic (1996) "Reinventing UNHCR: Enterprising Humanitarians in the Former Yugoslavia, 1991–95," *Global Governance*, 3:41–58.

Working Group on International Refugee Policy (1999) "Report of the International Conference on the Protection Mandate of UNHCR," *Journal of Refugee Studies*, 12(2):202–217.

Zieck, M. (1997) *UNHCR and Voluntary Repatriation of Refugees: A Legal Analysis*. The Hague: Martinus Nijhoff Publishers.

Section II

The ethics of intervention

6   The UN Security Council, indifference, and genocide in Rwanda

I was on the Delta Shuttle from New York to Washington on April 6, 1994 when I first learned, by way of the *New York Times*, that the plane carrying President Habyarimana of Rwanda had mysteriously crashed as it approached the Kigali airport. My first response was to study the photograph of the dead president; after closely covering his comings and goings for the past several months, it struck me as odd that the first time that I would see his face was in a newspaper article announcing his death. Then I felt frustration bordering on exasperation. As a political officer at the U.S. Mission to the United Nations who was assigned to cover Rwanda, I had spent the last part of March consumed by the negotiations on the mandate extension of the United Nations Assistance Mission in Rwanda (UNAMIR). Although many of the Security Council debates on whether to extend a mandate and under what conditions have a scripted quality that foreordain renewal, this instance was uncharacteristically lengthy and contentious.

UNAMIR was charged with overseeing the implementation of the Arusha Accords, the blueprint to end the civil war between the Tutsi-backed Rwandan Patriotic Forces (RPF) and the Hutu-dominated Rwandan government, and to install a new, more representative, government. For some months, the Rwandan government had been dragging its heels and failing to produce the transitional government, leaving many on the Security Council increasingly irritated. The U.S. position was that the Rwandan government should be notified that unless it quickly established the transitional government, the UN operation would be ended. How strong these signals should be, and how serious the threat to close the operation should be, was a principal point of contention during the negotiations over the mandate's extension. The Security Council approved an extension just as the mandate expired in early April, the United States was satisfied that its concerns had been communicated to the Rwandan government, and I was relieved to have Rwanda off my desk and be able to turn my attention to other matters. The president's death changed all that, for bad and for good. Exhausted from the hectic pace, I would now not have my long awaited break. Still, Rwanda rarely commanded front-page news as it was now doing, and I could look forward to a departure from the daily monotonous routine.

As it so happens, I was on my way to Washington to meet the various people in the State Department from whom I received my instructions on Rwanda and other peacekeeping operations. Beginning in January 1994, I had been assigned primary responsibility for the peacekeeping operations in Rwanda, Burundi, and Mozambique, and had become the backup officer for the rest of sub-Saharan Africa. Such responsibilities entailed a never-ending stream of phone calls to various parts of the State Department that had some input into these operations, primarily the Bureau of International Organization and secondarily the Bureaus of Central and East African Affairs and Political-Military Affairs. Before the death of Habyarimana, the agenda for my trip to Washington had been to make the rounds, meet my bureaucratic counterparts, and discuss the various operations. Now I was anxious to hear about what was happening in Kigali.

I was greeted by my contact person from International Organization, who had little news but was eager to bring me upstairs to the recently established Situation Room. The "Sit Room"—something assembled at the outset of any crisis as a nerve center for receiving and coordinating information—had three banks of phones, roughly 20 people milling in and out, and a makeshift map of Rwanda hung on the wall, the only marker of why we were all there. As we entered the room, my contact person requested everyone's attention to relay news of the current situation in Kigali, which was rather sparse and highly speculative. She then asked each of us to introduce ourselves. When my turn came, I was given a special introduction by my contact: I was the person at the U.S. Mission to the United Nations who followed Rwanda. The subtext was that I was a Rwanda expert. My credentials established, those nearest to me immediately asked me to provide basic background on the country, as well as information about the military locations and strengths of the government, RPF, and UN forces; their anticipated moves; and what the Security Council was likely to do. To my amazement, I handled these and other questions with a degree of assuredness and authority expected of someone of my position. I offered to call my contacts at the UN Department of Peacekeeping Operations (DPKO) in order to gather more information on developments on the ground; I did, and my UN contacts gave me what they had, which was more alarming and complete than what I just had heard in the Sit Room. I relayed the information to those around me, solidifying my credentials as an expert on Rwanda. I declined the invitation to stay for the night shift on the pretext that I would be of greater service in New York. My contact agreed, although I doubt she cared one way or the other.

That I might be presented as a Rwanda expert still strikes me as rather incongruous. After all, I teach international politics at the University of Wisconsin, feel most comfortable in the world of theory rather than in the world of facts, and any claim I have to regional expertise is limited to the Middle East. That I became an expert on Rwanda is thanks to the Council of Foreign Relations, which offers a fellowship program that places academics in the U.S. foreign policy bureaucracy to both carry out research and become part of the policy-making process. Building on a long-standing interest in Third World security, I had proposed to examine how such issues were being handled after the Cold War. The UN, through its peacekeeping operations, had become highly involved in Third World security; therefore, the U.S. Mission to the United Nations seemed to be the perfect venue for examining such matters. The U.S. Mission agreed to host my year, and I was placed in the Bureau of Political-Military Affairs, reporting directly to the ambassador who covered security affairs and to the Mission's Political Section. At the suggestion of my immediate superior, I adopted the title of Adviser for Peacekeeping Operations. I proudly accepted my security passes, the first tangible evidence that I was a bona fide member of the U.S. Mission to the United Nations.

When I arrived at the U.S. Mission in August 1993, I was assigned to help cover Somalia. After the United States announced in October its intention to withdraw from Somalia by March 1994, my responsibilities for Somalia rapidly shrunk, and in my position, there was little to do but pray that the United States might withdraw without incurring additional casualties or further harm to its reputation. Consequently, I was assigned to other parts of Africa. When Rwanda became part of my "account," I knew little more about it than how to find it on a map and that it was the country with the gorillas; my first association with Mozambique was the song of that title by Bob Dylan. My lack of knowledge seemed to trouble only myself. My superiors were, perhaps, reassured by the experience I had gained covering Somalia and the fact that they would closely supervise my activities, and they knew better than I that in-depth knowledge of the country was not necessary to carry out my daily activities.

Among my duties as a political officer were reading cable traffic on my issues, writing talking points for the U.S. ambassadors, hosting various Washington officials when they visited the UN, covering the Security Council when my issues were on the agenda and then writing cables on its proceedings, and generally acting as a conduit between Washington and the UN. Sometimes I would be asked to work on long-term "policy" issues, such as peacekeeping reform and Security Council expansion. These I felt more comfortable with because they were more consistent with my academic training and background. But the Mission had little real use for long-term policy planning and great demand for another political officer—that is, someone who could help with the overwhelming workload—and I recognized that I would learn much more by becoming integrated into the daily routines than by working on policy projects that would be disregarded. In any event, I was a seasoned veteran of Rwanda for nearly four months when President Habyarimana of Rwanda was killed and all hell erupted.

Becoming a bureaucrat

That I might be plausibly presented as a Rwanda expert can only be understood in the context of the culture of the foreign policy bureaucracy. Like all

bureaucracies, the foreign policy bureaucracy organizes and privileges knowledge in particular ways, and in this context the knowledge that mattered
most was not the particulars about Rwanda but rather the culture of the
policy-making process in the U.S. government and the UN. Specifically, my
standing as an expert derived from the following factors. As a political officer
I was, by definition, an expert. Rwanda was my account; I was its owner
and hence a Rwanda expert. It hardly mattered that when Rwanda became
part of my account I knew little of its political, economic, and social structures. Nor did my daily routine allow me to devote any real effort to "get
smart" on the subject; I was responsible for other operations and my days
were consumed with back-to-back "fires" that needed immediate attention.
No one ever asked me for my credentials and it would not have mattered.
The other political officer at the U.S. Mission who covered Africa could claim
greater expertise by virtue of having covered the topic in recent years,
not from any formal training or visits. That she had never visited Africa
was a legacy of post-Cold War budget cuts: travel money was becoming
increasingly scarce and largely consumed by those at the top. Expert status
had very little to do with areal knowledge and much to do with bureaucratic
position.

My status also derived from my possession of the "facts" of the bureaucracy: who handled what issues, who had access to key decision makers, who
my counterparts were in other missions to the UN and other departments
in Washington, what had transpired in the Security Council, and what the
precise language of past mandates was. Over time, I accumulated a stock of
facts regarding the issues that I covered, and I became fluent in the acronyms
of the UN and the policy process. Knowledge of some of these facts and
having the Rwanda account went some distance in defining me as an expert.

More fundamentally, my standing as an expert derived from my ability to
formulate questions and responses, to pose talking points, to use language,
and to carry on conversations in ways that were consistent with the understandings and discourses of my superiors and my colleagues. In other words,
I had to understand the subtext to conversations, what was said and not said,
how information was framed, the symbols that were emotionally charged,
what knowledge was relevant, and how arguments were constructed and
topics debated. The foreign policy bureaucracy, like all organizations, has its
own culture to the extent that it has its own discourse, symbols, and norms of
interaction, in both practices and language choice, that mark insiders from
outsiders. Whether I was accepted and effective was dependent on acting in a
manner that was consistent with that culture.

My socialization into this culture was a slow and often awkward process.
When I first arrived at the U.S. Mission, I knew little of the language and
understood few of the symbols. My colleagues could speak full sentences in
acronyms that I had never heard of, use slang that referred to events and
processes of which I had no knowledge, and easily transform nouns like
"demarche" into verbs. Being unable to speak the language or understand the

subtext to conversations left me feeling generally alienated and often confused. My exhaustion at the end of the day was a testimony not only to the grueling and charged pace, but also to my ignorance of the discourse and symbols that circulated as I went through the day. To constantly question all that passed before me proved tiring and quite frequently provided fodder for my colleagues' amusement, causing them to make playful but derogatory references to my "academic" status. Ironically, participants from peacekeeping operations who passed through New York would similarly comment that colleagues at the UN existed in an "ivory tower," while they lived in the "real world." Events that would make my colleagues at the Mission take notice would have little effect on me; other events that would cause me to panic would leave my colleagues simply bored. My only other experiences that nearly matched this sensation of being in another world was when I was in my first year in graduate school and when I was doing field research in Cairo for my dissertation. Still, within several months I became comfortable with the cultural terrain.

A good illustration of this was my experiences learning to write "reporting cables," one of my most important duties as a political officer. Reporting cables are accounts of events, meetings, and developments that might be relevant to U.S. policy or someone, somewhere, in the foreign policy bureaucracy. There are rules to cable writing, and junior officers take a detailed course in this craft (and other aspects of diplomatic protocol) before they are given their first post. Although my job entailed endless hours writing cables, I received little guidance on its ins and outs, and consequently, learned by trial and error. Some aspects of cable writing were relatively straightforward to learn, such as how to set up the cable, who should be on the distribution list, and its formal organization. Less straightforward but more central to the effectiveness of the cable, however, was articulating the bureaucratic culture that the cable was to reflect and represent.

A good cable has various characteristics, and at first my cables had few of them. Initially my cables were "academic," reminiscent of my notes from graduate seminars: exhaustive, analytical, dense, aspiring to reach some mythical archimedean point that was attentive to the complexities of the issue, the details of the meetings, and the views of all those in attendance. But this approach completely overlooked the basic point that cables are political documents. As political documents, cables are expected to provide a narrative that weaves together various perspectives that derive from personal, bureaucratic, and U.S.-centered positions. My task as a political officer was to report on events in which my immediate superiors were directly involved or interested, or for which they had bureaucratic responsibility. Simply put, I had to "clear" these cables by the same individuals about whom I was reporting or who had a direct interest in the issue. Not surprisingly, they were concerned not least as much with making sure that they were represented favorably and protected from bureaucratic rivals as with "getting the story right." A good cable, I learned, is not only clear and succinct; it also offers an account that is consistent with the interests, both personal and bureaucratic, of one's superiors. For instance, my cables had to portray the U.S. ambassadors as sharp, alert, and probing; on numerous occasions I had to rewrite a cable because it did not quite capture the language of a superior or place her or him in the best light. Rarely would I record the gaffes of my superiors, no matter how consequential, and I learned that I was free to rearrange the sequence of events if it served a political purpose.

My cables were also expected to reflect the bureaucratic interests and worldview of the U.S. Mission to the United Nations in general and of the Political Section in particular. Those in Washington believed that we in New York had "gone native"—that is, that we were unreflectingly pro-UN and pro-peacekeeping, insufficiently sensitive to U.S. "national interests," and naive about U.S. domestic and Washington politics. We in New York believed that those in Washington had little understanding of the "politics of the UN" or how resolutions were crafted and drafted, and saw our job as having to explain to Washington how the UN and the Security Council worked and how the policies we proposed were, in fact, consistent with the U.S. national interests. Therefore, my bureaucratic interests were not limited to defending and expanding my turf, but also included learning a definition of the "U.S. national interest" that was consistent with my bureaucratic position at the UN. Over time I learned a conception of the "U.S. national interest" that supported the UN and peacekeeping. In fact, "players" at the U.S. Mission achieved this designation not simply by virtue of their position in the bureaucracy, but also through their ability to translate between and articulate the views of the U.S. Mission and Washington.

Furthermore, my own assignment and position shaped the interests I reflected and promoted in my cables. My bureaucratic interests included protecting my turf, as well as looking for opportunities to increase my visibility or capture an additional high-profile policy issue. When I first began covering Somalia, I was "tagged" to follow closely the issue of the Somali police force. Specifically, there was considerable interest in "standing up" the Somali police force to, first, help the UN with its task of maintaining security and, second, expedite the return of "law and order" to Somalia and the withdrawal of the United Nations Operation in Somalia. Soon thereafter, my immediate superior and I began using our expertise on Somalia to highlight the importance of civilian police in UN operations more generally. Not only were these important issues that were generic to other operations, but the promotion of this issue also promoted our profile. We were good bureaucratic actors—that is, good entrepreneurs.

Weaving these various views—personal, bureaucratic, and U.S.-centered —into a coherent narrative was something that had to be learned. Over time I became quite capable of presenting information so that it paralleled how other bureaucrats understood and organized the world; slowly I learned how to couch and frame my issue in ways that made sense to those on the distribution list. An effective cable is one that is likely to be read, and a cable will only be read if it organizes knowledge in a manner that conforms to the intended reader's organization of knowledge.

Slowly I acquired more than the skills of a political officer; I developed the mentality and mindset as well. After several months, I became more comfortable with my position, and better able to understand and share in the symbols, gestures, and utterances of my colleagues. Said otherwise, not only had I entered the bureaucratic world, but the bureaucratic world had entered me. My long days of intense interaction with my colleagues were slowly transforming how I understood, identified, and presented myself. Whereas once I had effected certain practices and discourses because of their instrumentality and strategic value, now I did so because they felt comfortable and consistent with who I was and how I understood myself. At various instances when I comfortably effected the language and the practices of a political officer, my colleagues commented on my "socialization" with chuckles and tongue-in-cheek congratulations. If once I thought of "me" and "them," I now began thinking in terms of "us." Although my identity as an academic and a visitor never disappeared for either my colleagues or myself, my presentation and practices were less strategic and mimetic and more authentic.

My new identity was tied to a particular set of interests. Whereas once I was bewildered by my colleagues' logic as they defended or promoted a particular policy, I soon became sympathetic to and supported their positions. More dramatically, if once I judged, promoted, and criticized policies depending on how they related to my "academic" preferences, I now had "swallowed a dose of reality" and was situating policies according to whether they were good or bad for the interests and reputations of, first, the United States, and, second, the UN. I more fully identified with my role as a representative of the United States to the UN, and I slowly identified with, developed a greater loyalty to, and took my identity from, these entities. I began to defend the policies of the United States and the potential of the UN not simply because to do otherwise might cause my colleagues to sanction me for disloyalty, but because I came to identify with these organizations. I was now a Rwanda expert.

Rwanda

The 24 hours after the death of President Habyarimana on April 6 produced the feared bloodshed. With only 5,000 lightly-armed peacekeepers scattered throughout Rwanda, UNAMIR was unprepared to confront the wave of terror unleashed by Hutu extremists against Tutsis and Hutu moderates. UN troops were instantly confronted by two increasingly untenable tasks: protecting the lives of civilians and defending themselves. The tension between these two goals became immediately apparent when ten Belgian peacekeepers were brutally murdered while protecting moderate Hutu politicians during the first days of the violence; the remaining Belgian troops were widely believed by UNAMIR and the Security Council to be marked for assassination. Whether or not the non-Belgian peacekeepers were at immediate risk from Hutu forces, they were running dangerously low on fuel, water, and food; moreover, resupplying or rescuing them was becoming increasingly questionable as the airport became a major battleground, raising the real possibility that any approaching aircraft might suffer the same fate as Habyarimana's. To make matters worse, the RPF was now assembling and preparing to march on Kigali. Therefore, the meager and badly supplied UN forces were confronted by two wars: the Rwandan government's terror campaign against its "enemies" and the brewing civil war between the government and RPF.

Back in New York, the Security Council had to decide quickly about both the future of UNAMIR and the UN's response to the growing violence. The Security Council was in almost constant session, meeting sometimes twice daily and long into the night. As I watched and participated in the debate over the Security Council's response during this critical period, I (and others around me) came to believe that the only responsible decision was to reduce UNAMIR's presence and mandate. Three factors, in my view, were most important for producing this consensus.

First, the Secretariat, namely Boutros Boutros-Ghali's office and DPKO, gave an impression of distance and aloofness from the emerging tragedy, which only reinforced the disinclination among many member states in the Security Council to propose a greater role for UNAMIR.[1] During these first days of the crisis, one of my responsibilities was to meet with officials at DPKO to try and ascertain their thoughts on UNAMIR's future and on how the UN ought to respond. In doing so, I became increasingly alarmed by their "business-as-usual" approach. Few who I encountered displayed much urgency. Two other incidents also contributed to my view of a Secretariat that was not up to the task. During a meeting between DPKO and representatives of the member states contributing troops to UNAMIR, the latter bitterly complained that they were unable to receive any information on the whereabouts or safety of their troops—or even to get DPKO to return their phone calls. As they walked out of the meeting, many of those representatives grumbled that they could not afford to place the lives of their people in the hands of a cavalier UN. One story making the rounds was that a member of the Secretariat said that the UN need not be overly concerned with their troops since "they are not our boys." In the UN's world, according to the delegate who told me the story, jeeps are more valuable than people. Although I cannot say that the incident ever occurred, it sounded plausible to me and, more important, very plausible to others.

Boutros-Ghali also emanated indecision to the point of paralysis, if not complacency. He happened to be in Europe in early April and opted to stay there rather than return to New York. This decision, in my view at the time, reflected a disturbingly distant stance from the unfolding tragedy and demonstrated a troubling abdication of responsibility and leadership. A more distressing episode concerned a reported conversation between him and Belgium's former Foreign Minister Willy Claes. With ten peacekeepers already dead and its remaining soldiers at risk, the Belgian government was debating whether to withdraw its troops. Claes called Boutros-Ghali to ascertain the Secretariat's thinking and how Belgium's decision might affect the future of UNAMIR. According to an authoritative source, despite the urgency of the situation Boutros-Ghali responded by saying that he would "get back to him in four or five days."

Most consequential, however, was the failure of the Secretariat to offer any options to the Security Council regarding the future of UNAMIR. The Secretariat, through its recommendations and reports, shapes the Security Council's deliberations and potentially its decisions. The Secretariat's agenda-setting influence was potentially enhanced in this instance because few, if any, member states had independent sources of information, and they therefore relied heavily on the Secretariat for intelligence and policy recommendations regarding UNAMIR's future. Yet the Secretariat's reports were evasive and noncommittal. My overall impression, shared by others on the Security Council, was that the Secretariat was "not up to the task" of crisis management, being either overwhelmed or insensitive to the dead peacekeepers and the escalating violence. At that moment, I became convinced that the Secretariat should not be given the responsibility of commanding troops in dangerous situations and that UNAMIR's size and responsibility needed to be reduced.

A second reason for the consensus to reduce UNAMIR's role was that no country was willing to contribute its troops for an expanded operation or mandate. Although there was a brief discussion concerning the possibility of UNAMIR's intervening to halt the escalating bloodshed and to protect the civilian populations, I was (and still am) unaware of a single member state who offered their troops for such an operation. Consequently, those on the Security Council, largely the nonpermanent members, who were arguing for an intervention force had little ammunition: the Secretariat, who would be responsible for carrying out the mandate, was silent, and silence was widely interpreted as disapproval. No troop contributors were volunteering for an expanded force. Indeed, soon after the death of its soldiers, Belgium, which represented the backbone of UNAMIR, announced its immediate withdrawal, and no state offered replacements.

Third, with UNAMIR's mandate to oversee the Arusha Accords effectively over, with no country willing to send its troops into an increasingly chaotic environment, and with access to the airport increasingly precarious, the Security Council had to protect its peacekeepers and the UN's reputation. This was a line most forcefully argued by the United States; it and others consistently argued that the Security Council had a duty and obligation to protect the lives of the peacekeepers and that the failure to do so would make it harder to obtain troops for future operations and, perhaps, further the decline in the UN's reputation. Although the Security Council was divided over the extent and timing of the drawdown, there was a general recognition that peacekeepers, unprotected and exposed, could do little good and much harm both to themselves and the UN's reputation and future. I fully shared and supported this view. After nearly two weeks of endless and circular debate, on April 21 the Security Council decided to withdraw the bulk of UNAMIR and to leave in place a skeletal force to assist the valiant, but ultimately unsuccessful, efforts of UN Force Commander General Romeo Dallaire to fashion a cease-fire agreement between the RPF and the government.

No sooner had the Security Council voted to reduce UNAMIR's presence than it and Boutros-Ghali revisited whether and how the UN might respond to confront the increasingly evident genocide. Boutros-Ghali now began to take a visible lead, using his bully pulpit to formulate options and to urge the Security Council and the member states to respond vigorously to the continuing massacres. The Security Council, highly embarrassed that its only answer to the bloodshed was a reduction of UNAMIR, began to debate the possibility of an intervention force. But there were no volunteers for such a force. It seemed that the daily reports of carnage and brutality only contributed to the belief that it was highly improbable that a modest-sized outside force could halt the terror, and no member state was enthusiastic about sending its troops into such chaos.

When the Secretariat finally unveiled its long-awaited plan in late April, it was greeted with considerable enthusiasm by the Security Council, although more because it created an image of a UN that was poised for action than because the plan was likely to contribute to ending the genocide. Simply put, this proposal was merely symbolic and highly impractical: it proposed to dispatch 5,000 troops to Kigali, acknowledged that these troops might not be located for months (if ever), and confessed that it had no real idea what they would do once they arrived. The United States rightly criticized the plan as little more than smoke and demanded that the Secretariat and others on the Security Council design a realistic proposal rather than constructing a Potemkin village. The United States also circulated its own suggestions for protecting and providing relief to the growing number of refugees. Because the United States objected to this initial proposal, the United States was widely portrayed in the media as representing the sole obstacle to military intervention by the UN. But the U.S. position, in my view, only blocked the adoption of a proposal that was designed to save face for the Security Council and diverted energy away from alternatives that might actually have helped those on the ground.

No international action would be taken until late June, when a UN-authorized French operation went to southern Rwanda to protect the refugees. The Security Council was unenthusiastic about France's proposed intervention. France had long-standing ties to the very Hutu military that was now accused of genocide, and the Security Council feared that France would use the pretext of a humanitarian intervention to intervene on behalf of its Hutu allies. But the Security Council set aside these concerns and reluctantly approved what was its only real option, by a vote of ten in favor and five abstentions. Soon thereafter, the United States and other countries contributed humanitarian assistance (although outside the UN umbrella) to try and alleviate the suffering of an estimated 2 million refugees. And in the fall of 1994, UNAMIR returned to Kigali in greater numbers, long after the RPF had captured the country, between 500,000 and 800,000 people had perished, and 2 million had become refugees.

I left the U.S. Mission in June 1994 and returned to academic life. As I began to write on UN peacekeeping and its future, I highlighted the policy implications of Rwanda and other peacekeeping operations. Most of the lessons I drew derived from the need to protect the UN's resources and to better define the limit and scope of future UN operations in order to salvage its reputation and to ensure the continuation of the member states' support. Although troubled by the Security Council's failure to take even the most minimal steps to alleviate the suffering in Rwanda, I justified the lack of action by arguing that anything short of a massive and dramatic intervention would not have stopped the genocide, no states were offering troops for such a campaign, and another "loss" after Somalia would jeopardize the UN's future. Such horrors existed and would continue to exist, I told myself and others, and the UN could not be expected to intervene wherever danger and bloodshed occurred.

In April 1995, I was watching a television special commemorating the first anniversary of the genocide of Rwanda. The narrator emphatically contrasted the genocide and the refugee crisis with the minimal efforts of the international community. My first response was my standard line: there had been no effective basis for UN intervention, and the Security Council had a responsibility not only to Rwanda but also to the UN and its peacekeepers. Upon further reflection, however, I began to question why I, along with so many others in the Security Council and the Secretariat, had so quickly concluded that the needs of the UN overrode the needs of those who were the targets of genocide. Why, for instance, had neither the Secretariat nor any member state vigorously petitioned the Security Council to assemble an intervention force? Why were most member states apparently more exercised by the need to restrain the UN from any further involvement than they were by the need to dispatch assistance? How did the desire to protect the UN's reputation become a justification for not intervening? Raising such questions led me to pose the reason for inaction in a more brutal manner: the UN had more to lose by taking action and being associated with another failure than it did by not taking action and allowing the genocide in Rwanda. The moral equation was: genocide was acceptable if the alternative was to harm the future of the UN.

The bureaucratization of indifference

I am increasingly drawn to the conclusion that the bureaucratization of peacekeeping contributed to this indifference to the suffering of the very people peacekeeping is mandated to assist. As I, for one, more closely identified with the United States and the UN, I found it easier to remain indifferent to the occasional evil in deference to their "interests." There is, in my experience, an intimate connection between the discourse of acting in the best interests of the international community, the bureaucratization of peacekeeping, and the production of indifference.[2]

The traditional view offered by international relations scholars is that states pursue their "security interests," and thus no matter how grieved member states were by the genocide in Rwanda, they were unwilling to commit money and manpower to any operation because it remained outside their "interests." This is part of the answer, but it does not adequately capture the dynamics of the Security Council's debate over Rwanda, nor explain why the Security Council agonized over its decision, nor why I and others were adamant that the UN's reputation was part of the moral calculus. What is missing from the traditional approach is an understanding of how the decision not to halt the genocide came to be understood and defined as ethical and moral.

Michael Herzfeld's *The Social Production of Indifference: Exploring the Symbolic Roots of Western Bureaucracy* (1993) offers a conceptual apparatus that I find useful for thinking about these issues. Herzfeld opens with a succinct concern: "How and why can political entities that celebrate the rights of individuals and small groups so often seem cruelly selective in applying those rights?" (1993: 1). How is it possible, asks Herzfeld, for Western bureaucracies, which are supposedly rooted in a democratic context, to be so unaccountable to, and to demonstrate such little concern for, those they represent? Why, he continues, do citizens of a democratic society come to accept, if not expect, such arrangements? While I cannot do justice to the complexity of Herzfeld's provocative argument, he offers five observations that inform my discussion of the relationship between peacekeeping and indifference.

First, state bureaucracies are not only instruments of domination, but are also symbolic markers of boundaries between "peoples" and are expressive of the societies that produced those bureaucracies. As symbolic instruments of the nation-state, bureaucracies distinguish citizens from noncitizens, separate the "community of believers" from the "community of apostates," and articulate the criteria that define who belongs and who does not.

Second, identity is linked to the production of difference and indifference. Bureaucracies are constitutive of the identity of the community, differentiate between members and nonmembers of the community, and are expected to attend to members while ignoring nonmembers. "Compactly expressed . . . indifference is a rejection of those who are different" (Herzfeld 1993:33). The identity of the bureaucracy, in other words, represents the emotional and cognitive mechanism for producing exclusion and apathy. Bureaucrats use identity to determine who will receive their attention and who will not, and for national bureaucracies, the most straightforward marker is citizenship.

Third, bureaucracies will selectively apply rights even among the members of the community. It is not the case that all members of society are treated equally or receive the same privileges; some are more equal than others. Privileged status cannot be reduced to economic and political power, for it depends as well on identity criteria such as race, religion, and gender.

Fourth, bureaucrats exhibit selective attention because they identify not only with their fellow citizens but also with their bureaucracy. Bureaucrats, in this respect, have something of a dual identity: as members of a particular national community they draw symbolic boundaries between themselves and those outside the national state, and as members of a bureaucracy, they draw boundaries between the bureaucracy and society. Simply stated, bureaucrats will often privilege the needs of, and take their identity from, the bureaucracy rather than the society that they ostensibly represent.

Fifth, a final reason for bureaucratic indifference is that bureaucrats pursue not only a bureaucratic agenda but also a personal one. Following Herzfeld, successful bureaucrats may be cynically defined as those who are able to manipulate the bureaucratic culture to achieve their personal goals; that is, they twist the language and rules of the bureaucracy to make it appear as if they are following the societal or bureaucratic interests when, in fact, they are pursuing their own.

How is it that society and even bureaucrats themselves cope with and explain their indifference? To address this issue, Herzfeld deploys the concept of secular theodicy, building on Max Weber's concept of religious theodicy. Briefly, Weber was interested in how religious systems account, in Herzfeld's words, for the "persistence of evil in a divinely ordered world" (Herzfeld 1993: 5). Weber observed that the "legitimation of every distinctively ethical prophecy has always required the notion of a god characterized by attributes that set him sublimely above the world" (Weber 1963:138). The more a religion holds to a conception of a transcendental deity, however, the greater is the problem of how to reconcile the "problem of the extraordinary power of such a god ... with the imperfection of the world that he has created and rules over" (Weber 1963: 138–139). Different religions have offered different responses that allow them to maintain their belief in these transcendental principles, notwithstanding the existence of the occasional evil. Such responses constitute "theodicy," as Herzfeld uses the term.

Herzfeld transports the concept of theodicy from the religious to the secular domain of "Western" nation-states, suggesting that (1) these states exhibit a secular transcendentalism bound up with the nation; (2) individuals who are part of the nation-state must cope with evils committed and ignored by the state's bureaucracy that potentially call into question the nation's transcendental values; and (3) theodicy serves the pragmatic goal of providing "people with the social means of coping with disappointment" (1993:7). Both religious and secular theodicy, therefore, derive from the "principle of the elect as an exclusive community, whose members' individual sins cannot undermine the ultimate perfection of the ideal in which they all share"

(1993:10), and both exhibit their own forms of theodicy as a way of "propping up belief in a flawed world" (1993:7).

Herzfeld argues that Western societies and their bureaucrats explain the presence of evil, and even justify their own indifference, with reference to abstract moral principles associated primarily with their respective nation and secondarily with democracy. The citizens of these states are able to excuse acts of repression and accept daily bureaucratic indifference by maintaining a continuous belief in the transcendental purpose of their nation-state. Such faith, notes Herzfeld, "permits genocide and intracommunal killings, to be sure, but it also perpetuates the pettier and less sensational versions of the same logic" (1993:33). Indifference is excused and explained by members of society because of the operation of secular theodicy.

The very bureaucrats who are often responsible for dispensing such disappointments also exhibit secular theodicy. Bureaucrats are notorious for buck-passing, invoking bureaucratic rules as limits on their autonomy and responsibility, and authoring and authorizing various laws that seem far from the values that define the community. But bureaucratic indifference is almost never paraded as such. Rather, the bureaucrat, who is a representative of the collectivity, dismisses the needs of the individual and excuses the particular instance of indifference by referring to the sanctity of the transcendental. Sometimes bureaucrats will feign concern but will use the veil of transcendentalism and the common good to camouflage their unwillingness to act; they would do something or intervene if they could, bureaucrats will insincerely profess, but they must obey the rules of the organization that are designed to foster the common good even if it allows for the occasional injustice. But not all such appeals by bureaucrats to the transcendental are strategic. References to the transcendental also enable bureaucrats to live with themselves while acting indifferent and permitting injustices. To be a servant of the state that espouses transcendental values while following bureaucratic rules means that disappointments are delivered on a daily basis and the occasional sin is excused, ignored, or justified with reference to abstract moral principles. A secular theodicy, in other words, displays itself. As representatives of the common good, bureaucrats can remain comfortably indifferent to the individual under the cloak of community, and the existence of transcendental principles is not undermined by what they witness or dispense. Such indifference is a testimony to the dominance of the interests of the organization over those of the individual, a testimony to the primacy of the transcendental over the particular. In general, the notion that actions occur with reference to, and are embedded within, a community context allows bureaucrats and other members of society to accept disappointments, if not evil.

There are important differences between national and international bureaucracies, such as the UN, but the comparison between national bureaucracies and the UN is apt for three reasons. First, both the national and international community are invested with transcendental principles by their members;

where Herzfeld looks to the nation-state, I look to the international community. Indeed, UN officials, according to David Rieff (1996:20), often talk about the UN as if it were a church, suggesting that they are guardians of a religion whose tenets are transcendental. Second, the UN is founded on the "principle of identity" and the existence of a "community, whose members' individual sins cannot undermine the ultimate perfection of the ideal that they all share" (Herzfeld 1993:10). The UN symbolically defines who is and is not part of the "international community," selectively applies the rights of the community among its members, and produces difference and indifference by differentiating members of the community from nonmembers. Third, UN officials and member states identify with and protect the UN's interests and reputation, strategically and sincerely evoke the discourse of the transcendental while ignoring the plights of the individual, and express their own brand of indifference and secular theodicy. These three observations provide the starting point for revisiting the Security Council's debates on Rwanda.

A complex and contested feature of the UN is the definition of its constituency, that is, of the "international community." In the history of the UN, the "international community," and concomitantly the UN's constituency, has been defined in three often contradictory, yet often conflated, ways: in terms of individual persons, in terms of collective "peoples" (largely defined according to identity-based categories of nationality, ethnicity, or even gender), and in terms of sovereign states. The UN charter declares that it is accountable to individuals and peoples who have universal rights that are before and beyond the state. Consistent with this, throughout its 50-year history, the UN has claimed both that it represents the peoples of the world and that there exist universal rights and principles that defy state boundaries. At the same time, however, the UN Charter also observes that a guiding principle of international society is state sovereignty and the principle of noninterference. The UN is an intergovernmental organization, its membership is limited to states, only states are part of the General Assembly and the Security Council, and states alone determine its policies. Throughout its history, the UN has generally promoted and honored the principle of sovereignty, which has meant that any tension over the UN's constituency— that is, who constitutes the international community—has most often been resolved in favor of states and against individuals and peoples. This is evident in the UN's peacekeeping operations during the Cold War. The first peacekeeping forces and military observer missions were introduced in the context of decolonization. Decolonization potentially unleashed a Pandora's box of explosive questions concerning the relationship between the state and the nation, and peacekeeping operations and observer missions were designed and deployed with an eye to the politics of territorial restraint and juridical sovereignty. Reflecting a General Assembly that insisted on bracketing the domestic and honoring sovereignty, these UN operations did not concern themselves with human rights, ethnic conflict, or humanitarian missions.

Throughout the Cold War, the UN favored the security of states over the security of peoples and individuals.

As policymakers and scholars began to imagine the post-Cold War order, they, first, used the UN as a vehicle to contemplate a global order founded on non-threat-based principles, and, second, began to reconsider the UN's promise and possible contribution to global security. This debate over the post-Cold War order also involved a reconsideration of the concept of "international security." During the Cold War, the UN reflected and expressed a statist definition of "international security" that focused almost exclusively on interstate conflict. The end of the Cold War, however, unleashed a spiraling number of proposals and statements that called for shifting the definition of "international security" away from states and toward individuals and peoples. Those in and around the UN increasingly voiced the concept of "human security" in various guises, suggesting that what matters is the security of peoples and individuals and not states, that states are often a source of insecurity rather than protection, and that domestic rather than interstate conflict is a greater threat to most individuals' security in today's world. Boutros-Ghali, for instance, would frequently stress the "human" foundations of security, arguing that the UN must be as concerned with the security of peoples and individuals as it is with the security of states.

Tied to these questions of "whose security" was a reconsideration of the working definition of the international community, which resuscitated the tension between the community as defined by sovereign states and the community as defined by peoples and individuals. When the UN and member states focused on state security and interstate conflict, it generally reflected and forwarded a definition of the international community that was defined by and limited to sovereign states. But beginning in the mid-1980s and accelerating after the end of the Cold War in the face of the new security challenges, the working definition of the international community was expanded to more fully include individuals and identity-based groups residing within states. UN officials increasingly sounded the view that the UN's constituency was not only states but also the citizens of these states. There was, if you will, a shift of representation, as various statements from the Secretariat and the Security Council offered that the UN was to protect not only the community of states but also individuals and peoples.

Peacekeeping operations reflect the UN's growing prominence in global affairs, the reconsideration of the definition of security, and the debate over the UN's constituency and working definition of the international community. To begin with, the UN's post-Cold War popularity translated into an explosion of peacekeeping operations. There were just 11 operations between 1956 and 1988, and no new operation was authorized between 1978 and 1988. Between 1988 and 1995, by contrast, the Security Council authorized 24 new operations. The UN was anxious to prove its promise, and the permanent members of the Security Council, who now found the UN to be a useful place to dump intractable conflicts, encouraged that sentiment. These and other factors contributed to an explosion of peacekeeping operations.

Perhaps more impressive than the growing numbers were the ambitious tasks assigned to these "second-generation" peacekeeping operations that reflected a changing definition of security. Prior to 1988, peacekeeping concerned interpositioning lightly-armed UN troops between two states that had agreed to a cease-fire. Peacekeepers were now being deployed not to monitor a cease-fire between two states but to promote domestic conflict resolution and to facilitate the post-conflict process of "nation-building"; soon the UN was running elections, creating new police forces, repatriating refugees, and overseeing the demobilization of armies and the reintegration of deeply divided societies. "Operation Provide Comfort," the UN's assistance to the Kurds of Iraq, inaugurated a new chapter in humanitarian intervention, and crises in Somalia and Bosnia stirred further movement in this direction. Many UN officials with whom I spoke recalled a sense of excitement and exhilaration during these first post-Cold War days; not only were they unshackled from the Cold War, but their activism was directed at helping people rather than states. "There are greater rewards," recalled one official with whom I spoke at the time, "from helping the victims of political turmoil than its instigators." While some member states feared that the UN was now treading on state sovereignty, other member states and UN officials championed this more ambitious agenda and cosmopolitan outlook that suggested a UN that was on the verge of fulfilling its initial but long-delayed promise.

As the UN became increasingly concerned with human security, however, it continued to operate in state-centric terms: human security most often meant "saving failed states." For many member states and UN officials, "democratic" states became the type most worthy of emulation. States that conducted periodic elections, had a competitive party system, and had legal guarantees of press freedom were identified as "democratic" and were accorded legitimacy and prestige by many member states and UN officials. Democracy so defined was equated with being "civilized" and was said to be a foundation of "peace" and "security." That "democratic states do not go to war with one another" became a cliché for many member states and UN officials, and Boutros-Ghali himself stated that "democratic" states are more legitimate than others and are less likely to have domestic conflicts or become embroiled in regional wars (1995). It should come as no surprise, then, that UN officials were busily forwarding numerous proposals that concerned how the UN might help expand the number of "democracies." In sum, being a "democracy" came to define full membership in "the elect" of the UN's "international community."

Most of the post-Cold War peacekeeping operations have been a direct extension of the view that domestic stability in general and democracy in particular are related to international order and define membership in the international community. The operations in Namibia (UNTAG), Cambodia

(UNTAC), El Salvador (ONUSAL), and Haiti (UNMIH), for instance, aspired to end civil wars and to forward democracy. Indeed, as the UN looked to end an operation it deployed the symbol of a "free and fair" election. Few genuinely believed that one election at the end of a peacekeeping operation was enough to institutionalize "democratic" practices, but the ritual of the election symbolized how peacekeeping operations were to help rehabilitate fallen members of the international community.

This highly ambitious and increasingly crowded security agenda overwhelmed a bureaucratically and organizationally underequipped UN. The first formal statement by the Secretariat concerning the future of the UN was Boutros-Ghali's *An Agenda for Peace*, undertaken in 1992 at the request of the Security Council in response to the growing number of peacekeeping operations and security issues being handed the Security Council. *An Agenda for Peace* was soon followed by numerous reports, including those by the Clinton administration and the Contact Group on Peacekeeping Reform at the UN. The UN also undertook various reforms that were designed to rationalize and expand its activities, including an enlargement and reorganization of the Department of Peacekeeping Operations; the establishment of a Department of Humanitarian Affairs and Electoral Assistance Unit; and the creation of standby arrangements for military forces. These reforms and developments were absolutely essential if an antiquated and inefficient organization was to meet the challenges of the day and to carry out its mandated responsibilities.

This bureaucratization also encouraged member states and the Secretariat to develop a vested interest in peacekeeping and the UN. Some UN and member state bureaucrats championed UN operations because they benefited materially from their involvement in UN operations. But many also believed that peacekeeping represented an important instrument for interstate and intrastate conflict resolution, and came to identify with the idea of the UN as transcending power politics. The common denominator was an identification with the UN's interests and future. The UN now had a constituency.

The bureaucratization of peacekeeping also impacted on the UN's decision making about these operations. Whereas in the early 1990s, it seemed that no operation was too small, large, or complex for the UN's attention, by the fall of 1993, many member state and UN officials argued that the UN was stretched too thin and was increasingly ineffective; it was time, they said, to exhibit greater self-restraint. This sobriety was driven in part by the "failures" of Somalia and Bosnia, and the Security Council now began to develop criteria for deciding whether to approve or extend a peacekeeping operation. These included whether (1) there was a genuine threat to peace and security; (2) regional or subregional organizations could assist in resolving the situation; (3) a cease-fire existed and the parties had committed themselves to a peace process; (4) a clear political goal existed and was present in the proposed mandate; (5) a precise mandate could be formulated; and (6) the safety of UN personnel could be reasonably assured (UN 1994a). In short, with bureaucratization came rationalization.

The emergence of these criteria contributed to the production of indifference. Much discussion at the UN revolved around how to better publicize "success stories," how to portray so-called failures as successes (or at least to demonstrate that the UN was not to blame), how to promote greater sensitivity to the conditions under which peacekeeping was likely to be effective, and how to ensure that the UN was not saddled with operations that had little chance of success. There was an important shift in the discourse of peacekeeping, as officials in and around the UN took greater care to protect the organization's interests, reputation, and future. The desire by UN officials and member states to pick winners and to avoid failures meant that the UN was as interested in its own security as it was in human security.

The concern for the UN's reputation and interests affected the selection of operations. To begin with, the desire to identify the conditions under which peacekeeping was effective meant that it was less likely to be deployed during instances of humanitarian crises or severe domestic turmoil. Perhaps the first instance in which the needs of the organization were explicitly cited and used to justify inaction was the Security Council's decision not to intervene in Burundi in October 1993, when nearly 100,000 persons died in ethnic violence. Living in the immediate shadows of Somalia and President Clinton's 1993 address to the General Assembly in which he challenged the Security Council to just say no, many members of the Security Council argued against intervention on the grounds that there was "no peace to keep" and that the UN needed to avoid obvious quagmires. Many UN officials and delegates breathed a sigh of relief when the Security Council opted to abstain from the conflict, whispering that the UN had to conserve its energies for "winners." The decision not to intervene in Burundi symbolized a shifting sentiment at the UN concerning the feasibility and desirability of humanitarian intervention. Those who opposed intervention contended that such crises are a by-product of wars, wars are defined by instability, and a modicum of stability is a precondition for effective peacekeeping. The UN could only be effective when there was a "peace to keep."

Moreover, whereas once the Security Council and the Secretariat routinely noted that they had a responsibility to help those who could not help themselves, they were now suggesting that they could only help those who were willing to help themselves. The same UN officials who once had forcefully argued for the need to protect war's victims were now defending their inaction in Bosnia on the grounds of preserving the UN's neutrality and impartiality. The language that began to creep into nearly all Security Council statements was that an operation was justified only so long as the parties of the conflict demonstrated a resolve to work toward political progress; the Security Council, for instance, emphasized how "the people of Somalia bear the ultimate responsibility for achieving national reconciliation and for rebuilding their country" (UN 1994b). But who were the "people" of

Somalia? of Bosnia? of Rwanda? By and large, "the people" no longer meant the victims of violence but those who controlled the means of violence. The UN was stepping away from its initial post-Cold War concern for human security and returning to the traditional tenets of peacekeeping that stressed the need for stability as a precondition of deployment and the focus on state security. This shift, according to many, was defensible on the grounds that the UN could only help those who were willing to help themselves, and that it was absolutely necessary to protect the UN's reputation and future.

The siren of secular theodicy was detectable in these developments. Many at the UN appealed to the interests of the UN, represented as a symbol of both the international community and universal human rights, to reconcile the uncomfortable tension between the transcendental and their reluctance to act. While the UN was still committed to the same transcendental values, they argued, the conditions under which it would henceforth become involved in attempting to secure and promote those values had been justifiably tightened. The secular and politically expedient decisions that were being offered in place of action were clothed in universalism and the need to protect the international community's defining organization. The occasional evil could be tolerated so long as it did not damage the greater collective good. These developments and this discourse imprinted the Security Council's debate over its response to the violence in Rwanda in April 1994.

A return to Rwanda

Member states could not simply and silently watch the unfolding genocide from the sanctuary of the Security Council. Rather, as "agents" of the "international community," they had to negotiate the fluid and contested relationship between their respective "national interests" and the "international community." States serve on the Security Council and thus represent state interests. Delegates are, after all, citizens of their states and representatives of their governments, from which they receive their instructions. What matters to these states are national interests. Yet what are these "national interests," and are these "national interests" inconsistent with the concerns of the "international community"? I noted earlier that, from my bureaucratic position, I learned an interpretation of the "U.S. national interest" that supported a more prominent role for the UN and involvement in activities that were not directly connected to traditional understandings or core definitions of national security. Although there were numerous occasions when events that exercised the Secretariat remained outside my conception of what should animate and involve the United States, over time my understanding of U.S. interests became more fully connected to the UN and its operations. "Working" these UN issues had shaped my definition of U.S. interests, and my learning a definition of U.S. interests had shaped my support for the UN.

My experiences and observations thus suggest that members of the Security Council view themselves not simply as handmaidens of states but also as representatives of the international community. What is the "international community" and what are its interests? Earlier, I argued that there has been a continuous, although varying, degree of tension between the notion of the international community as comprised of sovereign states and the international community as comprised of peoples and individuals. One of my observations of the workings of the Security Council was that while its members pursue their state (or "national") interests, there also is a strong hint of cosmopolitanism in their language and movements. For instance, the Security Council's documents refer to itself as a representative of the international community. While it is easy to dismiss such language as diplomatic blather, states take such blather seriously and oftentimes shift their policies accordingly. The Security Council is not alone in presenting itself as the representative of the international community and as responsible for protecting its interests; other actors—notably the media, nongovernmental human rights groups, and other states who are not on the Security Council—also identify the Security Council in this manner. During the debate over Rwanda, those in the Security Council referred to themselves as the "international community," and when the meeting adjourned, the president of the Security Council greeted reporters who asked if the "international community" had formulated a policy.

In general, the existence of the UN and the participation by member states in the Security Council remind member states that they should avoid starkly self-interested strategies and pursue more enlightened policies that reflect a sense of cosmopolitanism. Interstate cooperation at the UN, therefore, is not merely a technical feat but is also, as Durkheim might suggest, a connection to a moral order (Zabusky 1995:23, 113). Through their discourse and practices, member states not only address particular problems but also connect themselves and their activities to a set of transcendental values.

Throughout the Security Council debates, there was a tension between, first, state interests and the obligations to the international community, and, second, the competing demands on the Security Council that derived from its responsibilities to the UN and the Rwandans. While pained by the unfolding bloodshed, member states did not view their interests as suitably engaged to justify the involvement of their own troops for a risky intervention. Rwanda was outside most states' understanding of their "national interests," at least to the extent that they were willing to sacrifice their troops for such a cause. For most members on the Security Council, and particularly for the permanent members, Rwanda was distant from any strategic considerations. Since this was an intra- rather than an interstate conflict, whether this crisis constituted a threat to international security was also an uncertain and contested point. Still, no state represented its unwillingness to get involved as a matter of strategic calculations; rather, member states couched their reluctance in terms of the needs of the UN.

The United States, for instance, argued that the Security Council's overriding responsibility was to its peacekeepers, and if there were more fatalities the consequences would be more criticism of, and a dimmer future for, the UN. To further support its case for withdrawal, the United States employed the previously discussed six criteria for whether the Security Council should approve or extend an operation. Although these criteria were not formally adopted by the Council until early May, they had become widely accepted informally during the previous several months. Consequently, the United States was able to argue persuasively that by the Security Council's own criteria, which were intended to rationalize and formalize its debates and decisions, UNAMIR had no business being in Rwanda. UNAMIR's immediate withdrawal was in the best interests of the UN.

The Clinton administration's stance was also designed to protect itself and the UN from a hostile U.S. Congress. During the earlier debate over the mandate extension in late March, the United States advocated reducing UNAMIR to send a strong signal to both the Rwandan government that it needed to establish a transitional government, and to Congress, which had declared open season on the UN, that the administration could be tough on peacekeeping operations. Such displays of "toughness," suggested one administration official at the time, would benefit the UN because the administration would better shield it from further congressional attacks. "Tough love," he offered.

Two points bear emphasizing. First, to make the case for intervention required connecting such action to interests. Yet the language of interests is largely the language of states, and state interests were hardly engaged by the unfolding tragedy in Rwanda. Indeed, member states and members of the U.S. Mission framed any prospective intervention in the language of obligation. I, for one, viewed the violence as tragic but could not make the necessary strategic link to justify the deployment of U.S. troops. Simply put, Rwanda activated the language of obligation rather than interests, but to expect and justify the possible sacrifice of one's troops generally demands a connection to the language of state interests rather than of international obligations. Second, those member states who opposed intervention for self-interested reasons were reluctant to publicly display such calculations; much more morally palatable and defensible was the argument that the Security Council had an obligation and interest to protect its peacekeepers, and, relatedly, the future of the UN. Moral oratory draped self-interested actions. Indifference was presentable through the appeal to the transcendental.

Some nonpermanent members of the Security Council, however, demanded robust action to protect civilians, couching their arguments in terms of the "international community," referring thereby to a moral order that transcended state boundaries. But at the time, I feared that such language was designed to lure the United States into doing the work of and for the "international community." Over the course of the year, I became increasingly frustrated by the fact that when a humanitarian nightmare unfolded somewhere in the world, the world looked to the UN, and then the UN looked to the United States. Accordingly, I was suspicious that when other states evoked the "international community," they were, in fact, pointing to the United States. New Zealand and Czechoslovakia, whom I often referred to as the "conscience of the Council" in both derision and admiration, supported robust action by the UN and were critical of those members who resisted intervention. While they were arguing for action, however, they were not volunteering their own troops and were insinuating that the United States should take the lead. As some of us at the U.S. Mission joked about other proposed and existing UN operations, the international community seemed willing to fight down to the last U.S. citizen. The rhetoric of the international community, then, became something to fear and reinforced my defense of U.S. interests. In general, member states used the language of the international community and the defense of the UN to hide their own unwillingness to get involved and sometimes to implicate others.

Where was the Secretariat during these discussions? Earlier, I noted that its comments were limited to sketchy and noncommittal appraisals, failing to offer any concrete recommendations and thus forfeiting its agenda-setting powers. At the time, I attributed its lack of direction to "not being up to the task" of crisis management. Yet a highly authoritative and exhaustive report on Rwanda suggests not amateur but instrumental and strategic behavior (Adelman and Suhrke 1996). During the first, highly critical days after Habyarimana's death, the Secretariat was receiving concrete recommendations from its Force Commander, General Romeo Dallaire, who was cautiously optimistic that a limited military intervention could halt the bloodshed. The Secretariat, however, did not communicate UNAMIR's recommendations to the Security Council. I can only speculate as to why the Secretariat failed to do so, but one very real possibility is that it feared becoming embroiled in a conflict that spelled failure. While the motives are unknown, the consequences of the Secretariat's noncommittal stance are more certain: its failure to offer any recommendations or to hint that an intervention had any possibility of success played directly into the hands of those in the Security Council who demanded UNAMIR's immediate withdrawal. Member states were not the only ones who could hide their agenda.

There was a second reason why these meetings were so volatile: as representatives of the international community, member states were having to choose between their responsibility to the Rwandans and to the UN. This tension, which was a central and underlying feature of the debate, slowly gravitated toward the view that, however tragic for the Rwandans, the only responsible and feasible option was to withdraw UNAMIR. To place peacekeepers in harm's way would not only betray a singular responsibility of the Security Council but potentially lead to a further deterioration in the UN's stature. In the shadow of Somalia and in the midst of the drama of Bosnia, there was little doubt that a failure in Rwanda would translate into even greater trouble for the UN. The Security Council's reluctance to act, in this view, was morally defensible because it protected the international community's organization.

Elevating the survival of the UN over the Rwandans was facilitated by two additional factors. First, those who were responsible for and oversaw Rwanda (and other operations) were "experts" in the same way that I was an expert on Rwanda; expertise derived from my bureaucratic roles and responsibilities rather than my intrinsic knowledge per se. My expertise concerned UN operations rather than Rwanda; my colleague had spent a career at the U.S. Mission covering Africa, but at the time had never stepped foot on the continent. Our expertise, then, derived from our knowledge of the UN rather than those countries that were part of our "portfolio." The result was that I was more committed to the survival of the UN than I was to the Rwandans.

Second, being able to elevate the UN's organizational needs over the events in Rwanda was also facilitated by distance: discussions were occurring among UN officials and member states in New York while the tragedy was unfolding in Rwanda. While those in New York expressed genuine anguish for what was occurring in Rwanda, it was easier for them to identify with those with whom they interacted on a daily basis. That Rwanda was a member of the Security Council did not help me bridge the distance; its representative was a member of the ruling coalition, and therefore linked to the architects of genocide. As the Security Council debated the unfolding genocide, I would glance at him sitting quietly and passively during the deliberations, wondering how the Security Council could tolerate his presence without dressing him down and desiring to see him evicted from the room as soon as possible. Looking back, he served as a reminder to me that the international community would have to tolerate the occasional evil in order to maintain its central organization —the UN.

After endless deliberations, the Security Council voted on April 21 to reduce UNAMIR's presence and mandate, and to leave in place only those troops that were required to assist General Dallaire's efforts to gain a cease-fire. For those who opposed this decision but failed to offer troops to back their diplomatic pleas, this was the best that could be gotten. And those who insisted on reducing UNAMIR were reluctant to demand a complete withdrawal for fear of portraying themselves and the Security Council as morally bankrupt. By maintaining a token presence, the UN was able to symbolize its continued concern and, perhaps, help effect a cease-fire.

Still, the Security Council remained "seized of the matter" (a phrase that ritualistically closes nearly all Security Council resolutions) and continued to meet on a daily basis. Sitting through these long-winded meetings could be tortuous: information could as easily have been distributed without convening the Security Council. Why then remain in almost continuous session?

One reason was to give all members the opportunity to express their moral outrage. At the end of each day's debate, the President of the Security Council would announce to the press that the Security Council was disturbed by the violence and would continue to follow events closely. Indeed, there was a nearly rhythmic quality to the deliberations during these first weeks. On any one day, hours would be spent by the Security Council exchanging information and extolling the need for concrete action; pleased that it had demonstrated sufficient concern, the following day's meeting would be highly abbreviated.

A second reason was that these meetings provided an opportunity for member states to proclaim that they represented the interests of the international community. Because such interests were now defined as keeping a safe distance, this language was evoked as often to argue for restraint as it was for action. This became painfully apparent as the Security Council continued to meet through April with growing evidence of genocide. At first, the Security Council was reluctant to utter the word *genocide*. Its very mention had the raw, discursive capacity to demand action; its mere rhetorical presence might be enough to shame and embarrass the Security Council into doing what it resisted. Accordingly, there appeared to be a tacit understanding to avoid such inflammatory language. As the days passed, however, a member state would occasionally implore action because of genocide, but soon thereafter the discussion slowly converged on the belief that little could be done, that the Security Council had to protect the UN's interests, and that no member of the Security Council should use such explosive—that is, irresponsible—language outside the room.

Third, to have Rwanda on the Security Council's agenda meant giving the appearance that the Security Council cared, thereby enabling it to veil its indifference. While member states were unwilling to assemble an intervention force they also did not want to appear indifferent. By filling the halls of the UN, remaining in constant session, and generating a flood of documents and statements, the Security Council could display the facade of action, when in fact few states wanted anything of the kind. This suggests that one function of the UN was to distribute accountability to the point that it becomes irretrievable. Who was to blame for the lack of response to Rwanda? Everyone. The mere presence of the UN allowed states (and the Secretariat) to shield themselves from responsibility, to point fingers in all directions, and to avoid accountability or culpability.

In this way, under the watchful eyes of the Security Council, 500,000 to 800,000 Rwandans fell victim to genocide. No one can be certain that a modest intervention at the outset of the crisis might have halted this tragedy, but the record is that the Security Council did little until it was too late and safe. And the stark truth is that while some states called for intervention, few if any volunteered their own services. In this regard, the UN's indifference reflects the indifference of the member states. Yet the bureaucratization of peacekeeping shaped the Security Council's debates and contributed to the production of indifference. The Security Council saw itself as a representative of the international community. One of the dilemmas it faced was choosing between its charge in Rwanda and its protection of the peacekeepers. Any more peacekeeping fatalities, I and many others argued in the halls of the Security Council, would undoubtedly mean more criticism and fewer resources for the UN. This was the moral equation and the justification for inaction. Such inaction was made palatable and morally tenable, invested with ethical distinction, as it was given support by appeals to the transcendental value of preserving the international community's central organization. Officials in and out of the UN were able to explain the evils of Rwanda and their own indifference by pointing to the secular religion of the international community and its cathedral, the UN.

Conclusion

As I continue to think about peacekeeping and the lessons of Rwanda, I do so differently than when I completed my tenure at the U.S. Mission. To be sure, many of my initial "policy-relevant" recommendations still inform my views of peacekeeping, its functions, and its future. On the one hand, I continue to recognize that professionalizing peacekeeping was absolutely necessary if peacekeeping was to have a future. But on the other hand, I now also perceive that this bureaucratization entailed that those in and around the UN come to have a stake in and identify with the bureaucracy, begin to evaluate strategies and actions according to the needs of the bureaucracy, and, accordingly, begin to frame discussions and justify policies in a different manner. I became part of this bureaucratization process. I, too, altered how I judged and evaluated UN peacekeeping. Sometimes this meant that I had a heightened awareness of the complexities of the issues involved and the stakes of the game. Yet at other times, this involved a shift in what I thought was desirable and valuable; I became as interested in protecting bureaucratic and organizational interests as I was in employing the UN to help those it was supposed to serve. The UN might be above power politics, but it is not above politics.

This rendition of the politics of international organizations is somewhat more complicated, therefore, than that offered by many political scientists who subscribe to a liberal view of international organizations. Self-proclaimed liberals and neoliberal institutionalists are interested in identifying the conditions under which states cooperate, eschew short-term gains for long-term benefits, and abide by international agreements. International organizations are identified as an important instrument in the search for interstate cooperation, as they increase transparency in actions, establish common norms of behavior, and contain monitoring mechanisms that allow states to overcome collective action problems associated with interdependence choice.[3] At the extreme, however, liberals equate international organizations with progress, and neoliberals celebrate their existence as evidence that states have been able to put aside immediate gratification for long-term harmony.

International organizations have certainly played an important role in encouraging states to cooperate, but that is not the only role they are capable of playing. International organizations can become, first, a site for new political identities and definitions of interests that are inconsistent with their original intent and, second, a locus of authority far removed from those whose lives they affect and in whose name they operate. I have no desire to essentialize bureaucracies or to suggest a global "banality of evil," but I do want to call attention to this often unrecognized feature of international organizations. Although Herzfeld limits his discussion to "Western" bureaucracies and is reserved about whether his discussion travels to non-Western or international contexts, there is evidence that his analysis and the story of Rwanda are not isolated phenomena. Stacia Zabusky's *Launching Europe* (1995) demonstrates how Herzfeld's analysis can survive the journey from state to interstate politics; Liisa Malkki's (1996) reflections on the UNHCR in Central Africa offer similarly disturbing observations about the relationship between international organizations and the individuals in whose names they act. And evidence from Bosnia, eloquently argued in David Rieff's *Slaughterhouse* (1995), also suggests a relationship between the bureaucratization of peacekeeping, the concern for the organization's interests, and the production of indifference. In general, an intriguing, though equally disturbing, implication is that the dynamics and developments that Herzfeld locates among "Western" states are increasingly globalized phenomena. A more nuanced understanding of the consequences of global bureaucratization should be on the intellectual agenda of an era defined by globalization-cum-bureaucratization.

But the UN is more than a site of indifference, a place where state inaction and organizational interests come to have an ethical content and moral luster. The Security Council and the UN are also sites of a struggle over individuation and connection, a place where member states define themselves and their interests through their engagement and confrontation with a set of transcendental values. In this regard, the UN offers sanctuary to contemplate a moral order that transcends local confines, a place where member states mimic, learn, and express a set of transcendental values that are above, beyond, and before the sovereign state. It is this UN, as the international community's secular cathedral, that allows many, including myself, to maintain a belief in the transcendental, even in the face of the occasional evil that exposes the sins of the members.

Acknowledgments

This article extends my earlier discussion of some of these events in Barnett (1996). This article has benefited from the reactions and observations of many colleagues in diverse fields, and to them I owe a collective thanks: Marty Finnemore, Michael Herzfeld, Victoria Shampaine, James Fernandez, Hugh Gusterson, Diana Saco, Mark Laffey, Jutta Weldes, Daniel Segal, and the participants at the workshop "Culture and the Production of Insecurity," held at the University of Minnesota, October 27–29, 1995. This article, finally, could not have been written without the support of the U.S. Mission to the United Nations, the Council on Foreign Relations, and the MacArthur Foundation's International Peace and Security Fellowship. The views expressed are strictly my own.

Notes

1 Because the UN is an international organization that is also representative of states, it can be understood as both the sum of its parts and as an independent actor. I will refer to the Security Council, the 15 member states who are designated to preside over matters of international peace and security, when discussing the UN as a representative of its member states. I refer to the Secretariat when considering the UN as an independent actor, and I refer most frequently to the office of the Secretary-General and DPKO.

2 I want to add two critical caveats. First, I am representing my personal reflections after a period of distance and attempting, as best as possible, to represent and interpret the events unfolding around me; I have no doubt that others would tell a different tale. I observed these events from the U.S. Mission to the United Nations, and I expect that those residing in Rwanda, the UN, or other delegations would offer a different view. Second, I have tremendous respect for the integrity and values of many of those with whom I worked; these were highly dedicated individuals who worked long hours and labored under difficult conditions. I have no doubt that they would object to my characterization of their supposed indifference.

3 For an overview of liberal theories of international relations, see Zacher and Matthews (1995); for a neoliberal statement, see Keohane and Martin (1995).

References cited

Adelman, Howard, and Astri Suhrke, with Bruce Jones (1996) Early Warning and Conflict Management: Genocide in Rwanda. Study II, Evaluation of the Emergency Assistance to Rwanda. CHR Michelsen Institute, Development Studies and Human Rights Project. Bergen, Norway: CHR Michelsen Institute.

Barnett, Michael (1996) The Politics of Indifference at the United Nations and Genocide in Rwanda and Bosnia. *In* This Time We Knew: Western Reactions to Genocide in Bosnia. Thomas Cushman and Stjepan Mestrovic, eds. Pp. 128–162. New York: New York University Press.

Boutros-Ghali, Boutros (1992) An Agenda for Peace. New York: United Nations Press.

—— (1995) Democracy: A Newly Recognized Imperative. Global Governance 1 (Winter): 3–12.

Herzfeld, Michael (1993) The Social Production of Indifference: Exploring the Symbolic Roots of Western Bureaucracy. Chicago: University of Chicago Press.

Keohane, Robert, and Lisa Martin (1995) The Promise of Institutionalist Theory. International Security 20 (Summer): 39–52.

Malkki, Liisa (1996) Speechless Emissaries: Refugees, Humanitarianism, and Dehistoricization. Cultural Anthropology 11: 377–404.

Rieff, David (1994a) Statement on the Conditions for the Deployment and Renewal of Peacekeeping Operations. S/PRST/1994/22, May 3.

—— (1994b) Security Council Resolution Renewing the Mandate of UNOSOM II until 30 September 1994. S/Res/923, May 31.

—— (1995) Slaughterhouse. New York: Simon and Schuster.

—— (1996) The Institution That Saw No Evil. The New Republic, February 12: 19–24. United Nations, Security Council.

Weber, Max (1963) Theodicy, Salvation, and Rebirth. *In* Sociology of Religion, by Max Weber. Ephraim Fischoff, trans. Boston: Beacon Press.

Zabusky, Stacia (1995) Launching Europe: An Ethnography of the European Cooperation in Space Science. Princeton, NJ: Princeton University Press.

Zacher, Marc, and Richard Matthews (1995) Liberal International Theory: Common Threads, Divergent Strands. *In* Controversies in International Relations Theory: Realism and the Neo Liberal Challenge. Charles Kegley, ed. Pp. 107–150. St. Martin's Press.

7 UNHCR and the ethics of repatriation

"We would never push refugees across a border at gunpoint," replied the UNHCR official.

I was in Geneva interviewing officials regarding what they saw as the environmental demands and organisational reasons that accounted for the evolution of the agency's repatriation policy. This particular official was slightly more vitriolic than most when it came to defending a policy that had been accused of playing fast and loose with traditional refugee rights. He readily agreed that UNHCR no longer clung to the original principles guiding voluntary repatriation and insisted that such departures were warranted because, firstly, states were demanding that refugees return as quickly as possible and, secondly, there was no objectively "safe" benchmark in many "post-conflict" settings. I conceded the broad point that if UNHCR had to wait for the ideal conditions before sponsoring a repatriation exercise then it might have to wait forever, yet wondered aloud about the opposing danger of sacrificing principles on the altar of pragmatism. "How does the agency know when it is about to go too far? How far would the agency go? At what point are principles stretched beyond recognition?" It was then that he revealed the ethical bottom line: the agency would never physically coerce a return. Certainly many UNHCR staff would repudiate this position and would draw the line closer to original rights and principles but his candidness and position within the agency suggested that his views were hardly unfashionable.

UNHCR's new thinking on repatriation

UNHCR's repatriation policy has shifted dramatically over the years. The crux of voluntary repatriation is that refugees cannot be returned against their will to a home country that in their subjective assessment has not appreciably changed for the better and, therefore, still resembles the situation that triggered their flight. Beginning in the 1980s, however, UNHCR began to weaken this categorical imperative as it developed new concepts like "safe return" and "voluntariness" that made repatriation possible and desirable under less than ideal conditions.

There is considerable debate regarding what provoked this change. One explanation is that states made UNHCR do it. By the late 1970s, it is argued, Western and Third World states were demanding relief from the heavy burdens placed on them by the refugee regime. Western states were growing agitated by the increasing number of asylum requests from the Third World; viewing many of these requests as bogus, Western states began denying asylum in greater numbers and demanding a change in refugee law. Third World states were also increasingly intolerant of refugee flows that were imposing heavy financial, environmental and political costs. The result was that Western and Third World states demanded that UNHCR become involved in what the High Commissioner referred to as a policy of "deterrence".[1]

The agency acquiesced because it had little alternative: patrons held the purse strings and were going to send refugees back whether UNHCR liked it or not. UNHCR could sit on the sidelines with its principles but would be of no help to refugees in danger. UNHCR had no real choice but to play ball and more fully reconsider its repatriation policy. Only a thick-skinned or self-destructive organisation would have been oblivious to the preferences of its patrons on whom its freedom to act depended.

It is worth pausing to consider the historical convergence between this state-induced pragmatism and the agency's 1990s presentation of itself as a humanitarian international organisation at the same time as it developed relief activities that were directed at, and situated in, refugee-producing states. Sweeping global changes prepared the groundwork for this humanitarianism. Most significant was a change in the sovereignty regime. In recent history states have leaned on the norm of sovereignty and its principle of non-interference to shield themselves against unwanted intrusions on their domestic affairs. Increasingly evident during the Cold War, and then bursting onto the scene after its end, was a growing acceptance that state sovereignty was conditioned by popular sovereignty. A key aspect of popular sovereignty was said to be the expectation that states should have a degree of domestic legitimacy and respect basic human rights. The implication was that governments could no longer behave monstrously toward their populations without fear of sanction by the international community. This was not only a normative issue but was also related to international peace and security. If illegitimate states were more likely to generate domestic conflicts that had regional and international implications, then domestic governance was related to international governance.

For reasons related to these developments, UNHCR became more deeply involved in the domestic affairs of states. The emerging belief that state sovereignty was conditioned by popular sovereignty permitted UNHCR to enter into once sacred domestic territory. UNHCR increasingly admonished those governments that were causing refugee flight and began to propose concepts such as "state responsibility". There were also security imperatives. Internal conflicts led to refugee flows which, in turn, triggered regional instability and challenged "human security".[2]

UNHCR's humanitarian discourse

UNHCR's growing interest in refugee-producing countries was accompanied and legitimated by a humanitarian discourse – warranted because of a principled concern for the fate of displaced peoples and the desire to relieve their suffering. The agency became increasingly involved in in-country protection, bringing relief to people (rather than waiting for people to reach relief). It widened the definition of refugee to include IDPs and supported development projects to provide refugees with a means of livelihood to ease reintegration back into their country of origin.

If the 1990s can be described as the dawning of the age of humanitarianism its theme song was sung with a statist inflection. UNHCR's expanded humanitarian space was legitimated with reference to a moral discourse around the assuagement of suffering and fostering of "responsible" states. However, states were willing to license these activities not because of an outpouring of generosity but because of its very deficit. States were retreating from their obligations to refugees at the same time that the end of the Cold War swelled refugee case-loads. Because they were less willing to house the growing number of refugees and more interested in seeing them speedily return home (and stay at home), states became receptive to the idea that UNHCR should become more involved in the affairs of refugee-producing countries. UNHCR was permitted to expand the humanitarian space in one area because it was being shrunk in another.

Humanitarianism and the risk to refugee rights

The distressing implication was that refugee rights were possibly at risk because of this actual, living humanitarianism.[3] In-country relief might be permitted because states were now backtracking on their obligations under asylum and refugee law. The desire to get refugees back "home", in itself unobjectionable, can lead to *refoulement* and involuntary repatriation. The desire to help all those displaced, regardless of which side of an international border they find themselves on, could mean that states are willing to help IDPs because they do not give individuals the opportunity to flee across a border and seek asylum. Though the desire to eliminate the root causes of refugee flows is undoubtedly noble, it could lead to individuals being discouraged from fleeing a country deemed to be "improving" or "safe".

Simply put, this expanding humanitarian agenda has potential to erode the traditional protection guarantees and rights given to refugees. Humanitarianism risks becoming implicated in a system of deterrence and containment which usurps refugee rights. The broad global context – including both state pressures and humanitarian imperatives – has shaped UNHCR's repatriation policy and explains how and why its humanitarian operations might represent a potential threat to refugees.[4]

The fundamentalist–pragmatist debate

The focus on global forces can obscure the fact that UNHCR is a relatively autonomous organisation. Although states place all kinds of shackles on international organisations such as UNHCR, the agency, nevertheless, retains some autonomy and operational discretion. Moreover, UNHCR is able to use its role as protector of refugee law to place some distance between itself and member states. UNHCR derives autonomy from its standing as a bureaucratic organisation that is increasingly viewed as the authority and the lead agency in refugee affairs. Even the most constrained international organisation has some autonomy and capacity for independent thinking and action.[5 & 6]

UNHCR may have its own reasons for adopting humanitarianism and pushing repatriation, reasons not simply determined by pragmatic compromise but based on moral considerations.

UNHCR staff have thrown light on why the agency has revised its "exilic" bias and promoted repatriation. In its infancy UNHCR favoured repatriation but was precluded from doing so because of the Cold War context and the circumstances of many refugees. Once the environment and circumstances became more favourable to repatriation UNHCR was ready, willing and able. Moreover, UNHCR was influenced by new developments in refugee law, refugee activities and ethical understandings that revolved around the discourse of "home" and the "right of return". Also, refugees were "spontaneously repatriating" and UNHCR began to initiate activities to hasten and ease their reintegration. UNHCR was not a reluctant advocate of repatriation.

A concern, however, was that this enthusiasm for repatriation might undermine the principles of voluntary repatriation and *non-refoulement*. Accordingly, it began to wrestle with how to reconcile its newfound preference for repatriation with its longstanding protection and assistance mission. Opinion within the agency was polarised. Fundamentalists maintained a more "legalistic" approach that suggested a human rights orientation toward refugee rights. They decried moves toward repatriation lest this new emphasis jeopardize UNHCR's unique role as the agent of refugees and compromise its independence *vis-à-vis* governments. Pragmatists argued for allying with governments. They held to a more expedient, political and pragmatic view of refugee law because they feared that ignoring systemic trends and pressures might compromise UNHCR's overall effectiveness. They believed that the organisational and doctrinal shift in favour of repatriation righted a defect in a system that had tended to privilege legally-oriented protection officers over those who had specific area expertise.

The ground shifted toward a pragmatic view. UNHCR became much more favourably disposed toward repatriation, convinced that return will inevitably happen under less than ideal circumstances, and that the agency must and should actively promote repatriation as soon as possible.

These changes showed up in various areas. UNHCR's organisational chart was restructured so that regional offices holding more more pragmatic views no longer had to report directly to a Protection Division that saw itself as the "priest of principles". The agency developed flexible new norms and rules on repatriation and introduced new terminology and categories of "safe" return that clearly differentiated repatriation under "ideal" conditions from repatriation under "less than ideal" conditions. "Protection" was increasingly married to repatriation. The "voluntary" in voluntary repatriation was also transmuted. Whereas once "voluntary" had implied that the refugee should consent to return to a country that in his/her view no longer represented a threat to personal safety, concepts like "voluntariness" meant that refugee consent was no longer necessary. All that was now required was that the situation in the country of origin had appreciably improved or held out the promise of improving. An immediate consequence of these changes was that the principle of voluntary repatriation was stretched to its finite limits.

UNHCR developed a "repatriation culture" characterised by an organisational discourse, bureaucratic structure and formal and informal rules that make repatriation more desirable, proper and legitimate under more permissive conditions.[7] The effect of this culture was to increase the danger that UNHCR would sponsor a repatriation exercise with potential to slide uneasily into involuntary repatriation and *refoulement*. This culture has its origins in a complex mixture of state pressures, pragmatic considerations and organisational learning. The existence of state pressures and the need to choose between the "least bad" of alternatives certainly forced UNHCR into areas that were not necessarily to its liking. But these pressures and momentary comprises also were institutionalised and legitimated with reference to new understandings. Policies in the 1960s that might have been viewed as a gross departure from acceptable practices increasingly not only became the norm (in its prescriptive meaning) but were also legitimated by a moral discourse.

Repatriation's ethical basis

We need to recognise that those in both the "principled" and "pragmatic" camps within UNHCR use ethical claims to support their positions. Pragmatists refer to a set of ethical principles to legitimate their position, principles largely founded on the desire to give refugees the ultimate form of protection – repatriation. Geneva, therefore, might reasonably decide to promote repatriation if, in its assessment, refugees were more likely to be safer at home than in the host country. In this view, the "principles" of the principled camp might expose refugees to greater harm in the long run. As one pragmatist said, "The priests care more about refugee law than they do about the refugees themselves."

Losing the refugee voice?

Yet the ethics of repatriation under less than ideal conditions is also accompanied by a discursive shift that makes it less likely that refugees themselves will have a voice in determining their future. Voluntary repatriation originally required that refugees give consent to their return. By many accounts this is less likely to be the case. As UNHCR officials concede, the decision to promote repatriation is based not only on the refugees' preference but more fundamentally on UNHCR's objective assessment of whether life is better at home relative to life in the camps (a calculation that can take into account the immediate situation and future circumstances). Where "protection" is increasingly tantamount to repatriation, UNHCR officials are disposed to the view that getting refugees home, even to highly unstable situations, is preferred and legitimate.

UNHCR might well be correct that refugees should repatriate under less than ideal conditions because their circumstances will become even less ideal if they remain in exile. But the issue at hand is whose voice counts and what calculations are used to determine the efficacy of repatriation. The shift away from absolute standards regarding the desire by refugees to repatriate given their assessment of the situation in the home country toward a comparative evaluation by agency officials regarding whether refugees would be more secure at home or in the camps has the direct implication of privileging the agency's knowledge claims over those offered by refugees. The ethics of repatriation under less than ideal conditions can be accompanied by a diminution of power accorded to refugees.

The impact of bureaucratic culture

UNHCR officials occasionally run roughshod over refugee rights – a callousness that some analysts see as a likely consequence of prolonged employment with the agency.[8] They imply that UNHCR staff appear, once socialised into the organisation, to embrace a different set of moral principles with which to guide and judge their actions.

Such observations relate to a broader literature on how bureaucratic culture is an incubator of indifference toward the targets of their policies.

A host of explanations can be offered. There is the possibility that because one's contribution is relatively small it cannot be related to the outcome. The sheer physical, psychological and social distance between the office holder and the subject can make it more difficult to fully comprehend or realise the effects of one's actions until after the event, if at all. If dissident voices are absent within the bureaucracy and complacency has become the norm, then those tempted to protest or dissent have a well-founded fear of ostracism and ridicule. There is evidence that the bureaucratic appeal to broad rules to generalise and find guidance reduces the concern for the particular and makes it more difficult to see and to act in extreme and extenuating circumstances.

Not to be forgotten is blind ambition: the belief that one's career prospects are best served by paying no heed to ethical dilemmas.[9] Also of importance is the influence of precedents that already departed from previous moral guidelines.

An ethnography of institutional ethics is required to understand the ethical reasons individuals use to guide and legitimate their actions; only after we try to recreate the moral universe as constructed by the participants themselves will we better understand the many ways that bureaucratic culture reorients practical and ethical reason.

Conclusion

There is a generalised concern that new humanitarians can be disturbingly disconnected from those in whose name they act. Whereas once we likened humanitarian agencies to white knights on muscled steeds charging to rescue the powerless and weak, we are now more likely to recognise that these knights are also interested in the mundane: career advancement, protecting the agency's reputation and cultivating the largesse of patrons. They are likely to use political and pragmatic considerations to navigate the moral dilemmas that populate complex emergencies and to develop ethical claims verging on indifference and callousness. None of this means that we need to be saved from our saviours. But it does mean that any discussion of humanitarianism requires a more thorough consideration of the multi-sided and polymorphous ethical field that underlies humanitarian action.

Notes

1 Executive Committee of the High Commissioner's Programme "Note on International Protection." 31 August 1983, p3.
2 Sadako Ogata "Half a Century on the Humanitarian Frontlines", lecture delivered at Graduate Institute for International Studies, Geneva, 25 November 1999.
3 The term is Alex de Waal's.
4 For a related critique, see B S Chimni "Globalization, Humanitarianism, and the Erosion of Refugee Protection," *Journal of Refugee Studies*, 13 (3), 1999, pp243–263.
5 B S Chimni "The Geopolitics of Refugee Studies: A View from the South," *Journal of Refugee Studies*, 11 (4, 1998), pp350–74; Michael Barnett & Martha Finnemore "The Politics, Power, and Pathologies of International Organisations", *International Organisation*, 53 (Fall 1999), pp699–732.
6 Marjorleine Zieck *UNHCR and Voluntary Repatriation of Refugees: A Legal Analysis*, Martinus Nijhoff Publishers, The Hague, 1997, pp438–39.
7 Michael Barnett "UNHCR and Involuntary Repatriation: Environmental Developments, the Repatriation Culture, and the Rohingya Refugees," presented at the 2000 International Studies Association meetings, Los Angeles, California.
8 See, for instance, Barbara Harrell-Bond "Repatriation: Under What Conditions is it the Most Desirable Solution for Refugees?", *African Studies Review*, 32 (1), 1989, pp41–69; Mark Walkup "Policy Dysfunction in Humanitarian Organisations:

The Role of Coping Strategies, Institutions, and Organisational Culture", *Journal of Refugee Studies*, 10 (1), 1997, pp37–60; Liisa Malkki "Speechless Emissaries: Refugees, Humanitarianism, and Dehistoricization", *Cultural Anthropology*, 11 (1996), pp377–404; and Fiona Terry "Condemned to Repeat?: The Paradoxes of Humanitarian Intervention", PhD thesis submitted to Department of International Relations, Australian National University, February 2000.
9 Mark Bovens *The Quest for Responsibility: Accountability and Citizenship in Complex Organisations*, Cambridge University Press, 1998.

8 Building a republican peace
Stabilizing states after war

Since the early 1990s, an impressive international apparatus dedicated to peacebuilding—that is, the attempt to build stable, legitimate, and effective states after war—has emerged.[1] The first sustained push in this direction came with the development of second-generation peacekeeping operations that both monitored cease-fires and attempted to help states emerging from civil wars develop the requisites for a stable peace. Over the decade various states, regional and international organizations, and international nongovernmental organizations dedicated more resources and developed more programs designed to help remove the root causes of conflict. The terrorist attacks of September 11, 2001, catalyzed an emerging view that weak states pose a major threat to themselves and to international security.[2] In response to the existing and anticipated demand for peacebuilding, the 2005 World Summit at the United Nations agreed to endorse UN Secretary-General Kofi Annan's proposals to create a peacebuilding commission, support office, and fund. Peacebuilding is now firmly established on the international security agenda.

Although peacebuilders do not operate with a single vision or from a single blueprint, liberal values so clearly guide their activities that we can call their collective efforts "liberal peacebuilding."[3] The explicit goal of many of these operations is to create a state defined by the rule of law, markets, and democracy. This objective is informed by the belief that, to have legitimacy, the state must be organized around liberal-democratic principles, and that because liberal democracies are respectful of their societies and peaceful toward their neighbors, they are the foundation of a stable international order. Toward that end, peacebuilders have developed an impressive range of programs. The United States pushes democracy promotion; the United Nations has extended its peacekeeping activities; the UN Development Programme attempts to nurture civil-society organizations and strengthen grassroots participation; international nongovernmental organizations run rule-of-law programs intended to enshrine basic human rights; and the World Bank promotes private sector reform and attempts to reduce levels of political corruption. All aspects of the state, society, and economy are to be rebuilt around liberal principles.

Peacebuilding, though, does not have an impressive track record. Certainly one reason is that it is virtually unimaginable that peacebuilders can create such a nearly ideal society with scant resources and little time under such unfavorable conditions.[4] Yet liberal peacebuilding might inadvertently be doing more harm than good. In their effort to radically transform all aspects of the state, society, and economy in a matter of months (and thus expecting conflict-ridden societies to achieve what took Western states decades), peacebuilders are subjecting these fragile societies to tremendous stress. States emerging from war do not have the necessary institutional framework or civic culture to absorb the potential pressures associated with political and market competition. Consequently, as peacebuilders push for instant liberalization, they are sowing the seeds of conflict, thereby encouraging rivals to wage their struggle for supremacy through markets and ballots.[5] Furthermore, peacebuilders have not given the state its due, a reflection of a liberal bias. Peacebuilders fear resuscitating a predatory state, presume that the best state is a limited state, and desire to create a strong society that can restrain the state. Those programs directed at the state are concentrated on helping it monopolize the means of coercion and develop its administrative capacity. The majority of activities, though, are intended to strengthen civil-society associations, the private sector, and societal organizations that can help individuals further their preferences and collective goals.[6] In short, peacebuilders have been more concerned with building a strong, liberal society than with developing state institutions. Yet liberalization prior to institutionalization can unleash societal demands before the state has developed the institutional capacity to channel, organize, and respond to those demands, thus triggering instability and conflict. Peacebuilders must recognize that peacebuilding is state building.[7]

These critiques of liberal peacebuilding point to the need for an alternative. Drawing from the central tenets of republican political theory, I develop a concept of republican peacebuilding—that is, the use of the republican principles of deliberation, constitutionalism, and representation to help states recovering from war foster stability and legitimacy. A central challenge of postconflict state building is to design states that contain the threats to stability posed by arbitrary power and factional conflict and to encourage society to begin conferring legitimacy on the new institutions. Republican peacebuilding's emphasis on the institutional foundations of stability and legitimacy is ideally suited to address these very concerns. Republicanism is attentive to the multiple threats to security.[8] There is the threat to liberty posed by the exercise of arbitrary power by the state. Factions, a permanent feature of any society, can create instability if not controlled; rivalry can explode into conflict or lead one faction to try to grab state power and deploy it against its enemies. To minimize these threats, republicanism identifies a package of institutional fixes that limits and distributes political power while restraining factions.

Republicanism also helps invest the state with legitimacy. Legitimacy, according to republicanism, is dependent on the use of proper means to arrive at collective goals. Proper means is dependent on a political process that considers the diverse interests of its citizens; that is, groups need to believe that their views are being incorporated. Although republicanism recognizes the potential centrality of periodic elections, it also suggests that alternative bodies can serve a representative function. Critical to republicanism is the concept of deliberation, which, at a minimum, requires individuals to give public reasons for their positions and decisions. This publicity principle encourages individuals and groups to find a common language, to generalize their positions, to incorporate the views of others, and perhaps even to discover common interests and develop a sense of community.

Republican peacebuilding has several advantages—especially over its liberal rival. It highlights how particular kinds of institutions might foster stability and invest the state with some legitimacy. It organizes into a coherent package emerging lessons learned from recent operations, particularly the emphasis on constitutions that distribute power and provide checks and balances on factions, and the utility of unelected assemblies of representation in the immediate postconflict environment. Not only does republican peacebuilding leave open the possibility of a liberal future, but those postconflict states that initially follow a republican path might be better positioned and more likely to develop liberal attributes if they first adopt a republican framework. It is modest. Unlike liberal peacebuilding, which uses shock therapy to push postconflict states toward some predetermined vision of the promised land, republicanism's emphasis on deliberative processes allows space for societal actors to determine for themselves what the good life is and how to achieve it. It is incremental. Unlike liberal peacebuilding, which has the vices of all grand social-engineering experiments, republicanism's emphasis on basic design principles and deliberative processes provides the shell for improvisation and learning informed by experience. Finally, republican peacebuilding offers principles not only for building states after war but also for conducting peacebuilding operations. The concern with arbitrary power extends beyond the postconflict state; it also includes the exercise of power by peacebuilders.

This article is organized as follows. The first section discusses the challenge of building stable, legitimate states after war. The next section sketches the salient aspects of republicanism and identifies important differences between republicanism and liberalism. The third section discusses the defining principles of republican peacebuilding, deliberation, representation, and constitutionalism. I illustrate the argument with references to various postconflict cases, with a particular eye toward either how republican principles aided the postconflict process or how following such principles might have helped international interveners avoid critical errors.[9] Before proceeding, though, an important disclaimer: I do not provide a "how to" manual for building states after war. One size does not fit all, and local circumstances must shape essential features of any operational strategy. A mandate or doctrine that established fixed rules would either become out of synch with a complex reality or would dangerously shoehorn that reality so that it fit the rules. Either way, it could be fatal for the operation.

State building after conflict

The modern state "exists when there is a political apparatus (governmental institutions, such as a court, parliament, or congress, plus civil service officials), ruling over a given territory, whose authority is backed by a legal system and the capacity to use force to implement its policies."[10] State building concerns how this process is accomplished. It has two elements. One involves the development of specific instruments states use to control society, that is, state capacity. Attention is directed to the monopolization of the means of coercion and the development of a bureaucratic apparatus organized around rational-legal principles that have the capacity to regulate, control, and extract resources from society. The concern, then, is with the degree of the state. The other element involves how states and societies negotiate their relationship, that is, the kind of state. Attention is directed to the organizing principles that structure the state's rule over society. States can be distinguished according to whether or not they contain institutions designed to incorporate diverse views, hold them accountable, limit their discretion, and safeguard basic individual rights and liberties. Those that do are inclusionary; those that do not are exclusionary.[11]

Although state building exhibits tremendous variation depending on the global context, the economic structure, patterns of authority relations and political power, and elite networks, arguably what distinguishes postconflict state building is the existence of a dual crisis of security and legitimacy. What makes postconflict state building necessary is the prior existence of conflict. Indeed, "postconflict" can be a misnomer for societies that are still experiencing violence. The legacy of conflict and the continuing climate of fear mean that individuals and groups are unlikely to trust the state to be an impartial force that can provide credible security guarantees. Until that happens, they will continue to seek protection from alternative security organizations, and these organizations will be reluctant to demobilize. In addition to being unable to provide physical security, the state also is hard pressed to deliver basic needs—such as food, medicine, and shelter—that are essential for human security. Indeed, in many instances the combination of conflict and a state's inability or unwillingness to provide these essential services compels local communities to develop and rely on parallel organizations. An immediate and critical challenge confronting the postconflict state, therefore, is demonstrating its utility by providing security for its population.[12]

International actors frequently perform these governance functions until the state is up to the task and then provide a range of assistance activities intended to help the state develop or recover these basic capacities. Most famous here is peacekeeping, which is expected to help maintain a cease-fire and give the parties to the conflict the reassurance that they will not severely compromise their immediate security if they take conflict-reducing measures.[13] In addition to this peacekeeping role, international actors provide security-sector reform packages to create a more professionalized military that subordinates itself to civilian control and respects basic human rights, as well as demobilization, disarmament, and reintegration packages to dismantle existing security forces and transform soldiers into productive, law-abiding citizens.

States after conflict also face a crisis of legitimacy. This is not terribly surprising. Domestic conflict usually erupts in illegitimate states, and the subsequent conflict rarely invests the postconflict state with legitimacy. The challenge, then, is to create public support and a modicum of legitimacy for the postconflict institutions. Not only does the effectiveness of the state's fledgling institutions depend on it, but a lack of legitimacy can contribute to the resumption of violence. In recognition of the intimate connection between legitimacy and stability, international peacebuilders have pushed for elections and liberal values, believing that this represents the surest and best way to invest the state with legitimacy. However well-meaning, such efforts potentially violate both the substantive and procedural dimensions of legitimacy.[14] What a Western audience defines as a legitimate value or institution might be viewed as illegitimate by the local community. The legitimacy of a decision also depends on the use of accepted procedures. Legitimacy, in other words, is not defined by liberalism per se but rather by societal agreement regarding the proper procedures for deciding and pursuing collectively acceptable goals.

A central challenge for postconflict state building is to create a state that can help further stability and has some legitimacy. Toward that end, peacebuilders have tended to concentrate their efforts on helping the state develop a monopoly of the means of coercion and organize itself around elections and liberal values. In this respect, they have attempted to increase the degree of the state and build a kind of state that is limited both in its functions and by a strong society. Missing from such efforts, though, is a proper recognition of the institutional foundations for postconflict stability and state legitimacy. This absence owes in part to the reining approach of liberal peacebuilding. Republicanism offers, as I argue below, a better way of developing a stable, legitimate state after conflict because it focuses on how institutions can address the multiple threats to security and help invest the state with legitimacy short of elections.

Republicanism and how it differs from liberalism

Liberalism and republicanism are frequently conflated, and with good reason.[15] Liberalism, as a political theory, derived from republicanism and thus borrowed various attributes that are now quite familiar, including the centrality of liberty and the need to check the power of the sovereign through elections, representation, constitutions, and laws. Yet liberalism slighted other concepts and dimensions of republicanism—namely, the conception of liberty as the freedom from arbitrary power, the threat posed by factions, the centrality of deliberation, and the constitutional restraints on arbitrary power—that not only clarify important differences between the two but also make clear why these features of republicanism match the challenges posed by the postconflict environment.

Republicanism has ancient and modern roots.[16] Its origins are in Greek and Roman philosophy. Aristotle contributed the core idea that individuals should be publicly minded if they are to develop a polity that will secure their individual freedoms and help them pursue justice and the good life. Cicero held that a principal virtue of the Roman Republic was that it minimized the dependence of citizens (propertied males) on each other, and described how this lack of dependence helped to minimize domination; he added, critically, that political institutions are required to secure individual freedoms. Modern republicanism is closely associated with the writings of Niccolò Machiavelli and James Madison. Specifically, where ancient republicanism tended to emphasize the importance of the state for promoting freedom, modern republicanism shifted attention to the dangers posed to liberty by the very state that is to promote it. In *The Discourses*, Machiavelli delivered a sophisticated argument regarding the ideal political arrangements, including forms of representation and deliberation, that were required to ensure liberty. Famously, he warned that allowing individuals to treat the polity in an instrumental manner would corrupt the body politic and threaten political stability. To tame the chronic tendency of individuals to pursue only their naked self-interest, he emphasized the domesticating influence of public deliberation; by compelling individuals to speak in the language of community, they might develop a greater sense of patriotism, that is, a love of country. In the *Federalist Papers*, Madison and his coauthors highlighted how factions, which are a permanent feature of political life, pose a danger to political stability and liberty; to minimize this threat, they proposed institutional arrangements to distribute and constrain power.

Modern republicanism, then, is concerned with how to develop a stable polity that lessens the threat posed by arbitrary power and factional conflict. Its concern with arbitrary power is tied to its conception of liberty. Liberalism focuses on the preservation of the autonomy of the individual from interference by others and the state. Republicanism offers a slightly different, and arguably more demanding, view of liberty and freedom—liberty as non-domination. Drawing from Roman law, it claims "that to be free mean[s] not to be dominated—that is, not to be dependent on the arbitrary power of other individuals, groups, or the state."[17] Domination occurs when an individual's activities or choices are subject to or threatened by the ever present possibility of arbitrary interference by other agents.[18] Power is arbitrary, therefore, when the interfering agent fails to consider the views of those potentially affected by its decisions.

Factions represent a second source of instability. Factions are a fact of life, but if uncontrolled, they can dominate a political system, threaten other factions, and undermine liberty. As Madison famously observed, factions—whether a minority or majority—that are united and actuated by some common impulse of passion or interest might eventually threaten the rights of other citizens or the political community.[19] Consequently, guarding against their pernicious effects was imperative. Notwithstanding republicanism's fear of factions, eliminating diversity is neither possible nor desirable. Individuals and groups cannot be expected to agree on all matters. Nor is it possible to erase diversity—and the attempt to do so creates a real threat to liberty. In general, supporters of republicanism worried about the threats to stability posed by arbitrary power and by a society unrestrained. As Machiavelli crisply summarized, "A prince who can do what he wishes is crazy; a people that can do what it wishes is not wise."[20]

Republicanism contains a set of principles that deal simultaneously with both challenges. Before republicanism, there was always the possibility that the medicine prescribed for one threat might unleash the other. After all, an antidote that concentrated on the dangers posed by a centralized state and arbitrary power risked loosening the constraints on factions; an antidote targeted at the dangers posed by factions risked creating a centralized state and arbitrary power. Republicanism's brilliance was to identify how specific institutional arrangements that dispersed political power and forced groups to negotiate could reduce the risk that the medicine would not kill the patient.

Republicanism also recognizes an intimate connection between state legitimacy and stability—an illegitimate state is an unstable state. Importantly, republicanism's view of what makes a state legitimate differs from that of liberalism. Liberalism provides a particular way of thinking about the means (i.e., democracy and elections) and the goals (i.e., progress, development, and rights). Republicanism, on the other hand, views the essence of legitimacy as the state's use of proper means to achieve collectively accepted goals.[21] No more, no less. The goals of the state can vary historically. Although currently most states pursue goals that are broadly liberal, because societies differ, so too can their goals. Proper means derives from a political process that incorporates the diverse interests of the state's citizens; that is, groups need to believe that their views are represented and considered. Periodic elections are generally considered the best, and possibly only, way to ensure that societal groups have their voices heard and views felt. Although republicanism, like liberalism, identifies elections as an important mechanism, it also acknowledges the possible incorporation of societal views in their absence. As I show below, critical for engineering a successful postconflict process is the principle of deliberation, which, at a minimum, requires that individuals provide public reasons for their positions and decisions.

Deliberation, representation, and constitutionalism

Republican peacebuilding promotes the foundations for postconflict stability by establishing the process for creating a legitimate state that is restrained in its ability to exercise arbitrary power and can minimize conflict among factions. Although various principles are associated with republicanism, the holy trinity of deliberation, representation, and constitutionalism is most important for promoting stability and legitimacy. Deliberation, a defining element of both representation and constitutionalism, facilitates both public engagement, and the accommodation and reconciliation among rival groups. Representation encourages the incorporation of diverse views and voices. Constitutionalism helps to distribute power across the political landscape. Below I discuss these principles and then illustrate their relevance for post-conflict reconstruction.

The taming effects of deliberation

The principle of deliberation is critical for the postconflict environment. Liberalism conceives of deliberation as little more than bargaining between utility-maximizing actors with fixed interests, or the very act of deciding.[22] Although republicanism recognizes this elementary feature of politics, its more demanding conception of deliberation concerns how individuals consider each other's views before making a decision. Aristotle initiated this tradition when he conceptualized deliberation as the process of forming the "general will." Modern republicanism, though, is concerned less with the discovery of a general will (in part because it doubts that one truly exists) and more with how individuals and groups must give public reasons for their positions and decisions. Republicanism postulates that this fairly modest act—the consideration of each other's views in a public setting—can have fairly significant and far-reaching consequences.[23]

To begin, public deliberation encourages individuals to "escape their private interests and engage in pursuit of the public good."[24] Individuals are self-interested. Allowed to pursue their selfish instincts, they would treat politics in an instrumental manner; such instrumentalism provides a climate for corruption and can endanger stability and political liberty. To domestic-ate these instincts and nurture an enlightened self-interest, republicanism recommends that political discussions be public. Such openness can compel individuals to consider the views of others, generalize their positions to widen their appeal, find a common language, articulate common ends, demonstrate some detachment from the self, and subordinate the personal to the community.[25] Of course individuals will frequently camouflage their personal interests in high-minded language, but the very act of public deliberation and the attending pressure on individuals force them to broaden their views and thus ameliorate conflict.[26]

Second, deliberation increases the prospect that the collective decision will have legitimacy.[27] Although the decisionmaking process does not require full, equal, and active participation (and thus does not demand direct democracy), it does contain mechanisms that compel those in power to consider alternative views. Deliberation and legitimacy, therefore, are inextricably intertwined. Third, because deliberation enhances the decision's legitimacy, it also increases the likelihood that the policy will be accepted, or at least not be met by passive or active resistance. Fourth, deliberation provides an opportunity for individuals to change their minds, to alter their beliefs, and to identify with the community.[28] The contrast with liberalism could not be greater. Because liberalism conceives of deliberation as the bargaining between actors in the pursuit of their preferences, the result of their exchanges, at best, encourages more astute strategic action. Although republicanism certainly acknowledges these enduring features of politics, it also recognizes that deliberation can affect not only individuals' strategies but also their interests and identities. Specifically, once forced to consider opposing views, individuals might begin to identify with each other and become more community minded. In this way, creating bridges between factions and individuals as they build a community might also produce a greater love of country and a sense of patriotism, understood as a sense of belonging that transcends race, ethnicity, or other groupings. In contrast to liberals, therefore, republicans are interested not only in what the country can do for the individual but also what the individual can do for the country.

The possibility that broader and more inclusive negotiations can encourage a sense of community and help establish a greater social identification with the state is an important theme in the history of Western European state formation. Consider Charles Tilly's narrative regarding the formation of the modern state. Although most analyses typically elevate the role of war, in my view what is more critical is how the state's need to mobilize access to the resources for war triggered negotiations between state and society, which in turn led to the "civilianization of government and domestic politics." Tilly summarizes the reasons for this process in the following way:

> Because the effort to build and sustain military forces led agents of states to build bulky extractive apparatuses staffed by civilians, and those extractive apparatuses came to contain and constrain the military forces; because agents of states bargained with civilian groups that controlled the resources required for effective warmaking, and in bargaining gave civilian groups enforceable claims on the state that further constrained the military; because the expansion of state capacity in wartime gave those states that had not suffered great losses in war expanded capacity at the ends of wars, and agents of those states took advantage of the situation by taking on new activities, or continuing activities they had started as emergency measures; because participants in the war effort, including military personnel, acquired claims on the state that they deferred during the war in response to repression or mutual consent but which they

reactivated with demobilization; and finally because wartime borrowing led to great increases in national debts, which in turn generated service bureaucracies and encouraged greater state intervention in national economies.[29]

The central mechanism here is negotiation. War caused state leaders to negotiate with their societies for access to the means of war. If states were going to survive, then they required men, money, and matériel. Because states were increasingly turning away from external sources of financing and foreign mercenaries, and were increasingly interested in securing these inputs from their societies, they had to negotiate with their societies to acquire them (or risk domestic rebellions if they attempted to use more coercive methods of extraction). In return for their sacrifices, societies expected to be able to make claims on the state. This process led to the expansion of the state apparatus and the development of representative institutions, which, in turn, increased the state's legitimacy. There is evidence from various postconflict cases, including those of South Africa and El Salvador, that negotiations and deliberations might also reconcile and create greater identification among former enemies.[30]

Deliberation occurs not in the abstract, but rather over specific public policies. In addition to the process of constitution making, which I discuss below, three policy areas are central for creating a sense of fate among the population and a greater connection between state and society. The first is public security. Peacebuilders have paid considerable attention to public security reforms, most evident in security-sector reform and demobilization, disarmament, and reintegration programs.[31] To the extent that these reforms reduce the number of independent and competing military organizations and professionalize the public security apparatus, they foster stability. Yet the process itself can also contribute to stability by encouraging a public debate regarding the collective purpose of military service and reconciling former combatants in the process of integration.[32] A second area is public finance and economic management. Presently, economic discussions are typically restricted to a handful of state ministries and international financial institutions. This exclusionary process forgoes an opportunity for state and society to debate what the state's budgetary priorities are and how to pay for them. Indeed, a recent World Bank meeting on postconflict economic reconstruction concluded that "*policy dialogue* between donors and recipients on governance reform must be honest, open and simple, leaving *space* for the recipient state to build itself in collaboration with and response to civil society and the private sector."[33] Deliberation principles are widely accepted as central to the third area, transitional justice.[34] Indeed, it is virtually an article of faith that any kind of transitional justice must involve a deliberative process defined by public activities that are designed both to hold accountable those accused of crimes against society and to give the victims of these crimes the opportunity to participate in a public healing process.[35]

Although deliberation is critical for promoting a more legitimate and stable polity, there can be too much of a good thing, especially in a postconflict context. Sometimes things are better left unsaid, and the less said the better. Responding to Thomas Jefferson's proposal that all of society routinely deliberate on constitutional questions, Madison averred that this would increase "the danger of disturbing the public tranquility by interesting too strongly the public passions." And "it is reason, alone, of the public that ought to control and regulate the government . . . while the passions ought to be controlled and regulated by the government."[36] Madison's fears seem particularly relevant for societies emerging from war. Relatedly, it may be best to remove some issues from public discussion, especially early in a postconflict process. For instance, trying to settle deeply personal issues in divided societies, including the role of religion in public life, might very well derail any reconciliation or reconstruction process. Deliberation also has extremely high transaction costs; sometimes decisions have to be made before all views can be considered. Indeed, in many postconflict settings, destroyed communication and transportation lines and continuing security problems make this physically impossible. That said, it is better to err on the side of inclusion, because deliberation between key societal groups can help them bridge differences, discover common interests, and develop a sense of community and common fate.

Representation beyond elections

Republicanism introduced the importance of representation, drawing from the idea in Roman law that "what affects all must be decided by all."[37] It was not, however, a "theory of direct participatory democracy but rather representative government within constitutional boundaries."[38] The scale of modern politics makes direct participatory democracy impractical and unnecessary. The geographic and demographic size of modern politics is too vast to expect citizens to participate actively in all affairs. Accordingly, representation meant that those in power spoke for and incorporated the interests of the citizenry. When considering mechanisms of representation, most discussions drift immediately to direct elections. Yet there are other ways to force state officials to consider the views of others, and thus meet minimal standards of representation. Indeed, the election or selection of an enlightened group relatively insulated from society might help it escape mob rule or particularly passionate factions and thus formulate generalized positions.

Republicanism's consideration of forms of representation outside of elections is of immediate relevance to postconflict settings. However desirable, elections can cause more troubles than they solve and potentially undermine the democratization process.[39] Consequently, there is a need for alternative, unelected arrangements such as consultative bodies and transitional governments that can perform the function of representation until elections are appropriate. If unelected bodies are to meet the principle of representativeness, though, they must fulfill two criteria: inclusivity, or incorporating diverse groups; and publicity, or making transparent their decisions and the reasons behind them. Satisfying these two criteria encourages those in power to broaden their perspectives, acknowledge the views of others, and meet minimal standards of representation. As such, these criteria help invest the political process with legitimacy, reduce the possibility of arbitrary power, and stabilize the postconflict setting.[40]

The contrast between Afghanistan and Iraq regarding the relationship between representation, legitimacy, and stability is particularly instructive. After the defeat of the Taliban in the fall of 2003, the immediate challenge was to construct a process to establish a new Afghan government. Under the auspices of various international sponsors, four central Afghan factions met in Bonn, Germany, to discuss the country's interim political authority and the process of establishing a new government. Although the meeting fell far short of any measure of inclusion, the Bonn agreement of December 5, 2003, did create a process that met minimal standards of participation, as it established the Emergency Loya Jirga (Grand Assembly of Elders), which would be responsible for selecting a transitional government until national elections for a permanent government could be held.[41] Although the delegates to the Emergency Loya Jirga were not formally elected, it was accorded tremendous legitimacy for two critical reasons. It had roots in Afghan history, reflecting local, not foreign, preferences. It also was impressively inclusive, comprising not only the major ethnic and religious groups but even some marginalized populations. There were two procedures for selecting the participants. At the local level, more than 1,000 delegates were selected by groups of elders, venerated elites, and powerful families; as a consequence, powerful interests were overrepresented, and women, poor, and minorities were underrepresented. To compensate for this predicted bias, another 500 delegates were appointed by the Loya Jirga Commission in consultation with various organizations, civil-society organizations, elites, refugees, and nomads. In early 2003 a second loya jirga was established through indirect elections to help draft the new constitution; it had all of the merits and deficits of the Emergency Loya Jirga. In general, although these bodies did not represent all views or encourage all those in attendance to speak their minds, arguably they met minimal standards of deliberation and representation. Importantly, this process is credited with helping to stabilize post-Taliban Afghanistan.[42]

The political process in the months following the fall of Baghdad in March 2003 traveled a very different path and contributed to a very different result. Unlike in Afghanistan, where the United States worked with the international community to begin the process of transferring authority to local elites, in Iraq it acted alone and continually resisted the idea of sharing authority with any Iraqi-grown transitional government. The United States arrived in Baghdad with only vague ideas regarding the transfer of authority to a new Iraqi government.[43] Although many Iraqis and State Department officials (especially those who ran the Future of Iraq project) urged the immediate creation of a broad-based interim authority, the White House and the Defense Department rejected the idea, believing that Ahmed Chalabi and other Iraqi exiles would easily and quickly take power.[44] The post-occupation chaos, however, destroyed this plan and led to the arrival of Paul Bremer in May as the head of the newly created Coalition Provisional Authority (CPA). Recognizing the need to establish some sort of governing body that included Iraqis, Bremer created the twenty-five-member Iraqi Governing Council (IGC) in July 2003. Not only did the handpicked body favor the Iraqi exiles and disadvantage the Sunnis, but it had little power.

In response to the IGC's failure to settle on a plan for creating a transitional government, on November 15 the CPA announced a schedule for ending the occupation by June 30, 2004, pivoting around a very complicated process whereby caucuses would select the members of the Transitional National Authority. Grand Ayatollah Ali al-Sistani, the most respected and popular religious figure in the Shia community, demanded the exact alternative: national elections. Officials in George W. Bush's administration objected for various reasons, including the fear that it might be unable to control the process or ensure an outcome consistent with its interests. The UN's Lakhdar Brahimi went to Baghdad to try to break the stalemate and establish a process to form a new interim arrangement.[45] Brahimi believed that it would be impossible to hold free, fair, and direct elections within a few short months because of the political, security, and logistical situation, and, drawing from his experience in Afghanistan, gave serious consideration to an Iraqi version of a loya jirga.[46] His position corresponded with those of some in the CPA, who strongly recommended that the process for selecting the interim authority be "as democratic and participatory as possible in order to give the government breadth, legitimacy, and popular support."[47] Reluctant to loosen its grip on the political process, the United States insisted on an interim government that was limited, comprised of technocrats, and selected through an exclusionary, complicated process using caucuses.[48] In the end, Brahimi convinced Sistani to agree to delay national elections; he also succeeded in convincing the United States to abandon the caucuses in favor of such elections.

Although the causes of the post-occupation violence in Iraq are over-determined, the Bush administration's failure to establish an inclusive Iraqi interim authority did not help. It certainly deepened Iraqi suspicions regarding the United States' intentions, failed to establish channels for allowing Iraqis to express dissent through nonviolent means, and increased the insurgency's power and popularity. Citing UN officials, experts on postconflict reconstruction, as well as dissident voices within the U.S. government, and drawing from his own experiences, Larry Diamond convincingly argues that if the United States had immediately established an Iraqi advisory body, been more inclusive of Iraqi voices, and spent more time encouraging Iraqis (especially Sunnis) to buy into the political process, it might have improved the prospects of stability.[49]

Constitutionalism and divided power

Republicanism introduced the importance of constitutions for establishing rules that restrain the exercise of arbitrary power, limit conflict between factions, and reduce the benefits of power. All constitutional systems have (1) an agreement over the rules of the game and the underlying principles that are to maintain the political order; (2) rules and institutions that limit the exercise of power; and (3) rules that are relatively difficult to amend.[50] If all three conditions are met, the constitution is more likely to be viewed by society as legitimate, have an enduring ability to limit the exercise of power and decrease the yields to power, and foster political stability.[51]

Republicanism identified a set of institutional arrangements that limit the exercise and the returns to power. Best known is the system of checks and balances—that is, the distribution of political authority that limits the possibility of either a centralized government exercising arbitrary power or a faction dominating the political system. The benefits of this kind of arrangement extend beyond the creation of a balance of forces within the political system to include compelling local actors to negotiate and compromise. In this way, divided government helps to further the goal of both political stability and legitimacy.

Practitioners and peacebuilders are coalescing around the need for divided government in postconflict settings. Although at first postconflict designers experimented with a variety of arrangements (including majoritarian democracy), soon they gravitated toward different forms of power sharing, reflecting the belief that the proportional inclusion of the most powerful elites and groups will help avoid a winner-take-all dynamic and thus reduce the likelihood that "losers" will become "spoilers" and return to war.[52] Although power sharing resembles divided government because both operate on the principle of a balance of forces, the latter is distinctive because of the self-conscious effort to distribute power across institutions and not specific groups.[53] This "power-dividing strategy" has several advantages, including the promotion of greater democracy, the separation of powers, the encouragement of crosscutting cleavages, and the establishment of an institutional setting that does not necessarily freeze particular coalitions of power.[54] In general, because constitutional orders can help promote postconflict stability, they are an essential part of postconflict state building.

In addition to the principles that define the constitution, what also matters is the process of making the constitution. The legitimacy of the constitution depends on the degree to which it allows for participation, dialogue, and deliberation.[55] Consequently, constitution making cannot be hurried by arbitrary deadlines but instead must provide a sufficient period to allow for broad participation, civic education and popular consultation, and a constitutional commission to incorporate a range of views. This deliberative process can do more than give legitimacy to the constitution; it also can help create bonds between former rivals. As Neil Kritz observed, "Where the constitution-making process has been sufficiently deliberative and has entailed broad public consultation, an intriguing result has repeatedly been the transformation of the members of a Constitutional Commission from serving primarily as advocates for their respective interest group into a more cohesive group with a greater focus on the needs of the whole society."[56]

The contrast, again, between Afghanistan and Iraq is instructive. Much like the Emergency Loya Jirga, the Constitutional Loya Jirga has been criticized for not being sufficiently participatory, for not engaging in civic education and outreach, and for compressing the process of deliberation into a fifteen-month period. These criticisms notwithstanding, it was a vast improvement over previous constitutional exercises in Afghanistan, and it did attempt to create meaningful deliberation.[57] Its accomplishments look all the more impressive when compared to the Iraqi constitutional process. The Iraqi Transitional Authoritative Law envisioned a transparent and widely participatory process that would lead to a constitution within seven months (there was a provision for extending the process, if needed). As the deadline neared, though, it became apparent that more time was needed. However, the Bush administration, mainly because it wanted to demonstrate progress to an increasingly impatient American public, forcefully intervened in the negotiations; conducted secret, exclusionary talks; and strenuously objected to any extension. Various consequences emerged from this rushed process. It restricted participation, making it more difficult to include the Sunni minority or to have genuine civic education engagement and public outreach (a difficulty compounded by the security situation). As the International Crisis Group summarized, "Regrettably, the Bush administration chose to sacrifice inclusiveness for the sake of an arbitrary deadline, apparently in hopes of preparing the ground for a significant military drawdown in 2006. As a result, the constitution-making process became a new stake in the political battle rather than an instrument to solve it."[58] The United States' heavy presence also fed into a popular view among Iraqis that the document was a creature of Washington. This hurried process also robbed the Iraqis of an opportunity to learn democracy and deliberation by doing.[59] Instead of the constitution process providing an opportunity for Iraqis to come together, it kept them apart.[60]

Although international peacebuilders are limited in what they can do to inculcate republican principles, they can make a difference.[61] They can help publicize decisions. They can try to avoid what has been called a "Linas-Marcoussis effect"—that is, giving incentives to rebels to attack civilian targets as a way to improve their position at the bargaining table.[62] They can try to encourage responsible members of the émigré community to reengage in politics. They can use political and financial levers to compel leaders to adopt republican principles, insisting that a condition of international assistance is the inclusion of otherwise marginalized groups.[63] Perhaps most important, though, they must demonstrate the patience and provide the resources required for a successful transition process.

Do as I say, not as I do

International peacebuilders need to do more than inject republican principles into postconflict societies; they also must live by these principles. They occupy positions of power—for good and necessary reasons. If the situation on the ground was stable, then they need not be there. Peacebuilders, presumably, are not imperialists with the desire to use their power to exploit, but rather public trustees with the desire to use their power for the public's benefit.[64] They also have expertise. Years of experience in the field and professional training give them the knowledge regarding what does and does not work in postconflict settings. International interveners are expected to operate with considerable discretion.

Yet whenever actors have power, abuse is always a possibility—and peacebuilders have been known to exercise arbitrary power.[65] The issue extends beyond the common charge by locals that much of the aid ends up in the pockets of foreigners who drive shiny Land Rovers, live in the choice residential areas, and wine and dine at the best restaurants. The heart of the matter is that they are unaccountable to the population in whose name they act. This lack of accountability has led to four distinct problems. One is that it increases the temptation to engage in exploitative and criminal behavior, most noticeable when peacekeepers are accused of rape and sex trafficking. This not only does incalculable damage to the victims; it also undermines the legitimacy and effectiveness of the entire operation. The crimes committed by U.S. soldiers at Abu Ghraib and other sites around Iraq further undermined the American occupation, and the political fallout from such crimes was compounded by the widespread perception by Iraqi society that the criminals went unpunished because of a "victor's justice." International peacebuilders must be held accountable and face real, not hand-slapping, punishment.

The failure of peacebuilders to incorporate the views of the local population also can lead to grave mistakes that otherwise might have been avoided.[66] The problem is more than the standard criticism that outsiders do not know the lay of the land, culture, language, networks, and cleavages (though this is a concern). Instead, it is their lack of knowledge about how to engineer a successful postconflict operation that poses the real problem. At present, many peacebuilders escape their uncertainty by relying on general models that frequently are developed from their most recent experiences in the field.[67] But universal models can be a false sanctuary. The danger posed by off-the-shelf templates is highly reminiscent of Albert Hirschman's confessional regarding the failures of development economics. Reflecting on policies that delivered growth without development and created the conditions for authoritarianism in South America and elsewhere, Hirschman damned the hubris of a field that assumed that generalized knowledge could be applied across diverse countries. The sin was falling in love with their models and assuming that these countries were so simple that those models told them all they needed to know.[68] The same hazard occurs in peacebuilding.[69] The only way out is for peacebuilders to acknowledge their uncertainty—and actively incorporate local voices into the planning process. As Noah Feldman recently warned, "The high failure rate [of nation-building exercises] strongly supports the basic intuition that we do not know what we are doing—and one of the critical elements of any argument for autonomy is that people tend to know themselves better than others how they ought best to live their lives."[70] This isolation from and dismissal of local knowledge and voices, as Larry Diamond's analysis suggests, led the United States to make several critical errors in Iraq, including a failure to recognize the incipient insurgency.[71]

Third, if peacebuilders are serious about preparing states for self-governance, then local elites must be included in the reconstruction process. Future leaders can learn as they share basic governance functions. A direct relationship characterized the success of the UN operation in East Timor and its willingness to give real power to the East Timorese; the increased participation of the East Timorese, in turn, provided a tremendous opportunity for the local elites to learn how to run a government.[72]

Fourth, encouraging local participation and accountability also helps build popular support.[73] Conversely, a population that feels alienated will become mistrustful, resentful, and potentially rebellious. Indeed, the U.S. experience in Iraq suggests that the more illegitimate the international presence is, as viewed by the local population, the more necessary it is to include their participation. The redress is not only to promote more inclusive interim bodies that allow locals to participate in the governance process; it also requires that the occupiers be prepared to listen and learn. How different might Iraq have been had the United States not affected the "same combination of arrogance, ignorance, and isolation that had plunged America into war in the first place."[74]

Peacebuilders must become more accountable to those in whose name they act, and the surest path to accountability is to adopt basic republican principles. They can create ad hoc and standing bodies that structure exchanges between the occupiers and the occupied. They can establish an ombudsperson to field complaints from the local population regarding the behavior of peacebuilders.[75] They can allow groups to air their grievances in the street and through the media, even if thin-skinned occupiers find such criticism unjustified and painful. They can encourage the development of ad hoc councils and citizens' organizations that are directed at the occupiers. They can interpret elections as a statement about their performance.[76] They must live up to the principles they espouse.

Conclusion

Republican peacebuilding is not the magic bullet for transforming a postconflict environment into a peaceful one. Whether republican peacebuilding—or any kind of peacebuilding—achieves even some of its lofty goals is highly dependent on various forces that are frequently outside the control of any single actor. Nor does republican peacebuilding specify the forms of institutions and deliberative mechanisms that are most desirable for a particular situation, how inclusive societal participation should be, or whether all issues should be open for deliberation. These and other concerns cannot be addressed in the abstract, but rather require judgment informed by a deep knowledge of local circumstances and views.

Yet republican peacebuilding is superior to the reigning alternative of liberal peacebuilding because it represents a better match for the nature of the postconflict environment. In the aftermath of conflict, an essential task is to help create the foundations for a state that (1) can contain the threats posed by factional conflict, (2) is restrained in its exercise of arbitrary power, and (3) has some semblance of legitimacy. Toward that end, republicanism emphasizes the necessity of creating mechanisms of representation, constitutional arrangements that distribute political power, and deliberative processes that encourage groups to generalize their views. This process can help foster stability and legitimacy.

Republican peacebuilding has a related advantage: it is incremental. A fundamental critique of contemporary peacebuilding is that peacebuilders do not know what they are doing. Grand plans can deliver grand failures, especially under such uncertainty. Current peacebuilding models do not give sufficient attention to context, incorporate all the relevant variables or account for their interaction effects, or prioritize the sequences of different activities. Instead of grand plans, peacebuilders should celebrate incrementalism.[77] Because republicanism emphasizes institutional mechanisms and deliberative processes, it helps slow the peacebuilding process and ensures that those with the knowledge have the ability to shape their lives.

The institutional mechanisms that help create stability in the immediate aftermath of conflict also provide the foundation for their institutionalization. An ever present danger is that agreements that are accepted for pragmatic reasons in the aftermath of conflict, agreements that privilege the powerful, will be frozen in time. Although this might lead to stability, it is a far cry from the open, inclusive democracy promised by peacebuilders. Although republican peacebuilding cannot override the necessity of shotgun weddings, it can establish principles that offer incentives for collaboration, compromise, and integration. Republican peacebuilding, therefore, can provide the foundations for the kind of society and state envisioned by liberal peacebuilders. If those committed to liberal peacebuilding want to further their cause, they might consider becoming more republican.

Acknowledgments

The article was written while the author was a Visiting Fellow at New York University's Center on International Cooperation. He thanks the Center for its support. For advice and comments, he also thanks Brian Atwood, Charles Call, Shepard Forman, Ronald Krebs, Madalene O'Donnell, Roland Paris,

William Scheuerman, Laura Sitea, Bernard Yack, and three anonymous reviewers. Many thanks, also, to Rebecca Cohen for her research assistance.

Notes

1 In *Agenda for Peace* (New York: United Nations Press, 2002), par. 21, UN Secretary-General Boutros Boutros-Ghali defined peacebuilding as "action to identify and support structures which will tend to strengthen and solidify peace in order to avoid relapse into conflict." Later, the Brahimi Report on Peace Operations refined the definition as "activities undertaken on the far side of conflict to reassemble the foundations of peace and provide the tools for building on those foundations something that is more than just the absence of war." Report of the Panel on United Nations Peace Operations, United Nations, A/55/305-S/2000/809, August 21, 2000. There are now many definitions, some of which are interchangeable with postconflict reconstruction. For a review of how different agencies conceptualize, operationalize, and prioritize postconflict activities, see Michael Barnett, David Kim, Madalene O'Donnell, and Laura Sitea, "Peacebuilding: What's in a Name?" *Global Governance*, Vol. 13, No. 3 (2007). For general statements on postconflict reconstruction, see Philip Roeder and Donald Rothchild, eds., *Sustainable Peace: Power and Democracy after Civil Wars* (Ithaca, N.Y.: Cornell University Press, 2005); Jennifer Milliken and Keith Krause, "State Failure, State Collapse, and State Reconstruction," *Development and Change*, Vol. 33, No. 5 (September 2002), pp. 753–774; Ashraf Ghani, Clare Lockhart, and Michael Carnaham, "Closing the Sovereignty Gap: An Approach to Statebuilding," Working Paper No. 253 (London: Overseas Development Institute, September 2005); Ho-Won Jeong, *Peacebuilding in Postconflict Societies* (Boulder, Colo.: Lynne Rienner, 2005); Simon Chesterman, Michael Ignatieff, and Ramesh Thakur, eds., *Making States Work: From State Failure to Statebuilding* (New York: United Nations University Press, 2005); and Charles T. Call with Vanessa Hawkins Wyeth, eds., *Building States to Build Peace* (Boulder, Colo.: Lynne Rienner, forthcoming).

2 For various statements, see International Commission on Intervention and State Sovereignty, *The Responsibility to Protect* (Ottawa: International Development Research Centre, 2001); Stuart Eizenstat, John Edward Porter, and Jeremy Weinstein, "Rebuilding Weak States," *Foreign Affairs*, Vol. 84, No. 1 (January/February 2005), pp. 134–147; Center for Global Development, *On the Brink: Weak States and U.S. National Security* (Washington, D.C.: Center for Global Development, 2004); *A More Secure World: Our Shared Responsibility* (New York: United Nations Press, 2004), a report of the Secretary-General's high-level panel on threats, challenges, and change; and Stephen D. Krasner and Carlos Pascual, "Addressing State Failure," *Foreign Affairs*, Vol. 84, No. 4 (July/August 2005), pp. 153–163.

3 This argument is most closely associated with Roland Paris. See his *At War's End: Building Peace after Civil Conflict* (New York: Cambridge University Press, 2004); Roland Paris, "International Peacebuilding and the 'Mission Civilisatrice,' " *Review of International Studies*, Vol. 28, No. 4 (October 2002), pp. 637–656; and Roland Paris, "Peacebuilding and the Limits of Liberal Internationalism," *International Security*, Vol. 22, No. 2 (Fall 1997), pp. 54–89. See also Oliver Richmond, "The Globalization of Responses to Conflict and the Peacebuilding Consensus," *Cooperation and Conflict*, Vol. 39, No. 2 (2004), pp. 129–150; Allen Lens, "From Peacekeeping to Peace-building: The United Nations and the Challenge of Intrastate War," in Richard Price and Mark Zacher, eds., *The United Nations and Global Security* (New York: Palgrave, 2004); Jens Meierhenrich, "Forming States

after Failure," in Robert Rotberg, ed., *When States Fail: Causes and Consequences* (Princeton, N.J.: Princeton University Press, 2003), pp: 155–156; and International Peace Academy, "The Future of UN Statebuilding: Strategic and Operational Challenges and the Legacy of Iraq," executive summary from a conference held in Tarrytown, New York, November 14–16, 2002.

4 Robert C. Orr, "The United States as Nation Builder," in Orr, ed., *Winning the Peace: An American Strategy for Postconflict Reconstruction* (Washington, D.C.: Center for Strategic and International Studies, 2004), p. 12.

5 Fareed Zakaria, *The Future of Freedom: Illiberal Democracy at Home and Abroad* (New York: W.W. Norton, 2003); and Paris, *At War's End*.

6 Barnett et al., "Peacebuilding."

7 Paris, *At War's End*; Chesterman, Ignatieff, and Thakur, *Making States Work*; Call with Hawkins Wyeth, *Building States to Build Peace*; and Simon Chesterman, *You, the People: The United Nations, Transitional Administration, and Statebuilding* (New York: Oxford University Press, 2004).

8 In this view, the first case of modern peacebuilding was the early United States, where the federalists invented new governance principles to confront the threats posed by factions and arbitrary power. For relevant discussions, see David Hendrickson, *Peace Pact: The Lost World of the American Founding* (Lawrence: University of Kansas Press, 2002); and Daniel Deudney, "The Philadelphian System: Sovereignty, Arms Control, and Balance of Power in the American States-Union, circa 1787–1961," *International Organization*, Vol. 49, No. 2 (Spring 1995), pp. 191–228.

9 My focus on postconflict activities suggests that there is a sharp break between the conflict and postconflict phases. Yet in many cases, conflict continues to define the "postconflict" stage. In these instances, republican peacebuilding, like any peacebuilding, will face a high degree of difficulty because of the need for some stability.

10 Anthony Giddens, *Sociology*, 2d ed. (New York: Polity, 1993), p. 309.

11 On inclusionary versus exclusionary institutions, see David Waldner, *State Building and Late Development* (Ithaca, N.Y.: Cornell University Press, 1999). See also Michael Mann's related distinction between infrastructural and despotic power. Mann, "The Autonomous Power of the State: Its Origins, Mechanisms, and Results," *Archives Europa Sociologica*, Vol. 25 (1984), p. 185.

12 For related arguments, see Paris, *At War's End*; Orr, "The United States as Nation Builder," p. 11; and Meierhenrich, "Forming States after Failure."

13 Michael Doyle and Nicholas Sambanis, "International Peacebuilding: A Theoretical and Quantitative Analysis," *American Political Science Review*, Vol. 94, No. 4 (December 2000), p. 779; and Page Fortna, "Inside and Out: Peacekeeping and the Duration of Peace after Civil and Interstate Wars," *International Studies Review*, Vol. 5, No. 4 (December 2003), p. 97.

14 On the procedural and substantive dimensions of legitimacy, see Mark Suchman, "Managing Legitimacy: Strategic and Institutional Approaches," *Academy of Management Review*, Vol. 20, No. 3 (1995), p. 517.

15 Political theorists debate the differences between liberalism and republicanism, the critical divides, and even whether they might be merged into either a liberal republicanism or a republican liberalism. See Richard Dagger, *Civic Virtues: Rights, Citizenship, and Republican Liberalism* (New York: Oxford University Press, 1997); Quentin Skinner, "The Republican Ideal of Political Liberty," in Gisela Bok, Quentin Skinner, and Maurizio Viroli, eds., *Machiavelli and Republicanism* (New York: Cambridge University Press, 1990), pp. 293–309; and Charles Taylor, "Cross-Purposes: The Liberal Communitarian Debate," in Nancy Rosenblum, ed., *Liberalism and the Moral Life* (Cambridge, Mass.: Harvard University Press, 1989), pp. 159–182.

16 For overviews of republican political theory, see Maurizio Viroli, *Republicanism* (New York: Hill and Wang, 2002); Maurizio Viroli, "Machiavelli and the Republican Idea of Politics," in Bok, Skinner, and Viroli, *Machiavelli and Republicanism*, pp. 143–171; Alan Patten, "The Republican Critique of Liberalism," *British Journal of Political Science*, Vol. 26, No. 1 (January 1996), p. 25; Skinner, "The Republican Ideal of Political Liberty"; Taylor, "Cross-Purposes"; Michael Sandel, "The Procedural Republic and the Unencumbered Self," *Political Theory*, Vol. 12, No. 1 (February 1984), p. 81; Dagger, *Civic Virtues*; and Philip Pettit, *Republicanism: A Theory of Freedom and Government* (New York: Oxford University Press, 1999).

17 Viroli, *Republicanism*, pp. 8, 11.

18 John Maynor, *Republicanism in the Modern World* (New York: Polity, 2003), p. 37; and Viroli, *Republicanism*, p. 41.

19 Quoted in Cass Sunstein, "The Enduring Legacy of Republicanism," in Stephen Elkin and Karol Soltan, eds., *A New Constitutionalism: Designing Political Institutions for a Good Society* (Chicago: University of Chicago Press, 1993), p. 181.

20 Quoted in Viroli, *Republicanism*, p. 58.

21 Bernard Manin, "On Legitimacy and Political Deliberation," *Political Theory*, Vol. 15, No. 3 (August 1987), p. 359; and Bernard Manin, Elly Stein, and Jane Mansbridge, "On Legitimacy and Political Deliberation," *Political Theory*, Vol. 15, No. 3 (August 1987), p. 338.

22 Sunstein, "The Enduring Legacy of Republicanism," p. 176. See also Pettit, *Republicanism: A Theory of Freedom and Government*, p. 130.

23 The literature on deliberative democracy offers a conception of deliberation that is related to, but goes considerably beyond, what I have in mind. The strong claim is that it is both desirable and possible to construct a nearly idealized communicative setting in which diverse groups listen patiently to each other, are willing to change their positions, and can eliminate even the most intractable differences. See Amy Guttman and Dennis Thompson, *Why Deliberative Democracy?* (Princeton, N.J.: Princeton University Press, 1996); James Bohman and William Rehg, *Deliberative Democracy: Essays on Reason and Politics* (Cambridge, Mass.: MIT Press, 1997); and James S. Fishkin and Peter Laslett, eds., *Debating Deliberative Democracy* (Malden, Mass.: Basil Blackwell, 2003). Among the criticisms of deliberative democracy are that the conditions under which it presumably works are so restrictive that few marriages would measure up; dialogue can harden positions and inflame conflict; sometimes decisions must be made before everyone's views can be acknowledged; and the weapons used to win an argument include not only logic but also character assassination, dirty tricks, and strategic action. See Ian Shapiro, "Enough of Deliberation: Politics Is About Interests and Power," in Stephen Macedo, ed., *Deliberative Politics: Essays on Democracy and Disagreement* (New York: Oxford University Press, 1999), pp. 28–38; and James Johnson, "Arguing for Deliberation: Some Skeptical Considerations," in Jon Elster, ed., *Deliberative Democracy* (New York: Cambridge University Press, 1998), pp. 161–184.

24 Sunstein, "The Enduring Legacy of Republicanism," p. 176. This view informs a distinctive meaning of corruption—the failure to subordinate private interests to public interests, and thus the desire to use politics for private gain.

25 James Fearon, "Deliberation as Discussion," in Elster, *Deliberative Democracy*, p. 54; Jon Elster, "Deliberation and Constitution Making," in Elster, *Deliberative Democracy*, p. 104; Pettit, *Republicanism: A Theory of Freedom and Government*, pp. 188–190; Thomas Christiano, "The Significance of Public Deliberation," in Bohman and Rehg, *Deliberative Democracy: Essays on Reason and Politics*, pp. 243–277; and Shelley Burtt, "The Politics of Virtue Today: A Critique and a Proposal," *American Political Science Review*, Vol. 87, No. 2 (June 1993), p. 361. Publicity is not always preferable to secrecy: individuals might be deterred from changing their minds or adopting more flexible positions if they believe that there

is an audience that might judge them harshly; and politicians are infamous for outbidding each other by staking out extreme positions.

26 Maynor, *Republicanism in the Modern World*, p. 125; and Manin, "On Legitimacy and Political Deliberation," p. 359.

27 Manin, "On Legitimacy and Political Deliberation"; and Pettit, *Republicanism: A Theory of Freedom and Government*, p. 169. Deliberation requires and is nearly synonymous with civic virtue. Recently, communitarians have pushed the concept of civic virtue in their desire to counteract the perceived decline of a sense of community. Although republicans agree that civic virtue is necessary for the development of community, their concept is more restrictive, related to the goal of minimizing arbitrary power, and increasing the ability of individuals to listen respectfully to the views of others and to appreciate how their actions affect society. Maynor, *Republicanism in the Modern World*, p. 56.

28 Cass Sunstein, "Beyond the Republican Revival," *Yale Law Journal*, Vol. 97, No. 8 (June 1988), p. 1549; and Frank Michelman, "Law's Republic," *Yale Law Journal*, Vol. 97, No. 8 (June 1988), p. 1528.

29 Charles Tilly, *Coercion, Capital, and European States, A.D. 990–1992* (Malden, Mass.: Blackwell, 1990), p. 206.

30 Mark Peceny and William Stanley, "Liberal Social Reconstruction and the Resolution of Civil Wars in Central America," *International Organization*, Vol. 55, No. 1 (March 2001), p. 149.

31 Albrecht Schnabel and Hans-Georg Ehrhart, eds., *Security Sector Reform and Postconflict Peacebuilding* (New York: United Nations University Press, 2006).

32 This applies not only to military but also to police forces. See Charles Call, "Police Reform and Political Reconciliation: The Case of El Salvador," workshop on democratization and internal security, MacArthur Consortium on International Peace and Cooperation, Stanford University, Stanford, California, February 1996.

33 Summary of Conference and Workshop on the Political Economy of Governance Reform, Copenhagen, Denmark, June 23–24, 2004, hosted by the World Bank's Public Sector Governance Group and the Danish Ministry of Foreign Affairs (emphasis in original).

34 For national-level activities, see Priscilla Hayner, *Unspeakable Truths: Facing the Challenge of Truth Commissions* (New York: Routledge, 2002). For national and local activities, see the War-Torn Societies Project, http://www.wsp-international.org.

35 Republicanism also differs from liberalism on the issue of rights. Liberalism embraces the language of universal, natural rights, holding that because of their common humanity all individuals have basic human rights that are intended to protect their autonomy and dignity. Republicanism views rights as emerging from the local community. Accordingly, because different communities have different histories and deliberative processes, they are likely to have different conceptions of rights, different understanding of how these rights are connected to the good life, and different views of which institutions and informal norms are necessary to protect them. Although different communities might converge on a common conception of basic human rights, this comes from human agreement, not by baptism.

36 Alexander Hamilton, James Madison, and John Jay, *The Federalist Papers* (Cutchogue, N.Y.: Buccaneer, 1961), pp. 315–317, cited in Joshua Cohen, "Deliberation and Democratic Legitimacy," in Bohman and Rehg, *Deliberative Democracy: Essays on Reason and Politics*, p. 89 n. 28.

37 Machiavelli, codex 5.59.5, quoted in Viroli, *Republicanism*, p. 4.

38 Ibid., p. 6.

39 For a general review of issues concerning elections after conflict, see Benjamin Reilly, "Postconflict Elections: Constraints and Dangers," *International Peacekeeping*, Vol. 9, No. 2 (Summer 2002), p. 118; and Terrence Lyons, *Demilitarizing*

Politics: Elections on the Uncertain Road to Peace (Boulder, Colo.: Lynne Rienner, 2005). For the possibility of democracy among nondemocrats after conflict, see Leonard Wantchekon, "The Paradox of 'Warlord' Democracy: A Theoretical Investigation," *American Political Science Review*, Vol. 98, No. 1 (February 2004), pp. 17–33.

40 The legitimacy of these unelected bodies is further complicated when they are established either in the presence of or by international peacebuilders, creating the local perception that international actors have profoundly shaped the composition of these bodies and thus compromising their legitimacy. This is one reason why peacebuilders are anxious to hold elections as quickly as possible.

41 Bonn, formally known as the "Agreement on Provisional Arrangements in Afghanistan Pending the Reestablishment of Permanent Government Institutions," was brokered by the four major Afghan factions and thus fell far short of any measure of representativeness.

42 For discussions of the loya jirga, see Daud Saba and Omar Zakhilwal, *Security with a Human Face: Challenges and Responsibilities*, Afghanistan National Human Development Report, 2004 (Islamabad: United Nations Development Program, 2005), pp. 124–127; J. Alexander Thier and Jarat Chopra, "The Road Ahead: Political and Institutional Reconstruction in Afghanistan," *Third World Quarterly*, Vol. 23, No. 5 (October 2002), pp. 893–907; Antonio Giustozzi, " 'Good' State vs. 'Bad' Warlords? A Critique of Statebuilding Strategies in Afghanistan," Working Paper Series No. 51 (London: Crisis States Programme, London School of Economics, October 2004); and J. Alexander Thier, "The Politics of Peacebuilding Year One: From Bonn to Kabul," in Antonio Donini, Karin Wermester, and Norah Niland, eds., *Nation Building Unraveled? Aid, Peace, and Justice in Afghanistan* (Bloomfield, Conn.: Kumarian, 2004), pp. 39–60. For a critical commentary, particularly on the centralization of power in the hands of a few cliques, see International Crisis Group (ICG), *Afghanistan: The Constitutional Loya Jirga*, Asia Briefing No. 29 (Kabul/Brussels: ICG, December 12, 2003), p. 11; and Chris Johnson and Jolyon Leslie, *Afghanistan: The Mirage of Peace* (New York: Zed, 2004), chaps. 7, 8.

43 For discussions on the lack of planning, see George Packer, *The Assassin's Gate: America in Iraq* (New York: Farrar, Straus and Giroux, 2005); Larry Diamond, *Squandered Victory: The American Occupation and the Bungled Effort to Bring Democracy to Iraq* (New York: Times Books, 2005); and James Fallows, "Blind into Baghdad," *Atlantic Monthly*, Vol. 293, No. 1 (January/February 2004), pp. 53–74.

44 Diamond, *Squandered Victory*, pp. 28, 34–35, 37, 42.

45 Ibid., p. 246.

46 Ibid., pp. 79–80.

47 Ibid., p. 251.

48 Ibid., p. 255.

49 Ibid., especially p. 295. Although Diamond is sympathetic with the charge that the first sin was the invasion, he nevertheless says that the United States might have recovered had it "asked the UN to assume the responsibility for organizing a national conference in July 2003 to choose an interim government; if, instead of sanctioning what became an Anglo-American occupation of Iraq, [UN Security Council] Resolution 1483 had provided for a transfer of authority (at least over most matters) to an Iraqi interim government, which would then have had international recognition, the political corner might have been turned." Ibid., p. 302. These initial moves, moreover, might have either relieved the pressure by the Shia for elections or created a movement for holding local elections before national elections. Ibid., p. 310.

50 These three elements draw from G. John Ikenberry, *After Victory: Institutions,*

Strategic Restraint, and the Rebuilding of Order after Major Wars (Princeton, N.J.: Princeton University Press, 2001), pp. 30–31.

51 For discussions of how constitutions are akin to institutions that constrain actors, see Barry Weingast, "Constitutions as Governance Structures: The Political Foundations of Secure Markets," *Journal of Institutional and Theoretical Economics*, Vol. 149, No. 1 (1993), pp. 287–311.

52 For a discussion of power sharing, see Donald Rothchild and Philip Roeder, "Power Sharing as an Impediment to Peace and Democracy," in Roeder and Rothchild, *Sustainable Peace*, pp. 29–50.

53 The literature on constitutionalism is increasingly attentive to the relationship between postconflict and transitional settings, on the one hand, and the most functional electoral design, on the other. See Andrew Reynolds, "Constitutional Medicine," *Journal of Democracy*, Vol. 16, No. 1 (January 2005), pp. 54–68; and Benjamin Reilly, "Does the Choice of Electoral System Promote Democracy? The Gap between Theory and Reality," in Roeder and Rothchild, *Sustainable Peace*, pp. 159–172.

54 Donald Rothchild and Philip Roeder, "Dilemmas of Statebuilding in Divided Societies," in Roeder and Rothchild, *Sustainable Peace*, pp. 16–18. Roeder contrasts power sharing with power dividing in ways consistent with republicanism's emphasis on divided power. Roeder, "Power Dividing as an Alternative to Ethnic Power Sharing," in Roeder and Rothchild, *Sustainable Peace*, pp. 51–82.

55 Neil Kritz, "Constitution-Making Process: Lesson for Iraq," testimony before the U.S. Senate Committee on the Judiciary on Constitutionalism, Human Rights, and the Rule of Law in Iraq, June 25, 2003, http://www.usip.org/aboutus/congress/testimony/2003/0625_kritz.htm; Devra Moehler, "Public Participation and Support for the Constitution in Uganda," paper presented at Cornell Social Science Seminar, Cornell University, Ithaca, New York, November 2003; and Vivien Hart, "Constitution-Making and the Transformation of Conflict," *Peace and Change*, Vol. 26, No. 2 (April 2001), pp. 153–176.

56 Kritz, "Constitution-Making Process."

57 Saba and Zakhilwal, *Security with a Human Face*, pp. 127–130.

58 ICG, *Unmaking Iraq: A Constitutional Process Gone Awry*, Policy Briefing No. 19 (Amman/Brussels: ICG, September 26, 2005), p. 1. See also Nathan Brown, "Iraq's Constitutional Process Plunges Ahead," Policy Outlook series (Washington, D.C.: Carnegie Endowment for International Peace, July 2005).

59 Diamond, *Squandered Victory*, chap. 7; and Jonathan Morrow, *Iraq's Constitutional Process II: An Opportunity Lost*, Special Report No. 155 (Washington, D.C.: United States Institute of Peace, November 2005).

60 For a discussion of the relationship between the constitution process and the prospects of postconflict stability and democracy in Liberia, see Amos Sawyer, *Beyond Plunder: Toward Democratic Governance in Liberia* (Boulder, Colo.: Lynne Rienner, 2005).

61 For statements on how the local institutions and informal norms and rules limit what peacebuilders can accomplish, see Francis Fukuyama, *State-Building: Governance and World Order in the Twenty-first Century* (Ithaca, N.Y.: Cornell University Press, 2004); and Christopher Coyne, "The Institutional Prerequisites for Postconflict Reconstruction," *Review of Austrian Economics*, Vol. 18, Nos. 3/4 (December 2005), pp. 325–342.

62 ICG, "Liberia and Sierra Leone: Rebuilding Failed States," Africa Report No. 87 (Dakar/Brussels: ICG, December 8, 2004), pp. 21–22. The Accra accords of 2003 and the Lomé agreement of 1999, which ended the Liberian and Sierra Leone civil wars, respectively, might have rewarded and encouraged thuggery.

63 For a discussion of aid as leverage, see James Boyce, *Investing in Peace* (New York: Oxford University Press, 2002).

64 Nicholas Wood, "Can an Iron Fist Put Power in Bosnia's Hands?" *New York Times*, November 5, 2005.
65 Although various authors advocate a greater role for a more permanent international presence, they have failed to consider adequately the restraints on power. See, for instance, Stephen D. Krasner, "Sharing Sovereignty: New Institutions for Collapsed and Failing States," *International Security*, Vol. 29, No. 2 (Fall 2004), pp. 85–120; and James D. Fearon and David D. Laitin, "Neotrusteeship and the Problem of Weak States," *International Security*, Vol. 28, No. 4 (Spring 2004), pp. 5–43.
66 Chesterman, *You, the People*, pp. 128–134; and Wood, "Can an Iron Fist Put Power in Bosnia's Hands?"
67 In a report on Liberia and Sierra Leone, the International Crisis Group writes that peacebuilders possess an "operational checklist" that does not recognize the underlying political dynamics. ICG, "Liberia and Sierra Leone."
68 Albert Hirschman, *Essays in Trespassing: Economics to Politics and Beyond* (New York: Cambridge University Press, 1981).
69 For a related discussion of Peter Evans's concept of "institutional monocropping," see Evans, "Development as Institutional Change: The Pitfalls of Monocropping and the Potentials of Deliberation," *Studies in Comparative International Development*, Vol. 38, No. 4 (Winter 2004), pp. 30–53.
70 Noah Feldman, *What We Owe Iraq: War and the Ethics of Nation Building* (Princeton, N.J.: Princeton University Press, 2004), p. 69.
71 Diamond, *Squandered Victory*.
72 Chesterman, *You, the People*, pp. 135–143. See also Jarat Chopra, "The UN's Kingdom of East Timor," *Survival*, Vol. 42, No. 3 (September 2000), pp. 27–40.
73 Larry Diamond, "Lessons from Iraq," *Journal of Democracy*, Vol. 16, No. 1 (January 2005), p. 15; and Chesterman, *You, the People*, p. 153.
74 Diamond, *Squandered Victory*, p. 297.
75 Chesterman, *You, the People*.
76 Feldman, *What We Owe Iraq*, pp. 66–68.
77 Charles Lindblom, "The Science of 'Muddling Through,'" *Public Administration Review*, Vol. 19, No. 2 (1959), pp. 79–88.

9   Humanitarianism transformed

The global response to the devastation caused by the tsunami of December 26, 2004, was an extraordinary display of humanitarian action. Within hours of the disaster scores of nongovernmental organizations (NGOs) were providing life-saving medical attention, shelter, and water. Soon thereafter, though, compassion became a status category. Bristling from accusations that they were not doing enough, states began to outbid one another in order to avoid censure and gain stature. In addition to an unprecedented outpouring of financial support, states temporarily gave their militaries humanitarian assignments. The United States dispatched the U.S.S. *Lincoln* to the coast of the Indonesian province of Aceh to perform search-and-rescue missions and deliver relief. Businesses gave in-kind and financial contributions, and established links on their Web sites where customers could, with a click of a button, join the relief effort.

This global mobilization was made possible by the great expansion of the humanitarian system since the end of the cold war.[1] Many states have developed humanitarian units within their foreign and defense ministries and have increasingly accepted the legitimacy of humanitarian intervention. Official assistance skyrocketed from $2 billion in 1990 to $6 billion in 2000. A growing number of international organizations, including the World Bank, provide some form of assistance. There has been an explosion of non-governmental organizations dedicated to some aspect of humanitarian action. Perhaps more impressive than their proliferation is their growing sophistication. NGOs once operated with a relatively slow-moving machinery and were staffed by individuals who were expected to learn on the job. Now, however, most prominent agencies have a system of global positioning and delivery that allows trained professionals to get assistance quickly where it is needed. Médecins sans frontières (MSF), for example, grew from a two-room office in the 1970s into an international network of 19 semi-independent branches, with a combined annual budget of $500 million, running programs in over 70 countries, with 2,000 international and 15,000 national staff. Finally, the very meaning of humanitarianism has expanded. Humanitarian action was formerly recognized as a separate sphere of activity, defined by the impartial relief to victims of manmade and natural disasters; now the term, according to many, includes human rights, access to medicine, economic development, democracy promotion, and even building responsible states.

This article reflects on two defining features of this transformation of humanitarianism: the purpose of humanitarianism is becoming politicized, and the organization of humanitarianism is becoming institutionalized. Once upon a time humanitarian agencies used to define themselves largely in opposition to "politics."[2] Certainly they recognized that humanitarianism was the offspring of politics, that their activities had political consequences, and that they were inextricably part of the political world. Yet the widely accepted definition of humanitarianism—the impartial, independent, and neutral provision of relief to those in immediate danger of harm—emerged in opposition to a particular meaning of politics and helped to depoliticize relief-oriented activities.[3]

Many activities might alleviate suffering and improve life circumstances, including protection of human rights and economic development; but any actions that aspire to restructure underlying social relations are inherently political. Humanitarianism provides relief; it offers to save individuals, but not to eliminate the underlying causes that placed them at risk. Viewed in this way, humanitarianism plays a distinctive role in the international sacrificial order.[4] All international orders have winners and losers and thus require their quota of victims. Humanitarianism interrupts this selection process by saving lives, thus reducing the number of sacrifices. However, it does not aspire to alter that order; that is the job of politics.

Humanitarianism's original principles were also a reaction to politics and designed to obstruct this "moral pollutant."[5] The principle of humanity commands attention to all humankind and inspires cosmopolitanism. The principle of impartiality demands that assistance be based on need and not discriminate on the basis of nationality, race, religious belief, gender, political opinions, or other considerations.[6] The principles of neutrality and independence also inoculate humanitarianism from politics. Relief agencies are best able to perform their life-saving activities only if they are untouched by state interests and partisan agendas.[7] Neutrality involves refraining from taking part in hostilities or from any action that benefits or disadvantages either party to a conflict. Neutrality is both an end and a means to an end because it helps relief agencies gain access to populations at risk. Independence demands that assistance should not be connected to any of the parties directly involved in the conflict or who have a stake in the outcome. Accordingly, many agencies either refused or limited their reliance on government funding if the donors had a stake in the outcome. The principles of humanity, impartiality, neutrality, and independence thus served to depoliticize humanitarian action and create a "humanitarian space" insulated from politics.

Yet these Maginot line principles defending humanitarianism from politics crumbled during the 1990s as humanitarianism's agenda ventured beyond relief and into the political world, and agencies began working alongside, and with, states. During the 1990s humanitarian agencies began to accept the idea that they might try to eliminate the root causes of conflicts that place individuals at risk; this vision swept them up into a process of transformation and into the world of politics. Humanitarian agencies and states began to share agendas. States became more willing to act in the name of humanitarianism, fund relief operations, use their diplomatic and political power to advance humanitarian causes, authorize military troops to deliver relief, and consider the legitimacy of humanitarian intervention and the protection of civilian populations. Humanitarian organizations were torn by the growing presence of states, acknowledging their potential contribution but worrying about the costs to their principles. Because, in their view, there are no humanitarian solutions to humanitarian emergencies, many lobbied states to apply military and political muscle to stop the bloodletting. Relief agencies working in war zones had to confront warlords and militias that demanded a king's ransom for the assistance that was made necessary by their conflict and their intentional targeting of civilians; agencies occasionally sought outside intervention to provide armed protection and to help deliver relief. Yet the growing willingness of humanitarian organizations to work alongside states potentially undermined their neutrality and independence. Humanitarian principles were completely shattered in places like Kosovo, Afghanistan, and Iraq, where many agencies were funded by the very governments that were combatants and thus partly responsible for the emergency. The ever-present fear that fraternizing between politics and humanitarianism would corrupt this sacred idea and undermine agencies' ability to provide relief was becoming a daily reality. Reflecting the anxieties unleashed by this mixing of politics and principle, commentators spoke of humanitarianism in "crisis" and warned of the dangers of "supping with the devil," "drinking from the poisoned chalice," and "sleeping with the enemy."[8]

Institutionalization represents another aspect of the transformation of humanitarianism. Before the 1990s there were relatively few agencies that provided relief; they had few sustained interactions; and they hardly considered establishing, revising, or maintaining principles of action, codes of conduct, or professional standards that would define the boundaries of the field. In the field they operated according to very few standard procedures and drew very little from scientific knowledge as they set up, often quite literally, soup kitchens. Their operations were frequently staffed by individuals with little or no experience, who jumped into the fray believing that all they needed was a can-do attitude and good intentions.

Over the 1990s humanitarianism became more recognized as a field, with more donors, deliverers, and regulators of a growing sphere of action. Various developments and pressures propelled this institutionalization. The influx of new agencies, marching to their own drums, created confusion on the ground. Donors, who were providing more funds, expected recipients to be accountable and demonstrate effectiveness. Rwanda was a turning point.[9] A flood of agencies—many there simply to fly the flag and impress prospective donors— were feeding the architects of the genocide in camps in Zaire, fueling their rearmament, and potentially causing more harm than good. The Rwandan tragedy and other events caused the entire community to undergo painful introspection that raised troubling questions regarding the legitimacy and effectiveness of humanitarian action. States raised similar questions, leaving aid organizations worried about their funding base. In response, the field began to institutionalize. It became increasingly rationalized, standardizing basic codes of conduct for intervention, developing accountability mechanisms, and calculating the consequences of actions. It became bureaucratized, developing precise rules that ideally could be applied across different situations. It became professionalized, developing doctrines, specialized areas of training, and career paths.

The humanitarian sector welcomed elements of this institutionalization because they helped to standardize expectations, ease coordination in the field, enhance efficiency, and improve the quality of care to more populations. Yet other features were distressing, potentially changing not simply the organization of humanitarian action, but its very character. Many organizations were now demonstrating commonplace interests in self-preservation and survival, at times allowing these interests to overshadow their principled commitments. The development of standardized templates and guidelines made them less able to recognize and respond to local needs. Rising concerns with efficiency in getting "deliverables" to "clients" hinted of a growing corporate culture; participants increasingly worried about protecting their "brand" and referring to the field as an "industry," a "business," a "sector," and an "enterprise." There were palpable fears that material and discursive borders that distinguished humanitarian agencies from commercial firms and even military units were disintegrating. If commercial firms were really more efficient at saving lives, and if nonprofits were acting like corporate entities, then exactly what distinguished the two? Politicization and institutionalization, each in its own way, called into question the very marks of distinction of humanitarian action.

Drawing from various strands of organizational theory, I consider the causes behind the expansion and politicization of the purpose of humanitarianism and the institutionalization of the field. Various global forces created new opportunity structures for humanitarian action: states gave more generously because it furthered their foreign policy interests; there was a surge of emergencies in the early 1990s; and a change in the sovereignty regime reduced the barriers to intervention. Although the general trend was toward expansion and politicization, humanitarian organizations did not respond uniformly to these opportunities. To understand this variation in response requires a consideration of, first, the organization's identity and its initial understanding of the relationship between humanitarianism and politics, and, second, its dependence on others for symbolic and material resources. Although there were pockets of resistance to this politicization, arguably most existing and newly established organizations accepted these changes because they operated with a definition of humanitarian action that interfaced easily with politics and were dependent on states for their financing. The field's institutionalization was largely triggered by challenges to its legitimacy and effectiveness, challenges from donors and participants, challenges that threatened its bottom line, and challenges that were addressed by making the field more rational, bureaucratic, and professional.

I then examine some of the effects of this transformation on humanitarian action. Much of the discussion of the effects focuses on politicization, that is, how the growing involvement by states is potentially compromising or distorting the essence of humanitarian action, whether these changes have been generally desirable, pragmatic, or self-destructive, and whether it is possible or even desirable to put the political genie back in the bottle.[10] But the possible effects extend beyond what humanitarian agencies do to include what they are. Any discussion of effects, of course, turns on some baseline understanding of humanitarian action. Such an analysis does not need to essentialize humanitarianism, to suggest that there was a settled or fixed meaning that existed for decades until disrupted by the post–cold war period. Nor does such an analysis provide an evaluative judgment as to whether these changes are necessarily good, reasonable under the circumstances, or reckless. Instead, such an analysis merely needs to ask what was the general understanding of humanitarian action prior to the 1990s, consider how politicization and institutionalization has shaken that understanding, and, most importantly, explore whether such changes have potentially undermined the cornerstone principle of impartial relief.

Although humanitarianism is now firmly on the global agenda, the same cannot be said for academic research. Most research directly related to humanitarian action is produced by specialized agencies such as the Overseas Development Institute's Humanitarian Policy Group; it is almost always directed at the policy community. Some social science research is related to humanitarian action, including the literatures on humanitarian intervention, civil wars, democracy building, refugee studies, and peacekeeping. However, there has been remarkably little consideration of humanitarianism as an object of research. The body of the essay points to various lines of inquiry, and in the conclusion I link my account of the transformation of humanitarianism to a broader research agenda that concerns the relationship between international nongovernmental organizations and world order, including the purpose of humanitarian action and its functions in global politics.

Causes of transformation

Environmental forces played a central role in transforming humanitarianism. Several important developments encouraged humanitarian agencies to move away from relief alone and toward the transformation of local structures, and to become more willing to work alongside and with states. Such developments led to its politicization. Yet not all agencies responded uniformly to these opportunities; consequently, I examine features of the organization and its relationship to the environment to help to explain this variation. Environmental developments also played an important role in shaping the institutionalization of humanitarianism. Similarly, although those in the sector had their own reasons for rationalizing, bureaucratizing, and professionalizing their organizations, pressures from donors and new international standards of legitimacy also played a critical role in institutionalizing humanitarianism. Yet not all agencies responded uniformly, and we need to understand why.

Expansion and politicization

Four global processes created new opportunity structures that foregrounded the "civilian" as an object of concern.[11] Geopolitical shifts associated with the end of the cold war and the demise of the Soviet Union increased the demand for humanitarian action in several ways.[12] There appeared to be more humanitarian crises than ever before.[13] Whether in fact there were more crises or whether great powers were now willing to recognize populations at risk because their policies were no longer the immediate cause, the emergencies were on the international agenda.[14] As states paid more attention to them, they linked these populations at risk to an expanding discourse of security. During the cold war the UN Security Council defined threats to peace and security as disputes between states that had become or might become militarized, conflicts involving the great powers, and general threats to global stability.[15] After the cold war, and in reaction to the growing perception that domestic conflict and civil wars were leaving hundreds of thousands of people at risk, creating mass flight, and destabilizing entire regions, the Security Council authorized interventions on the grounds that these conflicts challenged regional and international security. Responding to both the post–cold war humanitarian emergencies and the growing prominence of the Security Council in this domain, the General Assembly passed a watershed resolution in 1992 that made the UN the new coordinating body for humanitarian action.[16]

States also warmed to the idea of humanitarian action. They were increasingly generous. Even more impressive was their increasing willingness to support operations whose stated function was to protect civilians at risk, and even to consider the legitimacy of humanitarian intervention.[17] States also began to treat humanitarian action as an instrument of their strategic and foreign policy goals. Since 9/11 many states, including the United States, have viewed counterterrorism and humanitarianism as crimefighting partners. In 2001 former Secretary of State Colin Powell told a gathering of NGOs that "just as surely as our diplomats and military, American NGOs are out there [in Afghanistan] serving and sacrificing on the frontlines of freedom. NGOs are such a force multiplier for us, such an important part of our combat team."[18] States also discovered that humanitarian action could help them avoid more costly interventions. For instance, the major powers authorized the United Nations High Commissioner on Refugees (UNHCR) to deliver humanitarian relief in Bosnia in part because they wanted to relieve the growing pressure for a military intervention. Regardless of their motives, states were providing new opportunities for humanitarian action.

The second development that propelled the encounter between politics and humanitarianism was the emergence of "complex humanitarian emergencies," that is, a "conflict-related humanitarian disaster involving a high degree of breakdown and social dislocation and, reflecting this condition, requiring a system-wide aid response from the international community."[19] These emergencies, which seemed to be proliferating around the world, are characterized by a combustible mixture of state failure, refugee flight, militias, warrior refugees, and populations at risk from violence, disease, and hunger. Such situations created a demand for new sorts of interventions and conflict management tools. Relief agencies were attempting to distribute food, water, and medicine in war zones and were frequently forced to bargain with militias, warlords, and hoodlums for access to populations in need. In situations of extreme violence and lawlessness they lobbied foreign governments and the United Nations to consider authorizing a protection force that could double as bodyguard and relief distributor.These emergencies also attracted a range of NGOs.[20] Relief agencies that were delivering emergency assistance, human rights organizations aspiring to protect rights and create a rule of law, and development organizations keen to sponsor sustainable growth began to interact and to take responsibility for the same populations. The growing interaction between different kinds of agencies that hailed from different sectors encouraged a relief–rights–development linkage within a humanitarian discourse that became tied to the construction of modern, legitimate, democratic states.[21] As international actors began to think about the causes of and solutions to these emergencies, "humanitarian" came to include a wider range of practices and goals.

A third factor contributing to politicization was the political economy of funding. Although private contributions increased, they paled in comparison to official assistance. Between 1990 and 2000, aid levels rose from 2.1 to $5.9 billion. Moreover, as a percentage of official development assistance, humanitarian aid rose from an average of 5.8 percent between 1989 and 1993 to 10.5 percent in 2000.[22] A few donors were responsible for much of this increase, and they also now comprise an oligopoly. The United States is the lead donor by a factor of three. In 1999, for instance, its outlays exceeded the total assistance of twelve large Western donors. Between 1995 and 1997 it provided 20 percent of total assistance; in the following three years its contribution rose to 30 percent. The second largest donor is the European Community Humanitarian Organization (ECHO), followed by the United Kingdom, several European countries, Canada, and Japan. Although various motives fueled this increase in giving, many states expected either something in return or evidence that their money was being well spent.

Finally, a change in the normative and legal environment also coaxed humanitarianism into the political world. State sovereignty was no longer sacrosanct; rather, it was becoming conditional on states behaving according to particular codes of conduct, honoring a "responsibility to protect" their societies, and having attributes such as the rule of law, markets, and democratic principles.[23] Their legitimacy became tied to their having the rule of law, markets, and democratic principles. These developments created a normative space for external intervention and encouraged a growing range of actors to expand their assistance activities. In some cases aid agencies were supposed to provide immediate relief during conflict situations, while in others, to eliminate the root causes of conflict and create legitimate states. Regardless of the pretext, the new normative environment greased the tracks for more wide-ranging interventions.[24]

A flourishing human rights agenda also left its mark. The logic of relief and the logic of rights share important elements: they place the human citizen and humanity at the fore; they use the language of empowerment in attempting to help the weak; and they reject power.[25] That said, they also demonstrate divisions; the relief community will nearly always privilege survival over freedom, while the rights community is sometimes willing to use relief as an instrument of rights, that is, make relief conditional on the observance of human rights—a move many relief agencies view as nearly incomprehensible.[26] In any event, the fast-growing human rights movement pulled humanitarianism from the margins toward the center of the international policy agenda, and many relief agencies, increasingly adopting the language of rights, were glad to ride its coattails.[27]

Growing cosmopolitanism was also a transformative factor, for it underpins humanitarianism. Cosmopolitanism maintains that each person is of equal moral worth and that in the "justification of choices one's choices one must take the prospects of everyone affected equally into account."[28] The principle of impartiality presumes that all those at risk, regardless of their identity, deserve equal attention and consideration. The desire to help those who are suffering regardless of place means that borders do not define the limits of obligations. This cosmopolitan ethos, however, leads to different schools of thought in humanitarianism, schools that can be in tension.[29] Some humanitarians believe aid should be restricted to the victims of man-made and natural disasters; this branch emerged in the mid-nineteenth century and is most closely associated with the International Committee for the Red Cross (ICRC). Another branch of humanitarianism extends assistance to all those at risk and imagines eliminating the conditions that are hypothesized to render populations vulnerable.[30] As one aid worker wrote, "[I]n terms of the destruction of human life, what difference is there between the wartime bombing of a civilian population and the distribution of ineffective medicines during a pandemic that is killing millions of people?"[31] If individuals are at risk because of authoritarian and repressive policies, then humanitarian organizations must be prepared to fight for human rights and

democratic reforms. If individuals are at risk because of poverty and depriv-
ation, then they must be prepared to promote development. If regional and
domestic conflicts are the source of violence against individuals, then they
must try their hand at conflict resolution and attempt to eliminate the underlying causes of conflict.

Variation in response

Although these changes in global politics created new openings for an
expanded meaning of humanitarianism, aid agencies were not uniformly
receptive. Many, including the IRC and Oxfam, were ready, willing, and able
to capitalize on new openings. They saw virtue in expanding their operations
to help the powerless, and instead of being satisfied to help the "well-fed
dead," they could eliminate the root causes of conflict. Other organizations
made a pragmatic decision to become more political, though they were
cautious about every step and mindful of possible consequences. Still others
clung to their principles and resisted what they viewed as the siren of politics.
The ICRC and MSF fought the international currents and stuck to their
"first principles."[32]

Two factors account for much of this variance. One was the congruence
between the organizational culture and these new openings. Humanitarian
organizations can be sorted into two types—Dunantist and Wilsonian—
according to their understanding of the relationship between politics and
humanitarianism.[33]

Named after Henry Dunant, the patriarch of modern humanitarianism,[34]
Dunantist organizations define humanitarianism as the neutral, independent,
and impartial provision of relief to victims of conflict and believe that
humanitarianism and politics must be segregated. In general, Dunantist
organizations, which are often accused of seeing themselves as the "high
priests" of humanitarianism, fear that the relaxation of their founding principles or expansion of their mandate will open the floodgates to politics and
endanger humanitarianism.

Wilsonian organizations, so named because they follow in the footsteps of
Woodrow Wilson's belief that is was possible and desirable to transform
political, economic, and cultural structures so that they liberated individuals
and produced peace and progress, desire to attack the root causes that leave
populations at risk. Although many of the most famous members of this
camp, including Save the Children, Oxfam, and Word Vision International,
originated in wartime and thus concentrated on rescuing populations at
risk, they expanded into development and other activities designed to assist
marginalized populations. Over time they also undertook advocacy—like
a growing number of human rights organizations that also belong to this
camp. Agencies involved in restoring and fostering economic livelihoods also
express a Wilsonian orientation. Wilsonian organizations are certainly political, at least according to the Dunantist perspective; however, even those who

have subscribed to a transformational agenda present themselves as apolitical to the extent that they claim to act according to universal values and avoid partisan politics.

Organizations' understandings of the relationship between humanitarianism and politics help to explain their response to the transformations of the 1990s. The greater the discrepancy between organizational culture and environmental pressures, the more an organization will resist change for fear of political contamination; the greater the congruence, the more it will conform because such conformity will not threaten the organization's identity. MSF and ICRC, the two best known Dunantist organizations, spent much of the 1990s unsuccessfully attempting to police the borders between humanitarianism and politics. Wilsonian organizations not only capitalized on these openings, they frequently lobbied for them. Many humanitarian international organizations such as United Nations High Committee for Reform (UNHCR) exploited these changes in sovereignty to venture carefully into domestic space while claiming that they were not being political because they shunned any involvement in partisan politics. In fact, UNHCR actively lobbied for these changes by encouraging states to embrace the humanitarian agenda on the grounds that this principled position would further international peace and security.[35]

The gap between the moral and organizational mandate also may have contributed to the expanding purpose of humanitarian action. Organizations may have felt the need to expand in order to resolve the contradiction between their broad aspirational goals and the more narrowly circumscribed rules that limit their action.[36] Humanitarian organizations are empowered by moral claims or aspirations. Limited organizational structures make it impossible to fulfill these mandates, creating a reason for expansion into new areas. In attempting to relieve suffering, it is natural to aim for more than temporary relief, that is, for eliminating the conditions that produce a demand for humanitarian services.[37] For instance, before the 1980s UNHCR leaped into action only after populations crossed an international border. Yet many UNHCR staff bristled at these restrictions, wanting to take on a preventive role. In the 1980s UNHCR began trying to prevent refugee flows—to get at their "root causes"—and to lobby for "state responsibility."[38] From there it was a small step for UNHCR to become involved in eliminating the causes of flight and ensuring that repatriated refugees stayed at home; toward that end, it began promoting human rights, the rule of law, and economic development.

Finally, resource dependence helps to explain organizations' different responses to a broader definition of humanitarian action.[39] Humanitarian organizations do not survive by good intentions alone. They also need resources to fund their staff and programs; these resources are controlled by others. The willingness of others to fund organizations' humanitarian activities is contingent, in part, on their perceived legitimacy and whether they are viewed as acting according to the supporting community's values.[40]

Existing organizations, especially those that were culturally inclined to expand, thus had every incentive to move in directions that were directly rewarded by states. Development organizations are exemplary here. By the end of the 1980s, development as a project had become increasingly discredited. Humanitarianism handed these agencies a new function and sense of purpose; they became necessary for post-conflict reconstruction and structural prevention—central to humanitarian action and international and human security.[41] Newly established organizations, some humanitarian and some less so, found it advantageous to present themselves and their activities as quintessentially humanitarian. Existing agencies also were rewarded by expanding their activities. For instance, by becoming the lead humanitarian agency, UNHCR was in a position not only to expand its responsibilities, but also to demonstrate its relevance to the very states who paid the bills.[42]

Expansion and institutionalization

Until the 1990s, humanitarianism barely existed as a field. There were only a handful of major relief agencies, including the ICRC, International Federation of the Red Cross, MSF, and various organizations such as Save the Children and Oxfam that began as relief agencies, moved into development, and then developed an emergency response capacity (though generally not adopting the discourse of humanitarianism). Although these agencies shared broad principles, such as humanity, impartiality, neutrality, and independence, there was no concerted effort to establish codes of conduct and standards of behavior to regulate the field and define membership. Those who participated in relief work treated it more as a craft than as a profession because, in the main, they did not claim that their qualifications derived from specialized knowledge, doctrine, or training, and did not see this as their life's work.

Yet in the 1990s humanitarianism became a field, with regular interactions among the members, an increase in the information and knowledge that members had to consider, a greater reliance on specialized knowledge, and a collective awareness that they were involved in a common enterprise. The field was becoming rationalized, aspiring to develop: methodologies for calculating results, abstract rules to guide standardized responses, and procedures to improve efficiency and identify the best means to achieve specified ends. Humanitarian organizations were also becoming bureaucratized, developing spheres of competence, and rules to standardize responses and to drive means–ends calculations. Professionalism followed, with demands for actors who had specific knowledge, vocational qualifications that derived from specialized training, and the ability to follow fixed doctrine.[43]

Sociological institutionalism helps to explain why humanitarianism developed in this manner. This branch of organizational theory emphasizes the "socially constructed normative worlds in which organizations exist and how the social rules, standards of appropriateness, and models of legitimacy will constitute the organization."[44] The environment in which an organization is embedded is defined by a culture that contains acceptable models, standards of action, goals, and logics of appropriateness. Organizations are constituted by, and will be compelled to adopt, this culture for a variety of reasons—though resource requirements figure centrally. As Scott and Meyer observe, this normative environment contains the "rules and requirements to which individual organizations must conform if they are to receive support and legitimacy from the environment."[45] In short, because organizations are rewarded for conforming to rules and legitimization principles, and punished if they do not, they tend to model themselves after organizational forms that have legitimacy.

The environment also helps to explain institutional isomorphism, that is, why particular models spread.[46] There are three mechanisms: coercive, mimetic, and normative. The first two are most relevant here. Coercive isomorphism occurs when powerful organizations, such as states, impose rules and standards on other organizations. Mimetic isomorphism largely occurs in situations of uncertainty, encouraging organizations to model themselves after others that they believe are successful. Normative isomorphism largely originates from professionalization—the attempt by members of an occupation "to define the conditions and methods of their work, to control the production of producers,"[47] and to establish the epistemic basis for their authority and the claim to occupational autonomy. In general, sociological institutionalism emphasizes how organizations, desirous of symbolic and material resources and exposed to the same environment, will tend to adopt the same organizational forms.

The institutionalization of humanitarianism was largely driven by challenges to the emerging field's legitimacy and effectiveness—challenges that emanated from donors that paid the bills and members who were experiencing a crisis of confidence in reaction to new circumstances and shortcomings. These challenges were answered by rationalizing, bureaucratizing, and professionalizing.

A major feature of the field's rationalization was the attempt to standardize relief activities.[48] In response to the influx of relief agencies that were operating according to varying standards—a situation made doubly dangerous for agencies in the context of providing relief during conflict—and the growing evidence that different populations were being differentially treated, humanitarian organizations attempted to establish professional standards and codes of conduct. Several such initiatives stand out. In 1992 the ICRC, the International Federation of the Red Cross, and the Red Crescent Society (in consultation with the Steering Committee for Humanitarian Response) began work on a ten-point code of conduct. Originally conceived as providing guidance during natural disasters, it was extended to cover conflict situations as well. The first four articles reaffirm the basic principles of the ICRC, and the last six identify "good practices" and methodology for relief operations. This document is used by various agencies to guide their actions in war zones.[49] Various NGOs also assembled what came to be known as the

Providence Principles, which also aimed to introduce standardized rules for delivering relief. The same desire led various NGOs to launch the SPHERE project to establish minimal standards in the areas of water, sanitation, nutrition, shelter, site planning, and health.[50] This development, in turn, led to the Humanitarian Charter, which endeavors to "achieve defined levels of service for people affected by calamity or armed conflict, and to promote the observance of Dunantist humanitarian principles." The sheer proliferation of principles and exercises to establish codes of conduct represented an attempt to standardize the rules governing humanitarian action.[51]

Another feature of rationalization was the introduction of systems of accountability.[52] This development was pushed by donors, who began to apply "new public management" principles as they expected humanitarian organizations to provide evidence that their money was being well spent. These principles originated with the neoliberal orthodoxy of the 1980s. One of neoliberalism's goals was to reduce the state's role in the delivery of public services and, instead, to rely on commercial and voluntary organizations, which were viewed as more efficient. Because government agencies justified the shift from the public to the private and voluntary sectors on the grounds that the latter were more efficient, they introduced monitoring mechanisms to reduce the possibility of either slack or shirking.[53] Until the 1990s, humanitarian organizations largely escaped this public management ideology. Because humanitarian assistance was a minor part of the foreign aid budget, states did not view humanitarianism as central to their foreign policy goals, and states trusted that humanitarian agencies were efficient and effective; there was little reason for states to absorb the monitoring costs. However, once funding increased, humanitarianism became more central to security goals, and states began to question the effectiveness of humanitarian organizations, they were willing to do so.[54] Toward that end, states introduced new reporting requirements, developed new kinds of contracts, and demanded greater evidence of results.

The drive toward accountability was not completely donor-driven, for those within the sector increasingly sought greater accountability—to recipients. It was not enough to be accountable to donors for how their money was spent; it shows it also was important to be accountable to the supposed beneficiaries of their activities. Accountability, therefore, increasingly meant identifying ways to improve agencies' policies. These developments led to various system-wide initiatives, including the Active Learning Network for Accountability and Performance in Humanitarian Action (ALNAP).[55] In addition, in 1999 various NGOs initiated the Ombudsman for Humanitarian Assistance to address their accountability to "clients."

Emblematic of bureaucratization was the effort by humanitarian organizations to develop technologies and methodologies to calculate the effects of their policies in order to demonstrate effectiveness and identify optimal strategies. Prior to the 1990s few humanitarian organizations even thought to measure the consequences of their actions, assuming that the mere provision of assistance was evidence of their good results. Two developments shattered this blissful assumption. The first was mounting evidence that some humanitarian interventions might be causing more harm than good. Rwanda, in particular, burst the confidence of the humanitarian community.[56] In addition, donors began demanding results-based evaluations.

Measuring impact and demonstrating that humanitarian organizations are responsible for success (or failure) is a demanding methodological task. Humanitarian organizations must define "impact," specify their goals and translate them into measurable indicators, gather data in highly fluid emergency settings, establish baseline data in order to generate a "before and after" snapshot, control for alternative explanations and variables, and construct reasonable counterfactual scenarios.[57] Nevertheless, they made considerable headway. Humanitarian organizations began to draw on epidemiological models in the health sciences and program evaluation tools of the development field. The United States pushed for creation of the Standardized Monitoring and Assessment of Relief and Nutrition (SMART). Care International's Benefits–Harms analysis, which borrows methodologies developed in the human rights field, helps relief and development organizations measure the impact of their programs on people's human rights.[58]

Humanitarian organizations also moved to professionalize. Although relief workers still learn on the job, organizations increasingly draw on the health sciences and engineering, extant manuals, and specialized training programs run by private firms, NGOs, states, and academic institutions. Agencies increasingly recruit relief workers who have training in specialized fields. Although relief workers still have a high burnout rate, and most organizations have an impressive degree of staff turnover, many agencies now have full-time staff, who draw salaries with benefits packages and treat the field as a career. In addition, many premier agencies underwent a major change in their bureaucratic structure. Although operational divisions still carry tremendous prestige and influence, they increasingly compete with newly established offices dedicated to fund-raising and donor relations, staffed by those whose primary field experience derives not from refugee camps, but from marketing campaigns and pledge drives.

Consequences of transformation

The transformation of humanitarianism has left its mark, and humanitarian organizations hotly debate whether it is a mark of Cain. At times this debate appears to devolve into two equally stylized camps: one waxing sentimental about some quasi-mythical golden age of humanitarian action in which relief agencies enjoyed a space of infinite expanse, and another suggesting that the golden age is around the corner because humanitarian agencies have never been better funded or better positioned to help more people at risk. Without getting pulled into this debate, I want to explore how the politicization and institutionalization of humanitarianism has left organizations more vulnerable to external control. States are now able to use direct and indirect means to constrain and guide the actions of humanitarian agencies in ways that agencies believe potentially violate their principles. The external environment more generally affects the organizational culture of humanitarian agencies—their identity, internal organization, practices, principles, and calculations. The discussion of the transformation of humanitarianism, in other words, forces us to consider the effects of power in terms of what humanitarian organizations do and what they are.

Power over humanitarian action

States and international institutions can now compel humanitarian agencies to act in ways counter to their interests and principles. Although states have historically vacillated in their desire to use humanitarian action to serve their interests, the 1990s were unprecedented to the extent that states attempted to impose their agendas on agencies.[59] Toward that end, states began introducing mechanisms that were intended to control their "implementing partners." Although such control mechanisms did not necessarily compel agencies to act in ways that they believed were antagonistic to their interests or principles, frequently they did.

The most important control mechanism came from the power of the purse. Sometimes donors make transparent threats. In 2003 U.S. AID administrator Andrew Natsios told humanitarian organizations operating in Iraq that they were obliged to show the American flag if they took U.S. funding. If not, he warned, they could be replaced.[60] One NGO official captured the U.S. message in the following terms: "play the tune or 'they'll take you out of the band.' "[61]

Sometimes donors use more subtle, indirect, methods, for example, by insisting that agencies submit to coordination mechanisms. Coordination can appear to be a technical exercise whose function is to improve the division of labor, increase specialization, and heighten efficiencies. Yet this coordination, like all governance activities, is a highly political exercise, defined by power. The power behind coordination has not been lost on humanitarian organizations, especially when the donors are parties to the conflict or have a vested interest in the outcome.[62] Most famously, NATO in Kosovo and the United States in Afghanistan insisted on coordinating humanitarian action.[63] Although they justified their role on the grounds that it would improve the relief effort, they had more self-interested reasons: in order to sell the war at home, the combatants wanted the favorable publicity that came with being televised delivering food to, and building shelters for, displaced populations. It also would help them win the "hearts and minds" campaign, integral to the war effort.[64] Humanitarian organizations, though, were now being coordinated by one of the parties to the conflict, compromising their neutrality and independence.[65]

The bilateralization of aid and the earmarking of funds also potentially

steers individual agencies, and has produced disturbing trends in the alloca-
tion of aid. Multilateral aid is technically defined as aid given to multilateral
organizations and not earmarked; these organizations, therefore, have complete discretion over how the money is spent. Bilateral aid can mean the state
either dictates to the multilateral organization how the money is spent or gives
the money to a nonmultilateral organization such as an NGO. Earmarking
means that the donor dictates where and how the assistance will be used, frequently identifying regions, countries, operations, or even projects; this is especially useful if governments have geopolitical interests or pet projects. Since the
1980s there has been a dramatic shift away from multilateral aid and toward
bilateral aid and earmarking. In 1988 states directed roughly 45 percent of
humanitarian assistance to UN agencies in the form of multilateral assistance.
After 1994, however, the average dropped to 25 percent (and even lower in 1999
because of Kosovo).[66] Accordingly, state interests, rather than the humanitarian principle of relief based on need, increasingly drives funding decisions. For
instance, of the top 50 recipients of bilateral assistance between 1996 and 1999,
the states of the former Yugoslavia, Israel/Palestine, and Iraq received 50 percent of the available assistance.[67] In 2002 nearly half of all funds given by donor
governments to the UN's 25 appeals for assistance went to Afghanistan.[68] If
funding decisions were based solely on need, then places like Sudan, Congo,
northern Uganda, and Angola would leapfrog to the top of the list.[69] In general, while there is more aid than ever before, it is controlled by fewer donors,
who are more inclined to impose conditions and direct aid toward their
priorities, undermining the principle of impartiality. Funding is now a
several-tiered system, with the least fortunate getting the least attention.[70]

Humanitarian organizations bristled at these control mechanisms. Any
organization will object to encroachments on its autonomy. Yet humanitarian
organizations feared not only less autonomy, but also having to compromise
their humanitarian principles. The language of principal–agent theory helps
explain why. States see themselves as principals that provide a temporary
transfer of authority to their agents, humanitarian organizations. Yet humanitarian organizations do not see themselves as agents of states or operating
with delegated authority; they see themselves as agents of humanity that
operate with moral authority. The very association with states and its pre-
sumption of delegated authority, then, potentially undermines the moral
authority cherished by most humanitarian organizations. Indeed, if states
fund humanitarian organizations in order to further their foreign policy
goals, then humanitarian organizations are justifiably concerned. States'
attempt to monitor and regulate humanitarian organizations almost by definition compromises their guiding principles.

Humanitarian action redefined

The new environment and the transformation of humanitarianism is also
leaving its imprint on the organizational culture of humanitarian agencies,

producing changes that potentially undermine the core principle of impartial relief. The transformation of humanitarianism, as already noted, includes an expansion of the practices and goals associated with humanitarian action. This logically means that many humanitarian organizations are, in other words, articulating an expanding set of goals. Goal expansion has several possible consequences. It can lead to traditional goals being displaced. Relief was formerly an end in itself, but agencies are increasingly considering its relationship to other goals. For instance, rights-based agencies have demonstrated a greater willingness to use relief in order to promote basic human rights. Not only does need cease to be unconditional, but aid organizations might now also be attempting to determine who is worthy of aid, thus acting much like the nineteenth-century relief workers interested in helping the "deserving poor."[71] There is growing anecdotal evidence, moreover, that as many agencies have increasingly emphasized advocacy, rights, and peace building, they have not maintained their capacity for emergency relief, harming their response capacity to situations like Darfur.[72]

Bureaucratization is associated with the growing priority of base organizational interests such as survival and funding.[73] Reflecting on the emergence of the "Humanitarian International," Alex de Waal argues that in the competition between "soft interests" such as performing relief well and "hard interests" such as organizational survival and prosperity, noble ideals increasingly lose.[74] Ideals are particularly threatened when agencies need to interact with new donor environments to fund their activities. States' new contract mechanisms, including short-term contracts, competitive bidding, and reporting rules, have introduced perverse incentives for agencies that care about funding as much as they do about protecting populations at risk. Humanitarian organizations might doctor their performance indicators in order to transform failure into success, compete in areas in which they do not have a comparative advantage in order to secure funding, or fail to report shortcomings or the misuse of funds by subcontractors in order to avoid jeopardizing their contracts.[75]

Furthermore, because visibility can be a prerequisite for getting funding, many organizations prefer publicity to critical but very unglamorous work.[76] In the camps in Zaire following the Rwandan genocide, humanitarian groups rushed to the scene in order to show the flag and impress funders back home. Working in an orphanage photographs well and brings in revenue, but building clean latrines and sanitation systems does not—even though it is equally if not more essential for saving lives. Such a set of incentives might create market failures. De Waal posits a Gresham's Law for humanitarianism: bad humanitarian action can crowd out good action because humanitarian organizations are rewarded for being seen rather than for saving lives.[77]

Evidence also points to agencies' shifting what they consider to be appropriate action, thus redefining their principles and practices. Relaxation or redefinition of neutrality and independence can introduce new rule-governed behavior that can compromise impartiality. For example, one former Oxfam official reflected that his organization had become so supportive of NATO intervention in Kosovo that it forgot that genuine impartiality demanded that Oxfam and other relief organizations should have been on both sides of the border—helping Kosovar refugees *and* Serbian victims of NATO bombing.[78] Humanitarian organizations also might develop new rules that potentially undermine the safety of populations. As it attempted to navigate state pressures, UNHCR altered its underlying rules and principles of action in a way that increased its propensity to put the lives of refugees at risk.[79]

This transformation also can subtly alter the ethical principles and calculations used by agencies to guide their policies. Humanitarian agencies are demonstrating a shift from deontological, or duty-based, ethics to consequentialist ethics. This development is driven partly by a growing concern with the negative consequences of humanitarian action and the related desire to measure effectiveness and impact.[80] Previously humanitarian organizations were instinctively guided by deontological ethics: some actions are simply good in and of themselves regardless of their consequences. Ethical action consists of identifying these intrinsically good actions and then performing one's moral duty. The growing concern with unintended consequences, however, has contributed to an ethic of consequentialism: whether or not an action is ethical depends on the outcome. The issue for humanitarian organizations is becoming not whether aid has negative and unintended consequences—for it almost always does—but whether, on balance, it does more harm than good.[81] Consequentialist reasoning requires agencies to identify the outcomes of concern—and as their goals expand, the outcome variables that must be considered expand, too. Accordingly, agencies have an incentive to consider how relief might affect development, human rights, and peace building—potentially eroding the idea that agencies should give on the basis of need and not on the basis of other goals.

The desire to measure impact and effectiveness also can abrade a central element of the humanitarian ethic: a desire to demonstrate solidarity with victims and to restore their dignity. Relief workers, in Rony Brauman's words, aspire to "remain close to people in distress and to try and relieve their suffering."[82] They do so by providing not only relief, but also compassion and caring. The ethic of humanitarianism, in this respect, includes both consequentialist and duty-based ethics—it seeks to provide life-saving relief and holds that the motives matter for assuring benevolence. Yet can such nonquantifiable values as compassion be operationalized when attempting to determine the effectiveness of humanitarian action? Is it possible to quantify, for instance, the reuniting of families, the provision of burial shrouds, or the reduction of fear and anxiety among people in desperate situations?[83] If they are omitted from the model, the model might redefine how humanitarian agencies think about impact, downgrading basic ethical motives in favor of measurable outcomes. If the measurable variables are no longer dependent on the subjective needs of the "beneficiaries," will they even be consulted?

Measures of effectiveness, then, and the growing reliance of agencies on rational-legal principles to generate their legitimacy, might undermine the moral authority of humanitarian organizations. If the legitimacy and value of humanitarian action is based strictly on deliverables and producing measurable outcomes—saving lives at the cheapest price—then why not hire a private agency, if available?[84] After all, the victim probably does not care if the blankets are delivered by a commercial firm or a nonprofit agency. If aid agencies are increasingly drifting toward rational-legal principles as a way of defending their legitimacy, they might not only have difficulty competing with commercial firms but also might undermine their moral authority. The presumed difference between the Wal-Marts and the World Visions is that the former does not have moral authority while the latter does. What happens, though, when humanitarian agencies increasingly base their legitimacy on their ability to measure up to standards set by modern, commercial firms? Such a development might very well undermine what makes humanitarian action distinctive.

Conclusion: humanitarianism and world order

Humanitarianism can only be understood in relationship to the world order that constitutes it. Although much scholarship has focused on how principled actors have changed world politics by pressuring states to take the high road and redefine their interests, I have inverted this claim in examining how global politics has reshaped the nature of humanitarian action.[85] The environment that surrounded humanitarianism changed in profound ways during the 1990s. The expanding scope and scale of humanitarian action created new opportunities for agencies to help more people than ever before. A practice that was once restricted to relief and emergency assistance has become—like communism, nationalism, liberalism—an *ism*, not part of this world but a project designed to transform it.

These changes in humanitarian action suggest that it has a new function in international politics. Originally its distinctive function in the international sacrificial order was to interrupt the selection process by saving those at immediate risk. It did not pretend to be anything but palliative. Yet this temperance movement also served an ideological function, helping to reproduce the geopolitical order because it reduced pressures that might have demanded its transformation. Consider modern humanitarianism's origins. By the mid-nineteenth century, changes in military technology were making war more brutal; there was little tradition of medical relief; and the emerging profession of war reporting was transmitting gruesome pictures and accounts of soldiers left to languish and die on the battlefield. Publics were beginning to rebel at these sights and to express pacifist sentiments. In response, state and military elites co-opted Dunant's platform, removed its more radical proposals, accepted new rules governing how to tend wounded soldiers on the battlefield, and thus demonstrated to their publics their commitment to humanize war. Humanitarianism, in other words, helped to rescue those on the battlefield—and the system of war. In fact, decades after founding the ICRC, Dunant concluded that humanitarianism had been co-opted by the states-system; he walked away from reformism and embraced pacifism.[86] Recent developments in international humanitarian law can be interpreted as serving a similar function for the war machine as they lessen the demand for more radical change in the global-military order.

The drift of humanitarian action from relief to root causes indicates a shift in its role in the international sacrificial order. No longer satisfied with saving individuals today so that they can be at risk tomorrow, humanitarianism now aspires to transform the structural conditions that make populations vulnerable. Toward that end, aid agencies desire to spread development, democracy, and human rights, and to join a peace-building agenda that aspires to create stable, effective, and legitimate states. They are carriers of liberal values as they help spin into existence a global liberal order.[87] Although their transcendental, universal, and cosmopolitan commitments might appear to threaten an international society organized around the nation-state, in fact most of their activities do not challenge the states-system, but instead are designed to create a more stable, legitimate state organized around these supposedly universal principles.[88] Humanitarian organizations may or may not be part of a neoliberal agenda, and they may or may not resemble the missionaries of the nineteenth century. But by their own admission, they view their social purpose as promoting liberal values in order to make the world safer, more humane, and more just.

Humanitarianism is now more firmly part of politics. Certainly it always was part of politics to the extent that its actions had political effects and relief workers saw themselves as standing with the weak and against the mighty. Yet humanitarian agencies restricted their ambition to saving lives at immediate risk in part to keep states at bay and preserve their goal for relief. They are now firmly, and in many ways self-consciously, part of politics. Humanitarianism no longer clings to principles of neutrality, independence, and impartiality as method of depoliticization, but increasingly views the former two principles as an (unnecessary) luxury. Humanitarianism and politics are no longer discursively constructed in binary, oppositional terms; instead, their points of intersection are many, and humanitarianism's meanings increasingly are defined by the sort of politics once viewed as its bête noire. Humanitarianism, in short, is self-consciously part of politics. It is increasingly an *ism* that is no longer satisfied with reforming the world, but now has ambitions about its very transformation.

This transformation is forcing humanitarian organizations to critically reexamine two defining self-images. One is the belief that they operate strictly on behalf of others, are devoid of power,[89] and are as weak as the individuals they were trying to save. Many humanitarian organizations now have annual budgets that rival those of the states that are the objects of their intervention, and they are no longer content to stand outside of politics but are increasingly part of governance structures that are intended to transform states and societies. Humanitarian organizations can no longer pretend that they lack power—including power over those with whom they stand in solidarity.[90]

These developments also challenge their self-image as representatives of humanity. As a recent report regarding the current and future challenges to humanitarianism puts it, "Many in the South do not recognize what the international community calls the universality of humanitarian values as such. . . . Humanitarian action is viewed as the latest in a series of imposition of alien values, practices, and lifestyles. Northern incursions into the South— from the Crusades to colonialism and beyond—have historically been perceived very differently depending on the vantage point."[91] Indeed, if humanitarianism increasingly reflects globalization and Westernization, then there are good reasons why those in the Southern hemisphere view these agencies as the "mendicant orders of Empire."[92] Although such observations are nearly as speculative as the claims to universality they are meant to replace, there has been little research into how the recipients view Western alms and whether other traditions of relief and charity also share values associated with the Western tradition of humanitarian action.

Humanitarianism is now balanced on the knife's edge of various tensions, tensions that have become more pronounced as it has become (more self-consciously) part of politics. Humanitarianism is now precariously situated between the politics of solidarity and the politics of governance. Humanitarian workers traditionally saw themselves as apolitical as they defied systems of power and were in solidarity with the victims of a sacrificial order. As they become increasingly implicated in governance structures, they find themselves in growing collaboration with those whom they once resisted. Whether they will be successful at this more ambitious agenda remains to be seen. Whether they are or not, though, humanitarian action might very well be an effect of the very circuits of power that they once viewed as part of the international sacrificial order.

Acknowledgments

The author thanks Bud Duvall, Kevin Hartigan, Martha Finnemore, Abby Stoddard, Ron Kassimir, Craig Calhoun, Jack Snyder, Adele Harmer, the participants of the Minnesota International Relations Colloquium, and three anonymous reviewers for their comments and corrections. Special thanks to the Social Sciences Research Council and the participants in its series on "The Transformation of Humanitarian Action."

Notes

1 On the recent expansion of the humanitarian system, see Blondel 2000; de Waal 1997, 68–72; Macrae 2002; Minear 2002, chap. 1; Roberts 1999. For an account of the growth of humanitarian organizations that focuses on external forces, see Lindenberg and Bryant 2001.

2 In this way, humanitarianism is a logocentric, which Jacques Derrida observes is in play whenever "one privileged term (logos) provides the orientation for inter-preting the meaning of the subordinate term" (Nyers 1999, 21). See also Cutts 1998, 3; Malkki 1995; Warner 1999; Minear 2002, 76.

3 This definition draws from Stockton 2004a, 15.

4 Bradol 2004.

5 Douglas 2002.

6 Pictet 1979.

7 The ICRC's principles are largely the industry standard, though there are debates about the priorities of these principles, their operational meaning, and even their relevance. Forsythe 2005; Terry 2002; Weiss 1999; Duffield 2001a; Minear 2002; Ramsbotham and Woodhouse 1996, 14–18.

8 Rieff 2002; Minear 2002; Donini 2004; Duffield 2001a, Slim 2004a, Leader 2000.

9 Terry 2002.

10 De Torrente 2004, Anderson 2004.

11 Slim 2004a.

12 De Waal 1997, 133–34.

13 On the epistemology of "humanitarian crisis," see Stockton 2004a.

14 Slim 2004a, 155–56.

15 White 1993, 34–38; Howard 1993, 69–70.

16 General Assembly Resolution A/RES/46/182, 19 December 1991, Strengthening of the Coordination of Humanitarian Emergency Assistance of the United Nations.

17 Lang 2003; International Commission on Intervention and State Sovereignty 2001; Holzgrefe and Keohane 2003; Wheeler 2000; Slim 2002c.

18 Secretary of State Colin Powell, remarks to the National Foreign Policy Conference for Leaders of Nongovernmental Organizations, October 26, 2001.

19 Duffield 2001a, 12; also see Edkins 1996; Weiss 1999, 20; White 2000.

20 Kelly 1998, 174–75.

21 Duffield 2001a.

22 Macrae et al. 2002, 15. For a good overview, see Randel and German 2002.

23 International Commission on Intervention and State Sovereignty 2001.

24 Macrae 1999, 6–7.

25 Chandler 2002, chap. 1.

26 See Bouchet-Saulnier 2000. See also Leader and Macrae 2000; Chandler 2002; Minear 2002, chap. 3.

27 Chandler 2002, 21.

28 Beitz 1994, 124. See also Linklater 1998, chap. 2.

29 Calhoun 2004.

30 Cosmopolitanism and the discourse of humanity have not always led to impartial-ity as understood today, because those who claimed to be "humanitarian" and act in the name of humanity also could reflect a discourse in which some peoples were more human than others and thus more deserving of assistance. See Finnemore 1996.

31 Bradol 2004, 9.

32 Sommaruga 1999; Tanguy and Terry 1999; Rieff 1999.

33 This classification derives from other taxonomies, including Minear 2002, 78; Stoddard 2002; Weiss 1999; Donini 2005. Feinstein International Famine Center 2004, 54, argues that how agencies position themselves around these categories is

determined by various factors, such as management and leadership, institutional culture, networks, and geographical and programmatic scope. Solidarist organizations are another branch; they openly identify with one party to a conflict and thus do not care about neutrality. Although I (and others) focus largely on international nongovernmental organizations, there are various international organizations whose principal mandate is humanitarian (and ICRC, the patriarch of the humanitarian community, is neither a nongovernmental or a international organization). Beginning after World War I and then increasing after World War II, states established various international organizations, including the UNHCR and the World Food Program, to help them carry out their humanitarian obligations. State sovereignty, though, significantly shaped their working definition of humanitarianism and its relationship to politics. At the beginning of the last century states cautiously evoked the language of humanitarianism for fear that such transcendental concerns might swamp their core interests and undermine their sovereignty; consequently, they used sovereignty to fence in what these international organizations could do and these organizations, in turn, cleaved to the principles of consent, neutrality, and impartiality in order to signal to states that they knew their place. The changing meaning of sovereignty, particularly noticeable after the cold war, though, opened up space for many international organizations to use a more expansive understanding of humanitarianism as they became more deeply involved in domestic space. See Barnett 2001 for a discussion.

34 Appalled by the carnage wrought by a fierce battle between French and Austrian forces in Solferino, Italy, in June 1859, Dunant, a Swiss citizen, appealed to the local population to tend to the thousands of suffering soldiers. Based on his personal experiences, Dunant wrote an account that became a bestseller in Europe and stirred European elites to consider his proposals for regulating war and administering to the wounded. These discussions produced both the Geneva Conventions, which established international humanitarian law, and the ICRC, which was to be an impartial, neutral and independent organization whose exclusive humanitarian mission is to protect the lives and dignity of victims of war.

35 UNHCR 1990.

36 Barnett and Finnemore 2004, chap. 6.

37 Another factor potentially influencing this expansion is psychological, deriving from personal strain of relief work. Relief workers migrate from one nightmare to another, comforted only by the fact that, at best, they provide temporary relief. This sort of existence takes a very high emotional toll. Wanting to believe that they are helping to build a better world, relief workers began to treat human rights, conflict resolution, and nation building as extensions of humanitarianism. See Rieff 2002.

38 Chimini 1993, 444; Coles 1989, 203.

39 The heart of the resource dependence approach is that "organizations survive to the extent that they are effective. Their effectiveness derives from the management of demands, particularly demands of interest groups upon which the organizations depend for resources and support. . . . There are a variety of ways of managing demands, including the obvious one of giving in to them" (Pfeffer and Salancik 2003, 2).

40 Meyer and Scott 1983, 140.

41 Duffield 2001a; Donini 2004; Duffield, Macrae, and Curtis 2001.

42 Loescher 2001.

43 For definitions of rationalization, see Weber 1947; for bureaucratization, see Beetham 1985, 69; for professionalization, see Ritzer 1975.

44 Orru, Biggart, and Hamilton 1991, 361. See also Scott 1987; Scott 1995; DiMaggio and Powell 1991; Meyer and Rowan 1977.

45 DiMaggio and Powell 1983, 140.
46 Ibid., 150–54.
47 Larson 1977, 49–52; cited from DiMaggio and Powell 1983, 152.
48 Leader 1999.
49 International Conference of the Red Cross and Red Crescent 1995.
50 Gostelow 1999.
51 Another innovation was the Consolidated Appeals Process, established in 1991 by the UN General Assembly in response to the growing perception that there were too many agencies appealing to too many donors for too many different sectors in too many situations. In order to improve joint planning and quickly mobilize funds and target them for high priority areas, the UN decided to act as a coordinating mechanism. By 2002 there had been 165 different appeals. See Porter 2002 for a review.
52 Smillie and Minear 2004, 215–24; Slim 2002a; Mitchell, 2003.
53 Macrae et al. 2002, 18–21.
54 De Waal 1997, 78–79.
55 Slim 2002a.
56 Anderson 1996; Terry 2002; Slim 1997; Vaux 2001, chap. 3.
57 Humanitarian Policy Group 2004; Fearon 2004; Darcy 2005.
58 O'Brien 2002.
59 Feinstein International Famine Center 2004; Donini 2005. Smillie and Minear 2004, chap. 9. These claims are consistent with principal–agent analysis. See Bendor, Glazer, and Hammond 2001, 20. For applications to international relations, see Thatcher and Sweet 2002; Nielson and Tierney 2003; Hawkins et al. 2005.
60 Natsios 2003.
61 Quoted in Smillie and Minear 2004, 143.
62 Minear 2002, chap. 2; Macrae et al. 2002, chap. 3; Donini 2004.
63 Rieff 2002, chap. 6.
64 States also wanted to see for themselves what was occurring in the field. Toward that end, they began sending representatives to relay firsthand accounts of assistance activities and began developing the capacity for independent needs assessments and strategic analyses. An immediate consequence was that humanitarian organizations no longer benefited from having privileged and highly authoritative information. Because the authority of NGOs comes from their practical experience from "the field" (Slim 2002b, 4), this development might undermine their discretion.
65 A major controversy in this regard concerns whether the willingness of aid agencies to align themselves with the United States in Afghanistan and Iraq is one cause behind the growing perception that aid workers are no longer given immunity during war.
66 Randel and German 2002, 21.
67 Ibid.
68 Smillie and Minear 2004, 145. See also Macrae et al. 2002; Jeffreys 2002; Porter 2002.
69 Many in the humanitarian sector agree that while the global response to the tsunami was impressive, it was disproportionate in relationship to need. In fact, because MSF believed that it had more than enough, it asked donors to unrestrict the funds so that they could be channeled to another region in greater need; if they refused, MSF attempted to return the donations.
70 In response to the politicization of priorities, humanitarian organizations entered into a dialogue with the principal donors to try to establish more impartial standards. The result was the Good Donorship Initiative. See Harmer, Cotterrell, and Stoddard 2004.
71 Rieff 2002.

72 Interview with official from the UN Office for the Coordinator of Humanitarian Assistance, New York, March 8, 2005.
73 Harrell-Bond 2002; Barnett and Finnemore 2004.
74 De Waal 1997, 65–66.
75 Cooley and Ron 2002; Darcy 2005.
76 Smillie and Minear 2004, 143.
77 De Waal 1997, 138–39.
78 Vaux 2001.
79 Barnett and Finnemore 2004, chap. 4.
80 There also were growing calls to measure "need"—to replace subjective and emotional assessments with more objective criteria as a way to reinforce the impartiality principle and bring more attention to forgotten emergencies. In short, objective indicators are the best way to reestablish values and principles. See Oxley 2001.
81 Slim 1997; Duffield 2001a, 90–95; Gasper 1999. Because it is nearly impossible, if not slightly macabre, to try to calculate whether aid saves more lives than it takes, some organizations have reasserted the importance of the principles of independence, neutrality, and impartiality for determining whether they should provide aid. See Weissman 2004.
82 Brauman 2004, 400.
83 Darcy 2005, 8.
84 Hopgood (forthcoming).
85 Keck and Sikkink 1998; Risse, Ropp, and Sikkink 1999.
86 Hutchinson 1996.
87 Boli and Thomas 1999.
88 Duffield 2001a. See also Fox 2001.
89 Fisher 1997.
90 Kennedy 2004; Duffield 2001a.
91 Feinstein International Famine Center 2004, 55.
92 Hardt and Negri 200, cited in Donini 2005, 2.

References

Abbott, Kenneth and Duncan Snidal. 1998. Why states act through formal international organizations. *Journal of Conflict Resolution* 42 (1): 3–32.

Anderson, Kenneth. 2004. Humanitarian inviolability in crisis: The meaning of impartiality and neutrality for U.N. and NGO agencies following the 2003–2004 Afghanistan and Iraq conflicts. *Harvard Human Rights Journal* 17 (Spring): 41–74.

Anderson, Mary. 1996. Do no harm: Supporting local capacities for peace through aid. Cambridge, MA: Collaborative for Development Action.

Barnett, Michael. 2001. Humanitarianism with a sovereign face: UNHCR in the global undertow. *International Migration Review* 35 (1): 244–77.

Barnett, Michael, and Martha Finnemore. 2004. *Rules for the world: International organizations in global politics.* Ithaca: Cornell University Press.

Beitz, Charles. 1994. Cosmopolitan liberalism and the states system. In *Political restructuring in Europe: Ethical perspectives*, ed. Chris Brown, 123–36. London: Routledge.

Bendor, Jonathan, Ami Glazer, and Timothy Hammond. 2001. Theories of delegation. *Annual Review of Political Science* 4: 235–69.

Beetham, David. 1985. *Max Weber and the theory of modern politics.* New York: Polity.

Blondel, Jean. 2000. Is humanitarian action everybody's affair? Reflections on an overworked concept. *International Review of the Red Cross* 838: 327–37.

Boli, John, and George Thomas, eds. 1999. *Constructing world culture: International nongovernmental organizations since 1875*. Stanford: Stanford University Press.

Bouchet-Saulnier, Françoise. 2000. Between humanitarian law and principles: The principles and practices of "rebellious humanitarianism." *MSF International Activity Report*. http://www.msf.org.

Bradol, Jean-Herve. 2004. The sacrificial international order and humanitarian action. In *In the shadow of "just wars": Violence, politics, and humanitarian action*, ed. Fabrice Weissman, 1–22. Ithaca: Cornell University Press.

Brauman, Rony. 2004. From philanthropy to humanitarianism: Remarks and an interview. *South Atlantic Quarterly* 103 (2/3): 397–417.

Calhoun, Craig. 2004. A world of emergencies: Fear, intervention, and the limits of cosmopolitan order. Lecture at University of Southern California.

Chandler, David. 2002. *From Kosovo to Kabul*. London: Pluto Press.

Chimini, B.S. 1993. The meaning of words and the role of UNHCR in voluntary repatriation. *International Journal of Refugee Law* 5 (3): 442–60.

Coles, Gervase. 1989. Solutions to the problems of refugees and protection of refugees: A background study. Prepared for the Round Table on Durable Solutions and the Protection of Refugees, Convened by the Office of the United Nations High Commissioner for Refugees.

Cooley, Alex and James Ron. 2002. The NGO scramble. *International Security* 27 (1): 5–39.

Cutts, Mark. 1998. Politics and humanitarianism. *Refugee Survey Quarterly* 17 (1): 1–15.

Darcy, James. 2005. Acts of faith? Thoughts on the effectiveness of humanitarian action. Available at http://www.ssrc.org/programs/emergencies/publications/Darcy.pdf.

De Waal, Alex. 1997. *Famine crimes: Politics and the disaster relief industry in Africa*. Bloomington: Indiana University Press.

DiMaggio, Paul, and Walter Powell. 1983. 'The iron cage revisited: Institutional isomorphism and collective rationality in organizational fields.' *American Sociological Review* 48: 147–60.

DiMaggio, Paul J., and Walter W. Powell, eds. 1991. *The new institutionalism in organizational analysis*. Chicago: University of Chicago Press.

Donini, Antonio. 2004. *The future of humanitarian action: Implications of Iraq and other recent crises*. Medford, MA: Tufts University, Feinstein International Famine Center.

——. 2005. Humanitarianism in the 00s: Is universality under threat? Paper presented at the 2005 annual meeting of the International Studies Association.

Douglas, Mary. 2002. *Purity and danger: An analysis of the concepts of pollution and taboo*. New York: Routledge.

Duffield, Mark. 2001a. *Global governance and the new wars: The merging of development and security*. New York: Zed Press.

——. 2001b. Governing the borderlands: Decoding the power of aid. *Disasters* 25 (4): 308–20.

Duffield, Mark, Joanna Macrae, and Devon Curtis. 2001. Politics and humanitarian aid. *Disasters* 25 (4): 269–74.

Edkins, Jennifer. 1996. Whose hunger? *Concepts of famine, practices of aid.* Minneapolis: University of Minnesota Press.

Fearon, James. 2004. Measuring humanitarian impact. Unpublished manuscript.

Feinstein International Famine Center. 2004. *Ambiguity and change: Humanitarian NGOs prepare for the future.* Medford, MA: Tufts University, Feinstein International Famine Center

Finnemore, Martha. 1996. Constructing norms of humanitarian intervention. In *The culture of national security*, ed. Peter Katzenstein, 153–85. New York: Columbia University Press.

Fisher, William. 1997. Doing good? The politics and antipolitics of NGO practices. *Annual Review of Anthropology* 26: 439 n.64.

Forsythe, David P. 2005. *The humanitarians: The International Committee of the Red Cross.* NY: Cambridge University Press.

Fox, Fiona. 2001. New humanitarianism: Does it provide a moral banner for the 21st century? *Disasters* 25 (4): 275–89.

Gasper, Desmond R. 1999. "Drawing a line": Ethical and political strategies in complex emergency assistance. *European Journal of Development Research* 11 (2): 87–114.

Gostelow, Lola. 1999. The Sphere Project: The implications of making humanitarian principles and codes work. *Disasters* 23 (4): 316–25.

Hardt, Michael, and Antonio Negri. 2001. *Empire.* Cambridge: Harvard University Press.

Harmer, Adele, Lin Cotterrell, and Abby Stoddard. 2004. From Stockholm to Ottawa: A progress review of the Good Humanitarian Donorship initiative. *HPG Research Briefing* 18. London: Overseas Development Institute.

Harrell-Bond, Barbara. 2002. Can humanitarian work with refugees be humane? *Human Rights Quarterly* 24 (1): 51–85.

Hawkins, Darren, David Lake, Daniel Nielson, and Michael Tierney, eds. 2005. *Delegation under anarchy: States, international organizations, and principal–agent theory.* Cambridge: Cambridge University Press.

Holzgrefe, J. L. and Robert Keohane, eds. 2003. *Humanitarian intervention.* New York: Cambridge University Press.

Hopgood, Stephen. Forthcoming. *Keepers of the flame.* Ithaca: Cornell University Press.

Howard, Michael. 1993. The historical development of the UN's role in international security. In *United Nations, divided world: The UN's roles in international relations*, ed. Adam Roberts and Benedict Kingsbury, 63–80. New York: Oxford University Press.

Humanitarian Policy Group. 2004. Measuring the impact of humanitarian aid: A review of current practice. Humanitarian Policy Group Research Report 17. London: Overseas Development Institute.

Hutchinson, John F. 1996. *Champions of charity: War and the rise of the Red Cross.* Boulder, CO: Westview Press.

International Commission on Intervention and State Sovereignty. 2001. *The responsibility to protect.* Ottawa: International Development Research Centre.

International Conference of the Red Cross and Red Crescent. 1995. *The code of conduct for the International Red Cross and Red Crescent movement and NGOs in disaster relief.* Adopted at the 26th International Conference of the Red Cross and Red Crescent, Geneva, Switzerland, December 3–7.

Jackson, Robert. 1990. *Quasi-states*. New York: Cambridge University Press.

Jeffreys, Anna. 2002. Giving voice to silent emergencies. *Humanitarian Exchange* 20:2–4.

Keck, Margaret, and Kathryn Sikkink. 1998. *Activists beyond borders*. Ithaca. Cornell University Press.

Kelly, Charles. 1998. On the relief-to-development continuum. *Disasters* 22 (2): 174–75.

Kennedy, David. 2004. *The dark side of virtue: International humanitarianism reassessed*. Princeton: Princeton University Press.

Lang, Anthony, ed. 2003. *Just intervention*. Georgetown: Georgetown University Press.

Larson, Magali Sarfatti. 1977. *The rise of professionalism: A sociological analysis*. Berkeley: University of California Press.

Leader, Nicholas. 1998. Proliferating principles: Or how to sup with the devil without getting eaten. *Disasters* 22 (4): 288–308.

——. 1999. Codes of conduct: Who needs them? *Relief and Rehabilitation Network Newsletter* 13: 1–4.

——. 2000. *The politics of principle: The principles of humanitarian action in practice*. Humanitarian Policy Group Report 2. London: Overseas Development Institute.

Leader, Nicholas, and Joanne Macrae, eds. 2000. *Terms of engagement: Conditions and conditionality in humanitarian action*. Humanitarian Policy Group Report 6. London: Overseas Development Institute.

Lindenberg, Marc and Coralie Bryant. 2001. *Going global: Transforming relief and development NGOs*. Bloomfield, CT: Kumarian Books.

Linklater, Andrew. 1998. *The transformation of political community*. Cambridge, UK: Polity Press.

Loescher, Gil. 2001. *The UNHCR and world politics: A perilous path*. New York: Oxford University Press.

Macrae, Joanna. 1998. Death of humanitarianism?: An anatomy of the attack. *Disasters* 22 (4): 309–17.

——. 1999. *Aiding peace . . . and war: UNHCR returnee reintegration and the relief–development debate*. New Issues in Refugee Research, UNHCR Working Paper 14, December.

Macrae, Joanna et al. 2002. *Uncertain power: The changing role of official donors in humanitarian action*. Humanitarian Policy Group Report 12. London: Overseas Development Institute.

Macrae, Joanna, ed. 2002. *The new humanitarianisms: A review of trends in global humanitarian action*. London: Overseas Development Institute.

Malkki, Liisa. 1995. Refugees and exile: From "refugee studies" to the national order of things. *Annual Review of Anthropology* 24: 495–523.

McFarlane, Neil, and Thomas Weiss. 2000. Political interests and humanitarian action. *Security Studies* 10 (1): 120–52.

Meyer, John, and Brian Rowan. 1977. Institutionalized organizations: Formal structure as myth and ceremony. *American Journal of Sociology* 83 (2): 340–63.

Meyer, John, and W. Richard Scott. 1983. *Organizational environments: Ritual and rationality*. Newbury Park, CA: Sage.

Minear, Larry. 1999. The theory and practice of neutrality: Some thoughts on the tensions. *International Review of the Red Cross* 833.

——. 2002. *The humanitarian enterprise: Dilemmas and discoveries*. Bloomfield, CT: Kumarian Press.

Mitchell, John. 2003. Accountability: The three lane highway. *Humanitarian Exchange* 24: 2–5.

Moore, Jonathan. 1999. The humanitarian–development gap. *International Review of the Red Cross* 833: 103–7.

Natsios, Andrew. 2003. NGOs must show results; Promote U.S. or we will "find new partners." Available at http://www.interaction.org/forum2003/panels.html#Natsios.

Nielson, Daniel, and Michael Tierney. 2003. Delegation to international organizations: Agency theory and World Bank environmental reform. *International Organization* 57 (2): 241–76.

Nyers, Peter. 1999. Emergency or emerging identities? Refugees and transformations in world order. *Millennium* 28 (1): 1–26.

O'Brien, Paul. 2002. Benefits–harms analysis: A rights-based tool developed by CARE International. *Humanitarian Exchange* 20:29–31.

——. 2004. Politicized humanitarianism: A response to Nicolas de Torrente. *Harvard Human Rights Journal* 17:1–39.

Orru, Marco, Nicole Woolsey Biggart, and Gary Hamilton. 1991. Organizational isomorphism in East Asia. In *The new institutionalism in organizational analysis*, ed. Walter W. Powell and Paul J. DiMaggio, 361–89. Chicago: University of Chicago Press.

Oxley, Marcus. 2001. Measuring humanitarian need. *Humanitarian Exchange* 19:29–31.

Pfeffer, Jeffrey and Gerald Salancik. 2003. *The external control of organizations: A resource dependence perspective*. Stanford: Stanford University Press.

Pictet, Jean. 1979. *The fundamental principles of the Red Cross*. Geneva: Henry Dunant Institute.

Porter, Toby. 2002. An embarrassment of riches. *Humanitarian Exchange* 21: 2–4.

Ramsbotham, Oliver and Tom Woodhouse. 1996. *Humanitarian intervention in contemporary conflict*. New York: Polity Press.

Randel, Judith and Tony German. 2002. Trends in the financing of humanitarian assistance. In *The new humanitarianism: A review of trends in global humanitarian action*, ed. Joanna Macrae, 19–28. London: Overseas Development Institute.

Rieff, David. 1999. Moral imperatives and political realities. *Ethics and International Affairs* 13: 35–42.

——. 2002. *A bed for the night: Humanitarianism in crisis*. New York: Simon and Schuster.

Risse, Thomas, Steven Ropp, and Kathryn Sikkink, eds. 1999. *The power of human rights*. New York: Cambridge University Press.

Ritzer, George. 1975. Professionalization, bureaucratization, and rationalization: The views of Max Weber. *Social Forces* 53 (4): 627–34.

Roberts, Adam. 1999. The role of humanitarian issues in international politics in the 1990s. *International Review of the Red Cross* 833: 19–42.

Scott, W. Richard. 1987. The adolescence of institutional theory. *Administrative Studies Quarterly* 32 (4): 493–511.

——. 1995. *Institutions and organizations*. Thousand Oaks, CA: Sage Publications.

Slim, Hugo. 1997. Doing the right thing: Relief agencies, moral dilemmas, and moral responsibility in political emergencies and war. *Disasters* 21 (3): 244–57.

——. 2002a. By what authority? The legitimacy and accountability of non-governmental organisations. *Journal of Humanitarian Assistance*, March 10. http://www.jha.ac/articles/a082.htm.

——. 2002b. Claiming a humanitarian imperative: NGOs and the cultivation of humanitarian duty. Paper presented at the 7th Annual Conference of Webster University on Humanitarian Values for the Twenty-first Century, Geneva, February 21–22.

——. 2002c. Military intervention as a means of protecting human rights. *Journal of Humanitarian Assistance*, March 11. http://www.jha.ac/articles/a084.htm.

——. 2004a. Protecting civilians: Putting the individual at the humanitarian centre. In *The humanitarian decade: Challenges for humanitarian assistance in the last decade and into the future*. Vol. 2. Ed. Office of the Coordinator of Humanitarian Assistance, 154–69. New York: United Nations Press.

——. 2004b. Politicizing humanitarian action according to need. Presentation to the 2nd International Meeting on Good Humanitarian Donorship, Ottawa, October 21–22.

Smillie, Ian, and Larry Minear. 2004. *The charity of nations*. Bloomfield, CT: Kumarian Press.

Sommaruga, Cornelio. 1999. Humanity: Our priority now and always. *Ethics and International Affairs* 13:23–28.

SPHERE Project. 2000. *Humanitarian charter and minimum standards in disaster response*. Oxford: Oxfam Publishing.

Stockton, Nicholas. 2004a. The changing nature of humanitarian crises. In *The humanitarian decade: Challenges for humanitarian assistance in the last decade and into the future*. Vol. 2. Ed. Office of the Coordinator of Humanitarian Assistance, 15–38. New York: United Nations Press.

——. 2004b. Afghanistan, war, aid, and international order. In *Nation-building unraveled? Aid, peace, and justice in Afghanistan*, ed. Antonio Donini, Norah Niland, and Karin Wermester, 9–37. Bloomfield, CT: Kumarian Press.

Stoddard, Abby. 2002. Trends in US humanitarian policy. In *The new humanitarianisms: A review of trends in global humanitarian action*, ed. Joanna Macrae, 39–50. Humanitarian Policy Group Report 11. London: Overseas Development Institute.

Tanguy, Joelle and Fiona Terry. 1999. Humanitarian responsibility and committed action. *Ethics and International Affairs* 13: 29–34.

Terry, Fiona. 2002. *Condemned to repeat?* Ithaca: Cornell University Press.

Thatcher, Mark and Alec Stone Sweet. 2002. Theory and practice of delegation to non-majoritarian institutions. *West European Politics* 25 (1): 1–22.

De Torrente, Nicholas. 2004. Humanitarian action under attack: Reflections on the Iraq war. *Harvard Human Rights Journal* 17 (Spring): 1–30.

United Nations High Commissioner for Refugees. 1990. Note on international protection. August 27. Available at http://www.unhcr.ch/cgi-bin/texis/vtx/excom/opendoc.htm?tbl=EXCOM&id=3ae68c000.

Vaux, Tony. 2001. *The selfish altruist*. Sterling, VA: Earthscan Publishing.

Warner, Daniel. 1999. The politics of the political/humanitarian divide. *International Review of the Red Cross* 833: 109–18.

Weber, Max. 1947. *Theory of social and economic organization*. New York: Oxford University Press.

Weiss, Tom. 1999. The humanitarian identity crisis. *Ethics and International Affairs* 13: 1–42.

Weissman, Fabrice, ed. 2004. *In the shadow of "just wars": Violence, politics, and humanitarian action.* Ithaca: Cornell University Press.

Welch, John, and Nathalie Laidler-Kylander. 2006. The new global brands: Managing non-governmental organizations in the 21st century. United States: Thomson Southwestern.

Wheeler, Nicholas. 2000. *Saving strangers.* New York: Oxford University Press.

White, N. D. 1993. *Keeping the peace.* New York: Manchester University Press.

White, Philip. 2000. Complex political emergencies: Grasping contexts, seizing opportunities. *Disasters* 24 (4): 288–90.

10 Conclusion

Beyond the international humanitarian order?

The essays in this volume were written against the backdrop of an international humanitarian order that was simultaneously expanding dramatically and registering growing concerns and doubts. In this respect, they mirror a dominant narrative of the post-Cold War period: those who had long been championing for a world that cared as much about humanity as it did sovereignty began to wonder about the kind of world that was being created in the name of humanity. There are many ways to explain these highs and lows, including the simple fact that inflated notions of the "international community" will always disappoint and grandiose boasts such as a "responsibility to protect" without the appropriate muscle will always sound like cheap talk. Yet this contrapuntal rhythm might also result from tensions that are intrinsic to the international humanitarian order, a possibility I want to address in this concluding essay.

I begin by asking: What is the significance of an international humanitarian order that chronically disappoints but nevertheless retains a loyal following? One answer is that, however flawed, it is better than no such order at all. In this respect, it is akin to Winston Churchill's aphorism regarding democracy—the worst form of government, except for all the others. To give up on the international humanitarian order would be tantamount to abandoning all those in need, which is unthinkable. This certainly provides a powerful reason for its popularity. However, it is not only those in need who might find themselves increasingly fearful and vulnerable. So, too, would those who have the power and the privilege to choose compassion. The objects of humanitarianism rely on its material gifts; the subjects on its spiritual gifts. The international humanitarian order is not only a global soup kitchen, it also is a symbol of what the international community can and should be, representing the practice and the promise of the transcendental, connecting everyday acts of giving to a moral universe. Such transcendental meanings are most clearly evident in religiously-inspired acts of compassion, including, for instance, the nineteenth century anti-slavery campaigns led by a coalition of evangelicals in Britain. Yet it is not only the religious who are members of a community of faith and give their worldly actions spiritual significance. Members of human rights and relief agencies frequently refer to forms of the international community and humanity that appear to have a religious-like standing.[1] For many the transcendental pivots around God; for others, though, around a secularized humanity. In either case everyday practices of compassion are illuminated by the divine.

The international humanitarian order's intimacy with the sacred can obscure the existence of the profane that lurks within. To some extent this disregard owes to recent developments in the study of international relations. It was not until the last decade of the last century that the study of international norms, ethics, and principles became acceptable once again. For much of the Cold War period mainstream international relations scholars assumed that the world was defined exclusively by interests defined in terms of power, and power defined in terms of military strength and economic wealth. The major point of resistance to this view came from neoliberal institutionalism, and the resistance was only partial: while neoliberals differed with realists regarding the possibility of enduring cooperation, they accepted many of the same starting points, including a world of anarchy and states pursing base interests.

And then along came constructivism. This is not the place to review its history, but one part of its childhood is critical to the story of a discipline that routinely treated ethics and power as existing in separate worlds. As constructivists attempted to demonstrate the independent effects of norms they were compelled to present their claims in juxtaposition to the language of power and interests, resulting in various binaries, including norms/interests, principles/power, and logic of appropriateness/logic of consequences. As mainstream international relations theorists and constructivist scholars engaged in hand-to-hand combat, some of these skirmishes led to a discovery of areas of overlap and others to irreconcilable differences—and they seemed to agree that ethics and power inhabit different terrains, with constructivists emphasizing how the former can dissolve the latter and rationalists insisting that power always gets the upper hand.

The concept of paternalism provides one way of reuniting ethics and power. Paternalism can be generically understood as the belief that we can and should act in someone else's best interests and even without their consent; the combination of care and control means that paternalism offers a combustible mix of ethics and power. If the possibility of paternalism is present in nearly all acts of compassion, which I believe it is, then it is most certainly a clear and present danger once compassion becomes institutionalized and globalized. In short, paternalism is not an unfortunate legacy of nineteenth-century humanitarianism but rather is an enduring feature of the international humanitarian order. Not only is it impossible to remove the possibility and the presence of paternalism, it is also not necessarily desirable—there are moments when paternalism is highly defensible. Accordingly, the challenge is to consider whether and when forms of paternalism are warranted and how to safeguard against the ever-present possibility that those who are in positions to care for others do not unjustifiably violate the autonomy, dignity, and liberty of the vulnerable. The concept of paternalism challenges practitioners, forcing them into a world of greater uncertainty regarding whether they are truly doing the right thing. Anxiety need not be a prelude to ethical resignation; it also can generate an opening for a different kind of engagement with those in need.

The international humanitarian order challenges not only the world of practice but also the world of scholarship. The discipline of international relations, much like the social sciences, has a history of considering the study of ethics and practical engagement as compromising the quest for objective, value-neutral, knowledge. The explicit incorporation of the language of ethics often unnerves the professional and modern social scientist, trained to consider ethical theory as either irrelevant or worthy of a few sentences at the end of the research. Yet my experience, which tracks with many of my colleagues whose scholarship focuses on genocide, humanitarianism, human rights, and public health, is that our choice of research subjects owes not to abstract curiosity or the discovery of an untapped data set but rather because we feel passionately about the importance of the subject, and retain hope that our research might advance our understanding of important developments in global affairs and make a difference to those outside our professional sanctums. It is nearly impossible to study the circumstances of the radical poor and the victims of structural and lethal violence without also considering what kinds of practical interventions might improve their circumstances, interventions that invariably include the language of causation and ethics. A healthy, vibrant, and relevant social sciences can only exist with practical ethics and engagement.

A transcendent international humanitarian order

The news coming from the international humanitarian order can cause even the most incurable romantic to reach for anti-depressants. Those who volunteer to work in emergencies have witnessed the worst that humanity has to offer.[2] Even their best intentions can make things worse.[3] Peacekeeping operations have a relatively low success rate, and at times the international community might best help others by minding its own business.[4] There is a fierce debate in the world of development regarding whether the billions of dollars in aid have done more than fatten the budgets of the contracting agencies.[5] And humanitarians can be wolves in sheep's clothing; many are charged with using their positions of power to exploit those who are seeking their protection.[6] The international humanitarian community is hardly oblivious to these accusations and recriminations, knows that good intentions are no longer enough, and has become increasingly attentive to measuring outcomes and addressing basic questions of accountability. Indeed, it is frequently weighed down by this knowledge.

What enables those in the humanitarian community to soldier on notwithstanding disappointment and doubt? The more I heard of these dismal tales from the field and from aid workers who were vocally cynical about whether their on-going interventions were making much of a difference the more I wondered about the source of their stamina and their continued hope against experience and expectations. Over the years I have kept a log of the moves made by the aid community to keep hope alive: denial; rationalization; a cognitive dissonance that comes from trying to reconcile good intentions with bad outcomes; a willingness to value the occasional success more than the constant string of defeats; a readiness to blame others for their failures; a faith in the capacity to learn; and the conviction that surrender is no alternative. Yet in addition to the combination of pluckiness and pigheadedness, I also heard an unwilled belief in the possibility of moral progress.

Scholars and practitioners are uncomfortable using the discourse of progress. It is closely associated with nineteenth-century civilizing missions, Eurocentrism, vainglorious confidence in the superiority of the West, and the general belief that the West represents the "end of history" and shows the rest of the world its future. The meaning of progress is generally in the eye of the beholder, and those with the power usually define its meaning. Those who continue to insist on the possibility of progress have a remarkable capacity for forgetting a twentieth century defined by horrific episodes of mass killing, often engineered by those who claimed to be the paragons of civilization.

Many scholars also continue to refer, in knowing and unknowing ways, to the concept of progress. Liberal approaches suggest that the world is improving, largely because of the expansion of liberal democracies. Liberal states have various qualities that make them good neighbors: more transparent and thus more trustworthy, more inclined toward inclusive debate and dialogue, more likely to settle their differences through wordplay and not gunplay, and more inclined to respect and honor human rights.[7] A considerable body of constructivist scholarship tracks the steady evolution and institutionalization of "good" norms that countermand power politics.[8] English School theorists have identified a change from a system of states, to a society of states, to a global society with elements of cosmopolitanism.[9] Critical theorists are famous for demonstrating how power masquerades as progress, but they nevertheless stay on the lookout for evidence of emancipation.[10] Although international relations scholars do not have a consensus definition of progress, their writings suggest a strong normative preference for inclusive deliberation to decisions by fiat, for cosmopolitanism and humanity to chauvinism and discrimination, and for practices based on generalized ethics to a politics of the powerful.

Practitioners also apparently find progress to be a concept that they cannot live with and cannot live without. Over the years my conversations with aid workers on the topic have tended to run as follows: They recite their misgivings and doubts regarding whether their interventions have done much good. I ask if they believe in the possibility of progress. They become visibly uncomfortable. I break the awkward silence by suggesting that perhaps we can find some notion of progress in the expansion of institutions that protect the vulnerable and provide the powerless with new opportunities to determine their own fates. They seize on the opening and recite various milestones in their lifetime, including developments once unimaginable, including the International Criminal Court and a Responsibility to Protect, and vast improvements in the machinery of compassion and care that have saved lives. It is virtually impossible to engage the international humanitarian order without driving under the influence of some concept of progress.

What anchors this faith in the possibility of progress? There is no single answer, but I have been impressed by what can only be called the "transcendental." The transcendental should not be confused with more familiar concepts such as cosmopolitanism. When international relations scholars and political theorists refer to a global, transnational, or cosmopolitan society they typically have in mind a belief that we have obligations to others regardless of their identity or their location.[11] The discourse of humanitarianism connects to cosmopolitanism through the principles of impartiality and nondiscrimination. The transcendental, however, refers not to the material but to the metaphysical or supernatural. It recalls John Dewey's approving reference to William James' understanding of religious experience (as distinct from religion), in which the "self is always directed toward something beyond itself and so its own unification depends upon the idea of shifting scenes of the world into that imaginative totality we call the Universe."[12] Humans have a constant need to find "something beyond or transcendent to their lives."[13]

The capacity of individuals to link their everyday actions to the transcendental, to find meaning and enchantment in practical and worldly activities, is closely connected to the famous distinction between the immanent and the transcendental. There are various ways to think about their relationship, but for my purposes Charles Taylor's view works well:

> The great invention of the West was that of an immanent order in Nature, whose working could be systematically understood and explained on its own terms, leaving open the question whether this whole order had a deeper significance, and whether, if it did, we should infer a transcendent Creator beyond it. This notion of the "immanent" involved denying—or at least isolating and perhaps problematizing—any form of interpenetration between the things of Nature, on the one hand, and the "supernatural" on the other, be this understood in terms of the one transcendent God or of Gods or spirits, or magic forces or whatever.[14]

Processes associated with the enlightenment, modernity, and secularization have caused considerable disenchantment, but humans nevertheless demonstrate a remarkable ability for discovering enchantment in their daily lives and maintaining a faith in the divine.

The transcendental can be either religious or secular. International relations scholars have been notoriously slow-footed when considering the continued relevance of religion in world affairs, generally assuming that the world has been thoroughly secularized and religion has been put in its place. For them, this secularization is generally treated as a good thing; after all, modern international relations begins when a secular sovereignty silenced the religious wars and brought a modicum of stability to global affairs, and lately religion has grabbed their attention once again because religious fanatics are undermining domestic and international stability. Consequently, many international relations scholars operate with the narrative of the secular as superior to the religious, of the secular as part of the rational world and the religious as part of the irrational, and of the binary of the secular and the religious. Given these assumptions it has been difficult for international relations scholars to recognize religion's continued place in world affairs, the possibility that the "religious" has constituted elements of the "secular" international order, and that religion might be more than the root of all evil.[15]

Moreover, the transcendental can be intrinsic to seemingly secular projects, including nationalism, socialism, and liberalism.[16] Charles Taylor refers to the presence of the transcendental in what appears to be a secular world, including in British and American patriotism, in civilizing processes, and in a liberal order of equality, rights, and democracy that might be sustained by more than a Rawlsian "overlapping consensus" based on Kantian and utilitarian grounds.[17] Although Taylor argues that many modern beliefs and projects that appear to be quintessentially secular are in fact sustained and given meaning by religious discourses, Craig Calhoun rightly adds that the transcendental need not be limited to the religious but also can include activities that are designed to transform others and ourselves in ways that lift our spirits. Many who are part of the human rights movements speak of human rights as a "religion" and the Universal Declaration of Human Rights as their "bible."[18] MSF might appear to be the quintessentially secular organization, but they have many of the characteristics normally associated with an ecclesiastical order.[19] Transcendentalism can have religious and secular manifestations, embedded in a divine that refers to God or a secularized humanity, respectively.

After years of writing on the international humanitarian order in a critical voice, I confess that I, too, have an inexplicable need to believe in the possibility of progress and the existence of the transcendental. In "The UN Security Council, indifference, and genocide in Rwanda," I employed a secularized version of the religious concept of theodicy to explain how those at the UN found ethical meaning in their indifference to the genocide through their reference to the transcendental and the defense of the international community's church, the United Nations. In some respects mimicking their need to keep the flame alive, I ended this depressing story on an unexpectedly and defiantly up-beat note, confessing that I, too, had no alternative but to believe in the possibility of moral progress. I encountered a similar challenge when I wrote *Eyewitness to a Genocide*, concluding a book that began with the banality of indifference among international civil servants with the iconic case of Romeo Dallaire as evidence of the possibility of an ethic of responsibility.

In both of these instances and against my intellectual instincts, I felt a Spielberg-like need to find a glimmer of hope. My recent work on humanitarianism has also struggled to retain a space for genuinely emancipatory action in an otherwise deeply flawed and tragic world. The "audacity of hope" does not preclude level-headed analysis, and at the least it certainly cushions the blows delivered by reality.

Looking backwards it is now apparent that I have been articulating a meaning of progress that revolves around an expansion of the willingness of humans to incorporate the suffering and welfare of others into their everyday decisions. Progress, in other words, is not defined by sheer stocks of wealth but rather by social relations of care (though stocks of wealth can certainly enhance our ability to care). That the expanding international humanitarian order might be symbolic of international progress has been suggested by various scholars and practitioners, including most surprisingly Richard Rorty, who famously wrote against Kantian-inspired concepts of progress. He begins by suggesting that progress can best be understood as the ability of individuals to become aware of more alternatives. "It is the ability to come up with new ideas," he writes, "rather than the ability to get in touch with unchanging essences, that is the engine of progress."[20] But, he quickly adds up, the content of these ideas matter; specifically, it is ideas that widen sympathy for others and increase benevolence. "[M]oral progress occurs when benevolence is stretched to cover people whom those exercising power had never really thought of as members of the moral community."[21] Although there is no single cause for the expansion of benevolence, like many others Rorty is impressed by the tremendous outburst of humanitarian activity beginning in the nineteenth century, and he credits security, wealth, and education as the principal drivers of the expansion of sympathy over the last two centuries. In general, any meaningful notion of progress and a moral community requires a readiness to come to the assistance of those in need; benevolence is the surest sign of a moral community and the expansion of benevolence to incorporate those who were once considered outside that community is the surest indicator of progress.[22]

A view of progress that turns on social relations that leave a space for individual autonomy and expression denies the possibility that we can know the future and instead allows for a future that is influenced by an open-ended process of deliberation, contestation, and dialogue—and a healthy dose of imagination, the ability to connect through practical action the grounded reality of the present with the possibility of desired change. There are various notions of progress that presume a particular outcome, including a human mastery over nature, the democratic control over the means of production, and a perfected idea such as freedom. Although we can make general claims regarding the direction of history—and thus offer predictions how global relations might evolve, whether such evolutions are progressive or not depends mightily on the benchmarks used by society at any particular time. Ideally these culturally and historically produced notions of progress are increasingly shaped by more and more members of society. It is impossible to create a genuine deliberative process, but the burden is on society to try and ensure that public reason and not brute power are the tools of influence. It is impossible to create a genuinely representative decision-making process, but the burden is on those who have a seat at the table to ensure that those affected by decisions have their views represented. It is impossible to expect that individuals will change their minds when confronted by a better argument (I know of few scholars who have changed their minds on fundamental issues), but the burden is to cultivate a spirit of epistemological uncertainty.

Although deliberation, debate, dialogue, and doubt are probably essential to any meaningful notion of progress, such exchanges alone are unlikely to move society toward what counts as an improved future without the existence of moral imagination—a willingness to imagine the relationship between the here and now and what might be ultimately desirable. This moral imagination frequently derives not from some romanticizing of the past but rather from a fantasy about the future. As John Dewey defiantly and passionately wrote, it is not that:

> ideals are linked with existence and that they themselves exist, through human embodiment, . . . as if the efforts of human beings in behalf of justice or knowledge or beauty, depended for their effectiveness and validity upon the assurance that there already existed in some supernal region a place where criminals are humanly treated, where there is no serfdom or slavery, where all facts and truths are already discovered and possessed, and all beauty is eternally displayed in actualized form.

What moves us forward, Dewey continues, is an imagination that is rooted in the realities of the present but also imagines the possibility of changing the present to realize a different future.[23]

Humanity requires practice and the possibility of progress depends on individuals acting on the belief that it is possible. But, just like ideas, the transcendental, notions of progress, and concepts of humanity do not float freely. Instead, they are imagined and defined within a cultural and institutional milieu. What counts as moral progress is always constructed within a broader cultural-historical context, even if norm entrepreneurs, principled actors, and other traffickers of progress are treated by scholars as having created the vision of a more progressive international environment from Kantian cloth. A defining characteristic of the modern world order, moreover, is that definitions of progress and ethical principles are imagined and lived within an institutional context. The international humanitarian order is an increasingly institutionalized world order, and these humanitarian institutions, in turn, are given responsibility for helping make good on that order and further its institutionalization. Yet the Church can disappoint. Several of the essays in this volume speak directly to this issue, and in the next section

I want to suggest that one source of the disjuncture between principles and practices owes to how power defines principles.

Paternalism and world order

Nearly all humanitarians, regardless of their dialect, claim to be in solidarity with the objects of their compassion—yet the relationship between the deliverer and the recipient contains its own inequalities. Some can choose altruism; others have no choice but to play the role of the vulnerable but always grateful pauper.[24] Those that presume the authority to represent the suffering of others frequently (mis)appropriate the pain in ways that celebrate the deliverer and limit the capacity of the victims to express in their own words their suffering and sorrow.[25] The very cultivation of compassion can generate little more than feel-good moments that immunize on-lookers from real action that can have more tangible effects.[26] The "gift" often comes with obligations and generates new forms of dependencies.[27] The passion of compassion can lead to a politics of pity that creates a distance between the observer and the suffering object.[28]

While there exist various ways to dissect the power imbalance between the giver and the recipient, the concept of paternalism encapsulates its central ambiguities. There are various definitions of paternalism, but the general claim is that "the interference with a person's liberty of action justified by reasons referring exclusively to the welfare, good, happiness, needs, interests or values of the person whose liberty is being violated." Several features of this definition stand out. It involves benevolence and compassion and thus includes a genuine desire to help others. It is more than interfering in the lives of others to promote their welfare; it justifies suspending their liberty in some way in order to get them to act in ways that the intervener believes is more consistent with the needs of the object.[29] Importantly, then, paternalism is distinguished from naked expressions of power by explicit references to the needs, desires, and welfare of the subject. There is almost always a debate regarding the credibility of such pronouncements (we should worry whenever someone says that he is here to help us), but at a minimum it must include the combination of intentions and reasons that are concerned with the welfare of others.

The institutions that comprise the international humanitarian order are paternalistic. They aspire to relieve suffering and improve the welfare of others and frequently do so on the grounds that they know best. Those who engage in emergency relief typically must act in the heat of the moment and cannot begin to stop and ask for consent. Development agencies are staffed by individuals with doctorates in economics who opted for a career that helps others rather than maximizes their income potential, and claim to know better because of their training and education. International human rights activists will often make arguments regarding which rights should be prioritized and instruct local activists on how best to get there. As international public health experts deploy across the global South, dispensing medicine and advice, they often discover that their health recommendations require a change in lifestyles. In general, international humanitarian institutions are designed for the explicit purpose of improving the needs of others, and often claim to know what is in their best interest.

Paternalism has a bad name and for good reasons. It can be infantilizing. It rubs against liberal sensibilities that insist on the autonomy of the person. People know what is best for themselves, and the process of making these decisions, even if they are the wrong ones, is an important expression of their autonomy and dignity as humans. It is difficult to interpret the wishes, needs, and experiences of other populations, especially those experiencing tremendous hardship. International paternalism has a long rap sheet. Nineteenth-century humanitarianism was avowedly and explicitly paternalistic: it justified the violation of the autonomy of the colonized on the grounds that they were savages, barbarians, or children, incapable of making informed, rational, decisions. Famously, John Stuart Mill provided one of the earliest and most comprehensive defenses of liberalism and against paternalism, yet made exceptions in cases of children and barbarians. Much like the discourse of civilization in Mill's time, the contemporary discourse of humanitarianism can produce two kinds of actors: those who are subjects, who are good, who are expected to prevent human suffering, and who have the tools of emancipation; and those who are objects, whose humanity is to be secured or restored, and who are judged incapable of helping themselves.

Yet it is neither possible nor necessarily desirable to remove paternalism from the international humanitarian order. Paternalism is a latent or manifest feature of all relations of compassion. Accordingly, to end paternalism in our lifetime would mean to cleanse humanity of these other highly desirable human traits. Said otherwise, if paternalism cannot be avoided in most instances, then are we prepared to conclude that paternalism is a greater sin than not doing anything at all? Are we ready to watch others suffer and transform indifference into a moral virtue? And, while most of us prefer romantic notions of justice, in which the impoverished and the downtrodden storm the gates at Versailles, moral progress often depends on a revolution from above and on "condescension at the top."[30] Paternalism, then, can be instrumental for progressive change. Lastly, although Mill's defense of colonialism in the lands of "barbarians" offends our modern sensibilities, his substantive argument—that some populations are not competent to rule themselves—underlies the justification for modern-day trusteeships, transitional administrations, and other forms of international governance.

The ever-present possibility and occasional desirability of paternalism issues two challenges. One is to "reconcile our general repugnance for paternalism with the seeming reasonableness of some apparently paternalistic regulations."[31] The international humanitarian order challenges us to consider when and in what forms we are prepared to defend paternalism. Emergency relief is probably such a moment; in fact, to the extent that we can reasonably assume consent on the part of populations in need, relief might not even count as paternalism. Post-emergency and post-conflict assistance is a more complex case. As the relief and post-conflict recovery sectors links up with development they must consider whether the goal is to return the society to the (pre-war) status quo or to try and create the conditions for a more stable, durable, and desirable society; in either case there is the danger of paternalism precisely because these interveners are operating with visions of what they believe are in the local population's best interests. Certainly they do and will hear a clamor of demands from local elites regarding the need to return power, demands that might be reasonably ignored if they believe it is in the long-term interests of society.[32] But on what grounds do they claim to know better? On what grounds do they claim to able to articulate the general will and even a general will that cannot even be articulated by the public? These issues and questions are rife throughout the international humanitarian order.

Second, what kinds of mechanisms might guard against the abuse of power by those who claim to be acting in the best interests of others? Over the last several years this question has received more attention, especially as international agencies are being forced to wrestle with the relationship between their lack of accountability and the ineffectiveness of aid, charges of exploitation and criminal activity, and dereliction of their moral and professional responsibilities.[33] Their experience is not unique but rather is probably emblematic of the international humanitarian order—whereas once members of the order spent little time evaluating their effectiveness and assumed a near infallibility, they are now recognizing that they are not quite gods (even as they continue to surround their practices within a transcendental filament).

Their recognition that they and their profession are fallible is not only healthy, it also is essential for humanitarians to avoid the dangers of paternalism. Humanitarians at their best are skittish paternalists—wanting to do what is best for others but never quite confident that they know what is best. There are various ways to escape the anxiety that comes with uncertainty, including flights of denial, but the healthiest response arguably is a desire to check their beliefs against those they are trying to help. Such a move requires that the humanitarians do something that does not come easy to the paternalists—a willingness to place themselves in a position of epistemological and existential uncertainty, a move that questions what they believe they know and who they believe they are.[34] After two decades of working with Oxfam and in emergencies around the world, Tony Vaux writes:

> In order to understand the person in need and his or her full social, economic and political context we need to obliterate our own self. It is not a pleasant process because we have to question ourselves relentlessly. The advantage is that we will have a better chance of making the right decisions. If we allow ourselves to intrude on that judgment, we will

believe that we know the answers before we really do, and mistakes will
be made. . . . The issue is about "minimizing" the self and increasing
awareness of the "other".[35]

If humanitarian action has a saving dimension it is because those who act in
its name live an emancipatory ethos that forces them to constantly question
themselves and doubt whether they are truly doing good as defined by those
they want to help.

Ethics and scholarship

The social sciences were born in the late nineteenth century with a comfortable relationship to the world of ethics, the goal of harnessing science to
improve society, and the purpose of educating citizens and training public
servants. Many of the first social science departments were established in
institutions of higher learning that had a strong religious identity and in
which there was a foundational concern with what is the public good and
moral engagement in public life. A scientific method, initially drawn heavily
from the natural sciences and then influenced by the development of human
sciences, offered the promise of being able to address systematically and
rigorously the social problems of the day. Social science departments had
a mission to help citizens prepare for the demands of a rapidly changing
society, economy, and polity, and to train public servants who would be at
the controls.[36] The first generation of political science departments were
facsimiles of a social science that was keen to improve the world through a
commitment to scientific methods.

Reflecting these trends, international relations as a distinct field of study
emerged after World War One and in reaction to the horrors of the Great
War, and with a general commitment to trying to manage the effects of
anarchy, enhance the prospects of international governance and cooperation,
and reduce the chances of war. Although many of the early international
relations scholars were unfairly tarred with the brush of idealism, in the spirit
of the times they operated with a generalized notion of progress and the
confidence that it was possible to design an international governance system
that could improve global welfare.[37] World War Two shattered their confidence, but in the immediate aftermath of such horrors they felt compelled
to address the relationship between their theories and international public
policy. Such commitments were not monopolized by idealists. No lesser
figure than Hans Morgenthau aspired to explain international relations in
order to challenge the status quo, which necessitated a consideration of the
relationship between theory and practical knowledge and the existence of
transcendental moral ethics that can provide ballast for principled action.[38]

In the decades following World War Two, however, international relations
got "science": pursuing objectivity; embracing behavioralism and omitting
motives, beliefs, and reasons from empirical analysis; gravitating toward

economic theories of action which constructed an abstract, dehistoricized, individual; demonstrating a hyper attention to theory and methods for their own sake, and retreating into monastic life where the monks communicated through their version of ancient Latin or Hebrew—theory and numbers— and were increasingly unable to relate to the outside world.[39]

Practical engagement and ethics were casualties of this trend. Whereas once social science departments were committed to enhancing the "public good," scholars became increasingly autistic, removed from the world around them, and part of a sheltered community. Certainly global events influenced scholarly trends, but those scholars who wrote for a wider readership were frequently scorned for not doing "serious work," those that advised governments were accused of wanting to play philosopher to the prince, and those that worked with protest and resistance movements were accused of being ideological and sacrificing their academic credentials. The occasional calls for "usable knowledge" were lost in a discipline that became increasingly theory and methods-mad, obsessed with publication in top-refereed journals in order to gain status and ranking (notwithstanding the common refrain that the top journals fail to produce articles that anyone reads), and dedicated to training the next generation of scholars (and instruct those thinking of alternative careers to look elsewhere).[40] Academics had a remarkable capacity for translating disengagement into a heroic, self-justificatory rhetoric that nearly legitimated an intellectual narcissism.

International relations, and this is particularly true of American international relations, also disengaged from the study of ethics, in part because of the broader trend in the social sciences that treated normative and explanatory theory as incompatible. Even much of constructivism, especially those branches that developed in the United States, were attentive to causation to the neglect of ethics. The existing air pockets where ethics continued to be practiced had a European accent; some scholars followed trends in political theory and philosophy, most noticeably those influenced by Kantian approaches and the search for universal principles against which action might be judged.

Critical international relations theory remained one of the few places in the discipline where it was acceptable to address explicitly normative issues.[41] Yet a considerable body of critical theory operated with a rather severe view of what kind of ethical engagement was "acceptable." Robert Cox's distinction between problem-solving and critical theory is a touchpoint for many in this tradition: whereas critical theory unmasks relations of power with the hopes of bringing about an "alternative order," problem-solving theory takes the world as it is.[42] His differentiation encouraged many critical international relations theorists to act as if any proposal that was not sufficiently radical was virtually contemptible and to portray problem-solving theory as if it was a co-conspirator in all forms of oppression.

Consider the following example. Based on the secondary literature and four of the universe of cases of humanitarian intervention, Roberto Belloni assembles various well-known criticisms of humanitarian action into "nine theses" that he uses to indict virtually all forms of humanitarian action.[43] In his hands, humanitarianism might not be the root of all evil but it certainly is an accomplice. So, if humanitarianism is the road to hell, then to hell with humanitarianism. What are the preferred alternatives? Prevention—which fails to recognize that a fair bit of humanitarian action is already focused on prevention. A demand that Western states become less self-interested and halt weapon exports—which is like criticizing emergency room doctors for not abandoning gunshot victims to lobby for better gun control. And an insistence that Western societies practice human rights at home—which is unobjectionable on the surface but transforms isolationalism and indifference into cherished values.

Why is problem-solving theory the enemy? What, precisely, is ethically problematic with an engagement that aspires to make small but consequential changes in the lives of others? Are we to invert Max Weber's famous admonition that we should follow an ethics of responsibility and avoid an ethics of ultimate ends? Aid workers would certainly understand the distinction between critical and problem-solving theory—but would nevertheless have a difficult time suffering a critique that plans for the radical solution while the dying continues. Humanitarian actors might very well hold out the desire for a more just world, but that does not preclude them from acting to help those in life-threatening circumstances. Is the ICRC complicit in the legitimation of war because it tries to make the conduct of war a little less barbaric? If peacekeepers help to bring some stability, but fail to bring about a liberal peace, does that mean that there is no value in their interventions?[44]

International relations theorists must recapture ethics and engagement, not at the expense of social science but rather to generate a more vibrant and fulfilling social science.[45] Critique must be related to explicit notions of outcomes. Emancipatory critique cannot be left to one pocket of international relations theory but must become an explicit element of all international relations theory; to accept the claim that critique should be the monopoly of critical international relations theory is akin to saying that only clowns should make people laugh or only humanitarian organizations should be allowed to save people.[46] Among the possible ways of beginning to integrate theory with ethics and practice, two recent emerging developments appear particularly promising.

The first is the belated but welcome attempt by many constructivist scholars to marry empirical and ethical analysis. This outcome came as a consequence of a sequence of claims:

- actors are concerned not only with what are the consequences but also what is appropriate, and what counts as legitimate, just, and fair action;
- the reasons actors give for their actions are an important dimension to causal analysis;

- reasons derive not only from private but also from collective beliefs that situate decisions within an ethical universe;
- this ethical universe, in turn, arrays outcomes in terms of their inherent desirability;
- claims about what is desirable almost always must be judged in relationship to not what is the ideal but what is the possible; and
- evaluations of the possible require counterfactual analysis.

In this respect, constructivist scholars are finding themselves in a position familiar to those in the aid sector—leaning on consequentialism to defend the acceptability of certain kinds of outcomes. In general, resolving empirical questions about consequences is important for making normative judgments about desirable policies, which are themselves based on specifying the conditions under which different policies can lead to better or worse outcomes.[47]

Pragmatism represents a second possibility. There are various aspects and interpretations of pragmatism, but several of its features are particularly relevant. There is the conviction that politics is a practical activity to the extent that it is both most meaningful and useful when it is grounded in a particular time and place. As Friedrich Kratochwil succinctly summarizes, "Politics is inherently practical since it deals with doing the right thing at the right time in particular historical circumstances."[48] It recognizes that both the goals and the means of society can change. Change, however, can be most legitimately achieved through action that is grounded in democratic learning and practice, which, in turn, is consistent with what John Dewey called a "method of intelligence"—a "willingness to hold belief in suspense, ability to doubt until evidence is obtained; willingness to go where evidence points instead of putting first a personally preferred conclusion; ability to hold ideas in solution and use them as hypotheses to be tested instead of dogmas to be asserted; and (possibly most distinctive of all) enjoyment of new fields of inquiry and of new problems."[49] Doubt and skepticism become the epistemological foundation for the possibility of generating knowledge that can help solve problems that matter to human existence.[50]

The international humanitarian order poses a multitude of challenges to both scholars and practitioners. For both communities the idea of the good society, or at least a society that is better than the one that presently exists, remains a hopeful quest and gives meaning to their actions. For both communities the purpose of knowledge is the crafting of practical action, and they are enabled to argue in favor of some kinds of interventions because of their authority, in some cases a moral authority and in other cases an epistemic authority. These claims to authority can lead to forms of conceit and certainty, the belief that they do or can know better than others, including those who are supposed to benefit from their prescribed and implied interventions. For both, the challenge is to find a way to allow themselves to acknowledge their fallibility without succumbing to resignation and surrender; to acknowledge the politics and power that inheres in their interventions that are supposedly designed for the benefit of others. Ultimately, the possibility of progress in international relations depends not on the successful search for a space in which politics and power are removed, as if that was possible, but rather recognizing the politics and power that inhere in even the most seemingly ethical practices.

Notes

1 See Jonathan Benthall, *Returning to Religion: Why a Secular Age Is Haunted by Faith* (London: I.B. Taurus, 2008).
2 For a particularly moving account, see James Orbinski, *An Imperfect Offering: Humanitarian Action for the 21st Century* (Toronto, Canada: Walker and Company, 2008).
3 Fiona Terry, *Condemned to Repeat? The Paradoxes of Humanitarian Action* (Ithaca: Cornell University Press, 2002).
4 Jeremy Weinstein, "Autonomous Recovery and International Intervention in Comparative Perspective," Working Paper 57, Center for Global Development, Washington, D.C., 2005; Alex de Waal, "Mission Without End? Peacekeeping in the African Political Marketplace," *International Affairs*, 85, 1, 2009, 99–113.
5 Paul Collier, *The Bottom Billion: Why the Poorest Countries are Failing and What Can Be Done About It* (New York: Oxford University Press, 2007); Jeffrey Sachs, *The End of Poverty: Economic Possibilities for Our Time* (New York: Penguin Books, 2006); William Easterly, *The White Man's Burden: Why the West's Efforts to Aid the Rest Have Done So Much Ill and So Little Good* (New York: Penguin Books, 2007).
6 BBC, "Peacekeepers 'Abusing Children'," May 27, 2008. http://news.bbc.co.uk/2/hi/in_depth/7420798.stm
7 Anne-Marie Slaughter, "International Law in a World of Liberal States," *European Journal of International Law*, 6, 4, 1995, 503–539; Andrew Hurrell "Kant and the Kantian Paradigm in International Relations," *Review of International Studies*, 16, 3, July 1990, 183–205.
8 Richard Price, "Moral Limit and Possibility in World Politics," *International Organization*, 62, 2, April 2008, 191–220; Richard Price, ed., *Moral Limit and Possibility in World Politics* (New York: Cambridge University Press, 2008); Margaret Keck and Kathryn Sikkink, *Activists Beyond Borders* (Ithaca: Cornell University Press, 1998); Martha Finnemore and Kathryn Sikkink, "International Norms and Political Change," in P. Katzenstein et al, eds., *Explorations and Controversies in World Politics* (Cambridge, MA: MIT Press, 1999): 247–78; Martha Finnemore, *The Purpose of Force* (Ithaca: Cornell University Press, 2004).
9 Nicholas Wheeler, *Saving Strangers: Humanitarian Intervention in International Society* (New York: Oxford University Press, 2001); Andrew Hurrell, *On Global Order: Power, Values, and the Constitution of International Society* (New York: Oxford University Press, 2007), chap. 12; Robert Jackson, *The Global Covenant: Human Conduct in a World of States* (New York: Oxford University Press, 2000); Barry Buzan, *From International to World Society? English School Theory and the Social Structure of Globalisation* (New York: Cambridge University Press, 2004).
10 Andrew Linklater, *The Transformation of Political Community: Ethical Foundations of the Post-Westphalian Era* (Columbia: University of South Carolina Press, 1998); Robyn Eckersley, "The Ethics of Critical Theory," in D. Snidal and C. Reus Smit, *The Oxford Handbook of International Relations* (New York: Oxford University Press, 2008); Ken Booth, *Theory of World Security* (New York:

Cambridge University Press, 2007); Richard Sharpcott, "Anti-Cosmpolitanism, Pluralism, and the Cosmopolitan Harm Principle," *Review of International Studies*, 34, 2008, 185–205.

11 For statements on cosmopolitanism, minimal and otherwise, see G. Brock and H. Brighouse, eds., *The Political Philosophy of Cosmopolitanism* (Cambridge: Cambridge University Press, 2005). For a good discussion of the relationship between cosmopolitanism and the "harm principle," see Sharpcott, "Anti-Cosmpolitanism, Pluralism, and the Cosmopolitan Harm Principle."

12 John Dewey, *A Common Faith* (New Haven: Yale University Press, 1934), p. 19.

13 Charles Taylor, *A Secular Age* (Cambridge, MA: Harvard University Press, 2007). For a similar analysis of the concept of hope, see Patrick Deneen, "The Politics of Hope and Optimism: Rorty, Havel, and the Democratic Faith of John Dewey," *Social Research*, 66, 2, Summer 1999, 578–598. For Rorty, social hope revolves around the possibility that "unnecessary human suffering can be decreased, and human happiness thereby increased," Richard Rorty, "Hope and the Future," *Peace Review*, 14, 2, 2002, 154. Cited in Nicholas Smith, "Rorty on Religion and Hope," *Inquiry*, 48, 1, February 2005, 94. Also see Vincent Carpanzano, "Reflections on Hope as a Category of Social and Political Analysis," *Cultural Anthropology*, 18, 1, 2003, 3–32.

14 Taylor, *A Secular Age*, 15–16.

15 There is a growing literature on religion and world affairs, but very little on religion and international relations theory. For important exceptions, see Fabio Petito and Pavlos Hatzopoulus, eds., *Religion in International Relations: The Return from Exile* (New York: Palgrave 2003); and Scott Thomas, *The Global Resurgence of Religion and the Transformation of International Relations: The Struggle for the Soul of the Twenty-First Century* (New York: Palgrave, 2003). For a good overview of the challenge for theorists of IR and comparative politics, see Eva Bellin, "Faith in Politics: New Trends in the Study of Religion and Politics," *World Politics*, 60, 2, January 2008, 315–347; and J. Snyder, ed., *Religion and International Relations Theory* (New York: Columbia University Press, forthcoming).

16 Taylor, *A Secular Age*; Craig Calhoun, "Going Beyond." Retrieved from the SSRC blog, The Immanent Frame.

17 Charles Taylor, "Two Books, Yoked Together," http://www.ssrc.org/blogs/immanent_frame/2008/01/243shtwo-books-oddly-yoked-together.

18 See Nicholas Guilhot, "Secularism, Realism, and International Relations," http://www.ssrc.org/blogs/immanent_frame/2007/10/31/secularism-realism-and-international-relations/; Elizabeth Shenkman Hurd, "The Other Shore," http://www.ssrc.org/blogs/immanent_frame/2007/12/18/the-other-shore/

19 Benthall, *Returning to Religion*, chap. 4.

20 Richard Rorty, "Is Philosophy Relevant to Applied Ethics?" *Business Ethics Quarterly*, 16, 3, 372. This general orientation is shared by various scholars of the English School. For instance, *The Global Covenant*, Robert Jackson, following the work of Collingwood, defines human improvement and civilization as the ability to treat others as part of the moral community.

21 Rorty, "Is Philosophy Relevant to Applied Ethics?" 376.

22 Richard Rorty, "Who are We? Moral Universalism and Economic Triage," *Diogenes*, 173, 44, 1, Spring 1996, p. 13. Also see Richard Rorty, "Human Rights, Rationality, and Sentimentality, in his *Truth and Progress: Philosophical Papers* (New York: Cambridge University Press, 1998), pp. 167–185. For another argument regarding the possibility of developing universal moral codes around human suffering, see Andrew Linklater, "Towards a Sociology of Global Morals with an 'Emancipatory Intent'," *Review of International Society*, 33, April 2007, 135–150.

23 Dewey, *A Common Faith*, p. 49. Also see Richard Rorty, *Philosophy and Social Hope* (New York: Penguin Press, 1999).

24 Didier Fassin, "Humanitarianism as a Politics of Life," *Public Culture*, 19, 3, 2007, p. 507.

25 Elizabeth V. Spellman, *Fruits of Sorrow: Framing Our Attention to Suffering* (Boston: Beacon Press, 1997), pp. 7, 64.

26 Chandler, *From Kosovo to Kabul and Beyond*.

27 Marcel Mauss, *The Gift: The Form and Reason for Exchange in Archaic Societies* (New York: Norton Press, 2000).

28 Hannah Arendt, *On Revolution* (New York: Penguin Books, 2006); Leslie Butt, "The Suffering Stranger: Medical Anthropology and International Morality," *Medical Anthropology*, 21, 2002, 1–24.

29 Gerald Dworkin, "Paternalism," *The Monist*, 56, 1972, p. 65. Also see David Archard, "Paternalism Defined," *Analysis*, 50, 1, January 1990, 36–42; David Garren, "Paternalism, Part I" and "Paternalism, Part II," *Philosophical Books*, 47, 4, October 2006, 334–341 and 48, 1, January 2007, 50–59; Rolf Sartorius, ed., *Paternalism* (Minneapolis: University of Minnesota Press, 1983); Bernard Gert and Charles Culver, "Paternalistic Behavior," *Philosophy and Public Affairs*, 6, 1976, 45–58; Donald VanDeVeer, *Paternalistic Intervention: The Moral Bounds of Benevolence* (Princeton: Princeton University Press, 1986).

30 Richard Rorty, "Human Rights, Rationality, and Sentimentality," p. 183.

31 Joel Feinberg, *Harm to Self* (New York: Oxford University Press, 1986), p. 25. Cited from Peter de Marnefee, "Avoiding Paternalism," *Philosophy and Public Affairs*, 34, 1, 69–94.

32 See Paddy Ashdown, *Swords and Ploughshares: Building Peace in the 21st Century* (London: Phoenix Books, 2008).

33 Chesterman, *You, the People*; Feldman, *What We Owe Iraq*, pp. 66–68.

34 For a particularly moving account of the different possibilities that existed during the Spanish conquest of the Americas, see Stephen Greenblatt, *Marvelous Possessions: The Wonder of the New World* (Chicago: University of Chicago Press, 1991).

35 Tony Vaux, *The Selfish Altruist* (London: Earthscan Books, 2002), p. 7.

36 Dorothy Ross, *The Origins of American Social Science* (New York: Cambridge University Press, 1991); Anderson, *Pursuing Truth, Exercising Power*, p. 3; James Farr, John Dryzek, and Stephen Leonard, *Political Science as History: Research Programs and Political Traditions* (New York: Cambridge University Press, 1995). For the divorce in political science, see the essays by Gunnell, Kettler, and Barber in a special issue of the *American Political Science Review*, "The Evolution of Political Science," 100, 4, November 2006.

37 See Brian Schmidt, *The Political Discourse of Anarchy: A Disciplinary History of International Relations* (Albany: State University of New York Press, 1998).

38 Murielle Cozette, "Reclaiming the Critical Dimension of Realism: Hans J. Morgenthau on the Ethics of Scholarship," *Review of International Studies*, 34, 2008, 5–27. For an evocative study of post-war political scientists who felt compelled to use social science to address the challenges of their times, see Ira Katznelson, *Desolation and Enlightenment: Political Knowledge After Total War, Totalitarianism, and the Holocaust* (New York: Columbia University Press, 2004).

39 Ian Shapiro, "Problems, Methods, and Theories in the Study of Politics, or: What's Wrong with Political Science and What to Do About It," in Ian Shapiro, Rogers Smith, and Tarek Masoud, eds., *Problems and Methods in the Study of Politics* (New York: Cambridge University Press, 2005), 19–41; Lisa Anderson, *Pursuing Truth, Exercising Power* (NY: Columbia University Press, 2005).

40 Anderson, *Pursuing Truth, Exercising Power*, p. 3.

41 For good statements regarding critical international relations theory, see Robert Wyn Jones, ed., *Critical Theory and World Politics* (Boulder, CO: Lynne Rienner, 2001); Nicholas Rengger and Tristram Benedict Thirkell-White, eds., *Critical International Relations Theory After 25 Years* (New York: Cambridge University

Press, 2007); Steve Roach, ed., *Critical Theory and International Relations: A Reader* (New York: Routledge Press, 2007); Richard Devetak, "Critical Theory," in Scott Burchill et al, eds., *Theories of International Relations*, 2nd ed. (New York: Palgrave, 2001), 155–180; Andrew Linklater, "The Achievements of Critical Theory," in Steve Smith, Ken Booth and Marysia Zalewski, eds., *International Theory: Positivism and Beyond* (Cambridge: Cambridge University Press, 1996), 279–298; Andrew Linklater, "The Transformation of Political Community: E.H. Carr, Critical Theory and International Relations," *Review of International Studies*, 23, 3, 1997, 321–338; Andrew Linklater, *Beyond Realism and Marxism: Critical Theory and International Relations* (London: Macmillan, 1990); Andrew Linklater, *Men and Citizens in the Theory of International Relations* (London: Macmillan, 1990); Chris Brown, " 'Turtles All the Way Down': Anti-Foundationalism, Critical Theory and International Relations," *Millennium*, 23, 1994, 213–236; Jim George, *Discourses of Global Politics: A Critical (Re)Introduction to International Relations* (Boulder, CO: Lynne Rienner, 1994).

42 Robert Cox, "Social Forces, States, and World Orders: Beyond International Theory," *Millennium*, 10, 2, 1 June 1981, 126–55. For an updated statement, see Robert Cox, "The Point in Not Just to Explain the World but to Change It," in Chris Reus-Smit and Duncan Snidal, eds., *The Oxford Handbook of International Relations* (New York: Oxford University Press, 2008), 84–93.

43 Roberto Belloni, "The Trouble with Humanitarianism," *Review of International Studies*, 33, 2007, 451–474.

44 For a particularly eloquent plea for critical theorists to engage those outside the West in a more meaningful and inclusive way, see Craig Murphy, "The Promise of Critical IR Theory, Partially Kept," *Review of International Studies*, 33, April 2007, 117–133; and for an argument regarding the need of critical international relations scholars to go beyond critique and consider praxis, see Friedrich Kratochwil, "Looking Back from Somewhere: Reflections on What remains 'Critical' in Critical Theory," *Review of International Studies*, 33, April 2007, 25–45.

45 For an explicit and innovative attempt to bring ethics back into international relations theory, see Chris Reus-Smit and Duncan Snidal, eds., *The Oxford Handbook of International Relations* (New York: Oxford University Press, 2008).

46 I stole the analogy from Hugo Slim, "Humanitarianism with Borders: NGOs, Belligerent Military Forces, and Humanitarian Action," paper prepared for the ICVA conference on NGOs in a Changing World Order: Dilemmas, and Challenges, Geneva, February 14, 2003. http://www.jha.ac/articles/a118.htm

47 Kathryn Sikkink, "The Role of Consequences, Comparison and Counterfactuals in Constructivist Ethical Thought," in R. Price, ed., *Moral Limit and Possibility in World Politics* (New York: Cambridge University Press, 2008); Richard Price, "The Ethics of Constructivism," in Chris Reus-Smit and Duncan Snidal, eds., *The Oxford Handbook of International Relations* (New York: Oxford University Press, 2008), 317–326.

48 Friedrich Kratochwil, "History, Action, and Identity: Revisiting the 'Second' Great Debate and Assessing Its Importance for Social Theory," *European Journal of International Relations*, 12, 5, 2006, 6; Jörg Friedrichs and Friedrich Kratochwil, "On Acting and Knowing," forthcoming at *International Organization*; Molly Cochran, "Deweyian Pragmatism and Post-Positivist Social Science in IR," *Millennium*, 31, 3, 2002, 525–548.

49 "Liberalism and Social Action," in James Gouinlock, ed., *Excellence in Public Discourse: John Stuart Mill, John Dewey, and Social Intelligence* (New York: Teacher's College Press, 1986). Cited in Deneen, "The Politics of Hope and Optimism," p. 590.

50 For a clear methodological statement regarding what this might entail, see Peter Katzenstein and Rudy Sil, "Ecclectic Theorizing and the Study and Practice of International Relations," in Chris Reus-Smit and Duncan Snidal, eds., *The Oxford Handbook of International Relations* (New York: Oxford University Press, 2008), 109–130.

Index